D1263832

MURDER
IN THE
NEIGHBORHOOD

BOOKS BY ELLEN J. GREEN

AVA SAUNDERS SERIES
Twist of Faith
Absolution
Silent Redemption

STANDALONES
The Book of James

MURDER IN THE NEIGHBORHOOD

The true story of America's first recorded mass shooting

ELLEN J. GREEN

Thread

Published by Thread in 2022

An imprint of Storyfire Ltd.
Carmelite House
50 Victoria Embankment
London EC4Y 0DZ

www.thread-books.com

ISBN: 978-1-80019-807-4
eBook ISBN: 978-1-80019-806-7

For:
John Pilarchik
Orris Smith
Clark Hoover
James Hutton
Rose Cohen
Maurice Cohen
Minnie Cohen
Alvin Day
Emma Matlack
Helen Wilson
John Wilson
Tommy Hamilton
Helga Zegrino
And for the victims of gun violence everywhere

Foreword

All the characters depicted in this book are real. Some have passed away, a few are still living. This story has been crafted through meticulous research using newspaper articles, police reports, interviews that survived in both in print and on film, and the countless memories of relatives willing to share. The circumstances described are true. The contents of the encounters between characters and their exchanges have been pieced together from the patchwork of memories passed on by those who were involved, and gaps in the narrative have been plugged by the judicious use of artistic license. The clinical conversations that took place between the psychiatrists and Unruh have been pulled almost word for word from Howard Unruh's hospital records.

The story of Howard Unruh was first told to me by my mother. She spent some of her childhood years in East Camden, several miles from where the incident occurred, and vividly remembers the day of the shootings and the events that followed. She said the community was stunned, that stories and photographs filled the papers every day for months, as neighborhoods tried to make peace with what exactly had happened.

Gun violence wasn't unheard of in post-war America. What set this incident apart was that the shootings weren't sparked by a moment of passion, or secondary to another violent motive such as robbery; it was random and spontaneous and quick. Thirteen people were killed in twelve minutes—a few blinks of an eye had changed everything. It struck panic into small-town America, putting everyone on notice that nobody was really safe, and that we didn't really know one another as well as we thought we did.

Many years later I started working in the correctional system in the city of Camden and my interest in the story was reignited. Everything was right there—prosecutors who'd met Unruh, reporters who had investigated the case, the block where the shootings had taken place. I kept reading and researching. One afternoon I decided to drive to 32nd and River Road to see it for myself. The buildings are largely unchanged but the community there is vastly different and I wasn't sure if the people there would remember what had happened so long ago. It was serendipity that a woman had just purchased the Unruh and Cohen apartments that had been sealed for sixty-plus years, and offered a tour.

The apartments had many of the original fixtures—the closet door where Rose Cohen had hidden and lost her life was still there, although the door had been patched and painted. I had the opportunity to do a run through of the crime scene, to pace it out, see where it had all happened, to climb down a ladder into the basement and look for bullet holes from Unruh's shooting range, to stand in his bedroom where police had lobbed tear gas. It was then I decided that I needed to bring this story to the page. To bring post-war Camden back to life as best I could and tell the story from the beginning of what happened that day on September 6, 1949.

The story has everything: history, true crime, war, dysfunctional personalities, mental illness. And one unsolved mystery—the missing gate. The thing that is undeniable about the Howard Unruh story is that it opened the door to what has become a heartbreaking part of everyday life in America.

Prologue

That September morning started much like any other. Camden, New Jersey, the sparkling little sister of Philadelphia, connected by the high arches of the Delaware River Bridge, was waking up to heat nearing the mid-seventies—by nine o'clock the humidity was sitting high above the city, waiting to descend.

Cramer Hill, a small section of Camden, bound by the Delaware River to the west, the Pavonia Train Yard to the east, State Street to the south and 36th Street to the north—a grid of streets twenty-four blocks long, and about five or six blocks wide contained within—was about to draw the focus of the world but nobody knew it, not that morning at nine o'clock.

River Road cut a swath through Cramer Hill where open-bay trucks rumbled through all day long, overloaded with tomatoes headed for the Campbell's soup factory a few miles away. The clearly visible cargo was only held in place by wire mesh caging along the sides. The loud engine sounds called to children to get out of the street, to stand and watch, waiting for a tomato to break loose and fall into their small hands. They were often rewarded when a bump in the road threw a few of the greenish-red fruits into the street.

The smells of the river wafting in, the sounds of the boats, the hint of tomatoes cooking at Campbell's, the smoke from the stacks of Eavenson & Sons soap factory a mile away—it was all there. But mostly it was the shoemaker's pungent aroma of tannery oils, the lingering, savory fragrance from Latela's Italian luncheonette on the corner, the endless din of Engel's bar across the street, and the music that poured out of its doors after the sun went down that filled every home.

Five businesses shared one side of the small block—a cacophonic mix of a pharmacy, a barbershop, a cobbler, a tailor and a café. The other side only had two: a grocery and a bar. Most of the owners lived there, nestled in their small apartments above their establishments. They all knew each other well enough on that small stretch of River Road. Enough to pull a chair out onto the sidewalk on summer nights for a chat. Enough to get a drink at Engel's now and again. Enough to keep an eye on things and on each other. But not one of them saw it coming. Not the Pilarchiks, the Hoovers, the Hamiltons, the Zegrinos or the Cohens. They'd safely shared that space together for years, but not one of them was spared.

The sky was cloudless on that morning of September 6, 1949 when Raymond Havens stepped outside for some air. He had just turned twelve a few months earlier. His grandmother had sent him to get a haircut but he could see that the barbershop across the street was packed with waiting customers, kids overflowing outside, sitting on the steps. He wasn't getting a trim anytime soon. He debated going to the river to throw some stones but he knew he'd come back muddy. Instead, he just planted his feet at that corner and waited, trying to figure the best way to idle his time.

Mrs. Cohen, the pharmacist's wife across the street, was unlatching the heavy wooden door to the pharmacy—a dark space crammed with all sorts of odds and ends, complete with a six-stooled ice-cream counter. The Cohens had owned that pharmacy for as long as anybody could remember, perched right on the corner of the block at 32nd and River, where they got most of the kids walking home from Harry C. Sharp Elementary School two blocks away. Raymond liked them well enough, but never lingered inside. Quick and efficient, they took his money and sent him on his way. They had a son in the same grade at school, but Raymond barely knew him—a quiet kid named Charles.

Mrs. Cohen was busy that morning, in and out, around the side of the house and into the backyard, then back to the front again. She was a small dark-haired woman with a sharp tongue, and Raymond could hear her voice, crisp and exact. She wanted things just right. Her husband popped his head out, too, standing on the concrete steps, looking up and down the block. He was a large hulking figure of a man who seemed to get along with adults fine, but frightened children. Maybe it was because he was so big. Maybe it was the look he always wore on his craggy face. Raymond wasn't sure. He just knew he was sometimes terrified when he appeared, though to be honest, the man had never said or done anything to warrant that reputation.

The pharmacy was housed in a corner twin building—the business next door, having once been a butcher and then a produce store, was now empty, the apartment above rented to another family. They shared a common wall—the Cohens and this family—and a common backyard, split down the middle by a row of hedges and connected to one another by a gate.

Raymond crossed the street and peered through the plate-glass window into the barbershop. Mrs. Smith and her two children were in there, along with some older boys he didn't know. He hung by the doorway, half in half out, figuring out how much time he might have to whittle away. He couldn't go home uncut. Distracted by a loud sound behind him, he looked down the road to see a truck coming. He took a step back into the barbershop as it passed. The truck lurched by, the air from the exhaust launching a white paper napkin—the remnants of someone's Labor Day picnic the day before—into the air. It floated off the ground, skittering in the breeze. Raymond kept his eye on it. If he hadn't, he would have seen the man come onto River Road through the alleyway alongside the shoemaker's.

But he didn't see him. He kept his eye on that bit of paper, watching it twirl in the exhaust, rising about a foot above the pavement. It was in those few seconds, while the paper pirouetted, that time held its breath. Raymond saw the man walking now, his back erect, his legs moving but his torso remaining motionless as if they weren't connected. His brown worsted wool suit and bow tie were a common sight up and down River Road.

Raymond knew him better than most. His father traded stamps and embossing seals with the man, and Raymond was often used as a conduit for their exchanges. Cutting through that alley and over the rough lot between the buildings to his back door was an almost weekly chore. Their dealings became more protracted as Howard warmed to the boy, chatting about his interests—religion, guns, philosophy—and chewing over the latest developments of his life as if Raymond were already grown. He had a delicate way of speaking even when he described shooting Germans or manning tank guns during the Battle of the Bulge four years earlier.

This man, Howard—having made it through one of the Second World War's deadliest battles and surviving in one piece—was polite enough, soft spoken, bordering on kind but not quite reaching it. His apartment, only accessible from the backyard, had a kitchen entryway and a tiny living room, always cluttered with his bicycle, some books, his wooden trunk. Raymond had never seen the upstairs, but he knew it was bigger, with three good-sized bedrooms—almost the mirror image of the Cohens' apartment next door. His grandmother had described it in detail to her friend while folding laundry.

Howard had lived there with his mother for as long as Raymond could remember. Rita or Freda—she went by both— walked down River Road every day to get the bus to her job at the soap factory. Her gray coat bundled around her, she didn't talk to the neighbors much. She kept her head down, her arms crossed. She seemed nervous all the time. Odd and nervous, just like Howard.

But Howard didn't look scared or nervous to Raymond now. He disappeared into the cobbler's shop while Raymond kept his eye on the twirling paper. If only it had stayed suspended in the air things would have been different, he later thought, because when it landed, it was with a bang. It was the sound of a car backfiring, or a truck hitting the massive pothole up the street, or a firecracker. That's what he thought at the time. Then he saw the gun.

Raymond stumbled into the barbershop and landed in a vacant corner seat just before Howard burst through the door, the Luger in his hand held at hip level. It was all so fast. The barber Hoover moved behind the hobby horse where little Orris Smith was sitting, his face turning white, his hands starting to shake. He seemed to understand all too well what was about to happen. And it did. Two more blasts from the gun and Orris slid to the floor. Hoover too, only a few feet away.

Raymond didn't see the blood, not then. His eyes were locked on Howard's. And Howard's on his. But it only lasted a moment before Raymond freed himself from his seat and bolted through the door, making a right and heading towards Bergen. Legs pumping and shaking at the same time, he counted the sounds of the gunfire behind him. One, two, three…

When he'd circled all the way around the block and came back up 32nd Street towards River Road not even ten minutes later, he saw the pharmacist, Mr. Cohen, dead in the street, his face pressed to the pavement. Another man's feet dangled off the steps of the pharmacy, his head stretching into the doorway, a dark wet substance oozing onto the concrete steps on its way down to the sidewalk.

Raymond cut loose, ran back down to the barbershop and peered in through the big glass window. The white hobby horse was smeared with blood, so much so that it was dripping slowly onto the tile near the barber's feet. Mr. Hoover was stretched out across the floor, the back of his neck ravaged by a bullet that had entered on the other side, and the brush he'd been holding when he was shot had come to rest a few feet away in the middle of the floor.

A Nash automobile had run through a red light, the tires half up on the curb, the driver slumped forward, his head on the steering wheel, a bullet hole neatly between his eyes. A trickle of blood had danced down his face to his chin. Raymond was afraid to turn around. He knew there were more bodies, some inside the buildings and at least two more in another car a few feet away. He could hear the fading moans coming from the nearly lifeless woman slumped in the front seat. Instead of inspecting the inside of the car he rushed to the middle of the street, refusing to move. His eyes were peeled on Howard's upstairs window. He saw the shade flutter up, the lanky form filling the space. After dispensing all of his bullets, Howard had retreated to the comfortable safety of his second-floor flat.

Howard was looking right at him, but was motionless, blinking. There were sirens in the distance and adults pouring from houses into the street, trying to decipher the commotion and administer to the dead and dying. Raymond heard the screams from his lips: 'Why'd you do it, Howard? Why'd you shoot all those people?' But there was no answer. There never would be.

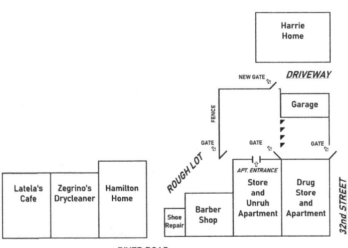

A plan of the neighborhood

Chapter One

Raymond

Thinking back on it, 1949 hadn't been a good year in any way at all for me. I was eleven, turning twelve, stuck in that in-between stage of feeling too old to be babied, but not old enough to be treated as an adult, that is until I got called to go to the police station in downtown Camden to give my testimony right after a series of killings happened in the neighborhood. That's what they called it—testimony. Really, they just wanted to know who I was and what I saw. I wasn't a person of interest, I was an eyewitness, but I knew the person of interest. That's what my father told me while he was brushing the sleeve of my good shirt to smooth the wrinkles. We couldn't go across town to be interrogated with me looking a mess.

I had never seen death before—not violent death anyway. I barely remember my mother's funeral with her being laid out in a coffin, her skin a waxy pale color, her eyes shut, hands folded; she was very peaceful but her body seemed empty, like a department store mannequin. She died from pneumonia when I was about three, and though those memories feel like clouds passing overhead that form fuzzy pictures and then break apart and move across the sky before I can grab them, the feel of her death has stayed with me.

Seeing the executions that happened right in front of me that day was very different. So sudden and unexpected, so fast that the thin line between life and death was nonexistent. One minute Mr. Hoover was alive, sweeping tufts of hair off the barber chair, the next he was dripping blood across the floor, half of his head gone. I crawled somewhere deep inside my brain in shock and had to hide my trembling hands inside my shirt sleeves so my father wouldn't see them.

He was probably shocked too, though you couldn't tell. His face was always like that—no expression, with his mouth pinched into a frown. My father was a lithographer at Printcraft here in the city. He would come home every night, his dirty hands filled with the rough bumps of callouses, his fingernails stained with ink and dyes that never cleaned off no matter how much or how hard he washed them. I'd never noticed the tired look in his eyes before but I saw it now. These murders had gotten to him. The truth was that he hadn't actually seen any of the killings. He was on his way to work at the time. His shock came from associating with the man who did the killing, of drawing me in, making me associate with him too. And that's maybe where this story begins. With Howard Unruh and the stamps.

I never liked stamps, not in a collecting kind of way. I didn't understand what the deal was of putting them in these big books and looking at them every now and again. But my father loved them. He had big catalogs of them all, separated by date and country, canceled, pristine, rare, historical. I could go on and on, but I won't. It's not that interesting. We lived at 835 Beideman Avenue in Cramer Hill. The neighborhood was crowded with all kinds of people and shops. It was about twelve blocks of congested chaos, and in all that mess my father found the one other person who was just as interested as he was in that old postage.

I remember the first time I met Howard. He was a tall skinny man who walked straight as if a string were attached to his head pulling him upwards, and wore the boots he'd used in combat when he killed Germans. That's what he told me but I don't know if it was true or if he was teasing me. I only knew he always had those boots on. It didn't matter if he was waiting for the bus to go to Philadelphia or if he was going to church, he had on his combat boots and a suit. And sometimes a bible under one arm.

He had a quiet face, and didn't smile much. His voice was so low and smooth when he was telling a story that I felt my eyelids grow heavy on more than one occasion. In a neighborhood that small you always knew someone by their face, but not always by their name or by their story. My father learned both of those things about Howard one day while waiting in the corner drug store to buy a soda. The two of them struck up some sort of conversation, and in a world of topics to choose from they settled on their hobby of collecting the things they mutually treasured.

After that I saw him at our doorstep many times. He hardly ever came in. He'd just stand there, book under his arm, or waxed paper envelope in one hand filled with the small squares of paper my father was waiting for. Back and forth they'd go, and that's how I got involved with Howard. That was maybe a good thing. Because if I had never got to know him the way I did, if I hadn't spent more afternoons than I could count sitting at his small kitchen table passing those stamps and seals as my father's courier, entertaining his ramblings about the war, then maybe I'd have a hole in my head from his German Luger P08 semi-automatic pistol too, like little six-year-old Orris Smith.

I thought about that a lot, especially when I was waiting on the long wooden bench by our front door, in my long-sleeved shirt and church pants. I didn't even know the kid, but I'll never forget his face now. The bullet must have hit him on the left side of his head, clean, leaving behind a hole about a quarter-inch wide. The blood mixed with his hair, taking it from a dusky blonde to dark maroon almost instantly. Then he must have slid sort of sideways off the little hobby horse and fallen on the floor because that's where I saw him on his side right below the pony's raised hoof. Then his mother swooped him up and started screaming.

I heard my father's deep voice and felt his hand on my arm tugging me up off the bench. It was time to go to the police station. When we got halfway down the block, there were so many officers in the streets, many of them walking in circles, keeping the gawkers back, talking to each other as if they didn't quite believe it themselves. Something like this had never happened before, not here, not anywhere really that I knew of. There were about eight hundred murders in the United States by the end of that year. But on that afternoon of September 6, those detectives only cared about these twelve, and they cared a lot about the man who had done the killing, the man who had barricaded himself in the upstairs rooms of his apartment.

I smelled something sharp in the air as we walked towards River Road. I coughed into my sleeve and then kept the fabric there against my nose.

"Tear gas," my father said, pulling me along to the bus stop. "They used tear gas on him to get him out. It'll clear in a bit."

The news of the shootings spread faster than word that the Japanese had surrendered, ending the war on VJ Day. My grandfather, who'd been on his way down to run some errands on Federal Street, had hopped off the bus and ran the seven blocks back to our house, frantic. He knew I was going to Hoover's barbershop to get a haircut. When I got through my front door, sweaty and crying, he was there. His face was a chalky gray color blending with his eyebrows and hair. He and my grandmother just wrapped me and my brother Milton up in their arms so tight my back hurt.

I think my father chose to walk this way to the bus stop, now that Howard was in custody and the threat had been secured, partly to satisfy his curiosity and partly to make his stand as one of the community. Practically every man in town was crowded around that intersection, looking, talking, pointing. In the ten minutes it took to walk that one block, with my father stopping and talking with anyone who muttered in his direction, letting his opinions blend and fold in with all the others, I realized that not one of them knew the truth.

I was trying to picture the Howard Unruh I knew with his religion and astronomy books all neat on his bookshelf, talking about the heavens and the stars as if those two disciplines had merged inside his head, all soft, eloquent and nonsensical at the same time. That man and the person they had flushed out of that upstairs apartment with gas and bullets couldn't exist in the same universe. They just couldn't. But they did. And the worst part of it for me was that Howard had clued me into that by looking me square in the eye as he was pulling the trigger.

Chapter Two

Raymond

I knew his name was Chief Doran because I heard my father call him that. I expected a big man in full police uniform with a gun attached to his holster, his badge right there on his shirt, or at least on the desk, but he wasn't like that. He was short with gray hair combed back off his forehead, wearing a wrinkled white shirt that was yellow along the collar and under the arms. He looked tired, like the pitted wooden desk in front of him, its entire surface covered with notes, papers and files.

He waved us in. "Come, sit down." He pointed to the two wooden chairs in front of his desk. "Now, Raymond," he began, staring me in the eyes for so long that I looked down at my sleeves, my fingers shaking. I held them together in my lap to keep them still. "I'm just going to ask you some basic questions. You just answer them the best you can. Okay? Just tell the truth, son, and everything will be fine. Got it?" I nodded. "So, I'm going to write as you talk. You might have to go slow." I nodded again.

I probably wouldn't have been so nervous if I'd known my examination was going to be so short. Less than thirty questions in all, I counted, and some of them were just repeating my answers and asking me if that's what I meant to say. I was up and out of that wooden chair in under twenty minutes. This Chief Doran didn't even know the important stuff to ask me and I wasn't going to prod him. He wanted to know how many shots were fired at the barber, who was killed first—little Orris or Mr. Hoover—and who else was in the shop. I was waiting for him to ask whether I even knew Howard, but he didn't. I'm not sure how I would have answered that anyway. The less people connected the two of us, the better.

It wasn't until the next day when I saw the newspaper my grandmother left on the kitchen table that I learned the whole story, not just my bits. Howard's kill count had gone up to thirteen people overnight—ten-year-old John Wilson died around 3 a.m. at the hospital. He was a boy I hadn't noticed, sandwiched between the two dead women I'd seen in the car. The paper said Howard did all this shooting in just about twelve minutes. It made me wonder how many of those minutes he had spent in the barbershop. Time became all balled up when I tried to figure it out. After he walked into that barbershop, minutes felt like hours and hours felt like seconds. It didn't matter. I just knew I'd never forget any of it.

The names of all the victims and their faces were spread across the page in black ink. The man I'd seen dead in the Nash, blood on his chin, was Alvin Day, a twenty-four-year-old veteran who just happened to be at that red light, or maybe went through it and slowed to see what the commotion was, and Howard blasted him in the temple. My eyes dropped from the page. Some teeny part of my mind wanted to make an excuse for what Howard had done—blame someone else—but I couldn't. He'd never laid eyes on Mr. Day before, as far as I knew.

Other than the two killings I'd witnessed, he'd also managed to take out Mrs. Zegrino in the dry-cleaning store just two doors over—shot her in the back room. She was pretty and nice, a schoolteacher in East Camden. She'd never hurt anybody. Whenever I saw her walking down the street she was always smiling. She hadn't even been married to the dry cleaner that long. I remember my grandmother talking about it just a month ago, how Thomas Zegrino had taken another wife. Her emphasis was on the word *another*. Mr. Zegrino was divorced and had a sixteen-year-old son, David, who lived with him, too. Mr. Zegrino and his son had somehow been spared.

I waited a minute before looking at any more pictures. That was four killings right there. I heard the scuffing of my grandmother's shoes on the floor and before I could turn around, she snatched the paper from my fingers.

She had on her blue house dress, an apron. Her hair was done, curled and pinned under her scarf. "I didn't know I left that out like that. I don't want you looking at those pictures." She folded it and tucked it under one arm. "Just because they canceled school on account of all this doesn't mean you can sit around all day thinking about dead people," she said bluntly. "And going outside might not be such a good idea either, unless you stay in the yard, but you need to find something to do."

I tilted my head. If I was old enough to be interrogated by the police, I was old enough to know the whole story. I was part of the story. "Who else died?"

My brother Milton came in, hands in his pockets. He was two years younger, ready to start fifth grade. "All of them died on that side of the street, Ray. The ones he could catch, anyways. Before he came into the barber's, he killed Mr. Pilarchik."

My head was shaking in a no-no way and I couldn't stop it. Mr. Pilarchik was the cobbler who had a shop right next to the barber. He was always fixing my cleats and he had a whole stash of comic books for kids to sit and read while he made the repairs. His store always smelled like really strong polish or turpentine—it was harsh and crawled up in your nose and stayed there for hours, but I liked it, and I liked when every now and then he would let me play with the big polishing wheel he used to buff out the finished products before returning them to customers.

"Then after he left the barber's, he went to the drug store. I think that's who he really wanted—"

"Milton, stop that," my grandmother jumped in.

"He's got to know, Grandma. He's going to hear it eventually. Then he killed our insurance man, Mr. Hutton, right there on the steps of the drug store. I think Mr. Hutton was in his way and didn't move or something. Then he went after the Cohens."

The only thing that popped into my mind at that minute was Charles, the Cohens' twelve-year-old son. He wasn't exactly my friend in school but we were in the same grade. We were both supposed to be starting middle school today. "He killed all of them? All the Cohens?"

"He got all of them but Charles. If you'd run out of the barbershop down 32nd Street instead of going the other way to Bergen you would have seen it all," Milton added. "They say he chased them upstairs into their apartment, shot Mr. Cohen off that little porch roof in the back. He landed half in the street, his face—"

"Milton, I said that's enough." Her voice was booming, loud enough that we both stopped talking. "If you need something to do, go hang the laundry. The basket is near the washer."

He turned and left the room quickly. He knew that tone and wasn't going to mess with her. She took the newspaper from under her arm and handed it to me. "Well, alright then, I guess you need to know sometime, and I'd rather you got it from here than your brother's gory mouth."

My grandmother no longer seemed irritated. She became very serious. "Ray?"

"Yes?" I hadn't unfolded the paper. I wanted to do it in private, where I could compare the details of what had been reported with what I had seen firsthand.

"Are you feeling funny about this because you knew him? I never thought anything about this man before, about your father sending you over there. Did he say anything about doing this? Did he ever... do anything to you?"

"No. Mostly he showed me his books. He liked to read."

Her hand was on her hip. "Are you sure? Did he tell you he was angry, or wanted to hurt anyone? Did he talk about this at all to you, Ray, because I've been up half the night just worrying about it..."

I stood up. "No, he didn't say anything to me. He didn't talk to me like that."

"Your father told me not to ask. He said to forget it, that things were bad enough. But I need to know. I don't want this preying on your mind. If he told you and you didn't tell anyone, it's not your fault. It's too much for an eleven-year-old. And nobody would have guessed he would go and actually do it."

"Grandma, I'm twelve, not eleven. And he never said anything about shooting people. He never told me. All he talked about was stamps." I stepped back and pushed the door open. I didn't want to hear my grandmother's words anymore. I didn't want to hear anyone's words anymore, not even the ones in my own head.

I started up Beideman towards River Road. I don't know why. It had been a day since it happened and I just wanted to go back and look around. Part of me thought that seeing it would make it better. That it might give me answers. Being totally honest, part of me just wanted to see where Mrs. Zegrino, Mr. Pilarchik, Mr. Hoover and Mr. Hutton died.

I fished in my pockets and felt a penny I didn't know was there. My first thought was that I'd stop at the drug store and get a piece of candy. Then I remembered, it wasn't open anymore and probably never would be again.

I flopped down on the steps of Miller's butcher shop just across 32nd Street from the drug store. Yesterday this street was filled with the sound of gunfire and the smell of tear gas. Now it was empty, and maybe because the sun ducked behind some clouds it suddenly looked sort of dark in a way, except for the hint of a light in the upstairs window of the Cohen apartment. It was creeping me out a little, like they were still up there, moving around. I opened the paper and looked at the picture of the Cohens, the two of them side by side. And then Mr. Cohen's mother, Minnie, she was there too, killed in her upstairs bedroom when she was trying to call the police. Charles lived though. Howard had let Charles live, just like he'd let me live. I wondered where Charles was, who was tending to him now that his whole family was dead.

When I glanced down at the paper again little Tommy Hamilton's face stared back at me. The Hamiltons lived in the bottom-floor apartment next to the cobbler's shop. They had a bunch of kids and Mrs. Hamilton was pregnant again. For whatever reason, Howard had pointed his gun at their living room window and fired, killing little two-year-old Tommy, hitting him right between the eyes while he was in his playpen. Mrs. Hamilton had grabbed him up and ran out back, trying to climb the fence with her swollen belly. It was a miracle she didn't get hurt. Tommy was dead before she'd even lifted him up in her arms.

In just twelve minutes he'd taken out the cobbler, the barber and Orris, the insurance man, Mr. Hutton, Mr. and Mrs. Cohen, Mr. Cohen's mother, Alvin Day in the car, the two women in the other car and ten-year-old John Wilson sitting in between them, Mrs. Zegrino and then Tommy.

I glanced across the street and suddenly thought about the Unruh apartment, wondering if it was empty and weird, like time stood still after they brought him out, and if there were tear gas canisters and spent shell casings strewn about the upstairs bedroom. Did they let him take his bible with him when they dragged him out?

My grandmother asking me about Howard, if he'd said anything to me, those words were circling around inside me, not because he did, but because he didn't. Something must have gone terribly wrong inside his head between when I last saw him on Wednesday and yesterday.

I walked across the street and down 32nd, a bit to the backyards of the apartments. I saw the policemen there, still guarding the property so the gawkers couldn't wander in and grab souvenirs. They weren't wearing uniforms, but they were acting official, going in and out of the back doors. I just stood there, hands in my pockets, then finally walked on down past the garage. I kept my eyes straight, not wanting to grab even a glimpse of where Mr. Cohen had fallen dead, his face half in the gutter.

When I reached the back of the property, I could see something was wrong. There was a fence that ran straight across the backyard enclosing the Cohens' yard and Unruh's in one straight line. But the fence on the Unruh's side had been ripped a bit and there was a gaping hole with nothing there.

A policeman, seeing me, wandered over. I knew him. It was Officer Ferry. He lived two blocks north, and was around the neighborhood a lot.

"Officer, what happened to the fence?" I asked.

His eyes flitted to the spot I was inspecting and then back again to me. "Someone stole his gate, ripped it right off the hinges and then broke some of the wire down, right here." He pointed.

"When was that?" I asked, expecting to be shooed away. "I never saw a gate back here. When'd they put it in?"

"Howard said he just put in it Monday. With his father and that friend of his mother's, Mr. Pinner. Worked most of Labor Day afternoon getting it all set. What's it matter to you, kid?"

"He put it in Monday and someone took it the same day?" I was starting to get a feeling about what had set Howard off. As Officer Ferry moved closer, I began to tense up, the same way I had when being interrogated by Chief Doran.

"Someone took it later on Monday night. It was gone by the time Howard got home early Tuesday morning. Left it just like this."

I wanted to leave, get out of there before he made the connection that I was friendly with Howard and began asking questions like my grandmother had. But this was starting to make some sense, and I needed more answers.

I ran my finger over the jagged metal. "But who—"

"Best you go on home now, Ray. I don't want you touching anything."

I was relieved that he had dismissed me, but was now even more curious than before. I put my hands in my pockets and started walking away, my fingertip running over the smooth curve of the penny. There were two things I was sure of. The first was that I was only six when Howard went off to fight the Germans. I was nine when he came home, and though it's true I didn't know him very well before he left—I wasn't spending much time with him that far back—I'm sure it wasn't the same Howard who returned to our neighborhood once the war had ended. He came back with those black combat boots on and he'd stopped carrying his bible everywhere he went.

The second thing I knew was that the installation of that gate probably meant everything to him. The fact that he built it with his father, and put it in right along the back-fence line. I'd heard most of it over the last several months. So, whoever was bothering Howard had picked at the wrong scab. When they took that gate, they'd lit a big, loud firecracker right in the back of this man's mind. And when it exploded, it took thirteen lives with it.

Chapter Three

Raymond

A gate is nothing. It's just a door that attaches with hinges to a fence to let you pass through. It could be made of all wood, or in this case it was just wire with two-by-fours all around the edges to frame it in. But that new gate at the back of Howard Unruh's property had a special meaning that had nothing to do with wire or wood. It wasn't so much the gate. It was what the gate meant to him.

The apartment where he lived was odd, let me start by saying that. That oddness maybe created all kinds of problems with no solution I could see. The building on that corner lot was a twin, meaning there were two store fronts facing River Road, with identical apartments nestled behind and over the top of each one. It probably worked well enough for the people living in the apartments before all those other businesses popped up around it. But when they did, it boxed in the second apartment.

The Cohens had the pharmacy and their apartment on the corner, so they had three ways to get out of their house—through their front business door, through a side door that led right out onto 32nd Street, and lastly through their back door into their yard and then through a gate to 32nd Street. They had control of the gate because of the way it was set up.

The Unruhs only rented the other apartment. They didn't have anything to do with the business in front of it, so they couldn't cut through the front way to get to the street. Their apartment didn't have a side door either, and if it did, it wouldn't have mattered because it would have let them out onto a dirt lot. The only way out for them was their back door. Which was the problem. When Howard and his mother came out of their house, they were stuck in that twenty-foot-long strip of their own backyard with no good option to get out to the street.

One day about six months ago I went to drop something off for Howard and we were sitting at his kitchen table by the window looking at his mother's little morning glory garden. He was quiet and I wasn't there too long. I was just about ready to go when his mother came home. She was carrying a small bag from the American Store with a few groceries in it. Her gray dress hung over her, half covered in some dark mess. Her hat, which looked like it was from the depression era, made out of straw and lace with a sad black bow, was in her hand. It was clear she was upset.

"I couldn't cross the Cohens' property, so I had to use the back way. It rained and it's filled with mud."

She looked all nervous and fluttery. I knew that if the Cohens wouldn't let her go across their backyard to get in, the only way she could get to the door was through the lot behind the barber and cobbler shops, which was always filled with water, mud, knee-high weeds or snow, depending on the season. It was pretty clear from looking at her dress and shoes that she'd fallen back there and got herself pretty dirty.

Howard's jaw moved back and forth, his teeth grinding just looking at her, but he didn't say anything. He just sat there. I started to get uncomfortable and stood up.

"Is there anything I can do, Mrs. Unruh?"

Howard had my little parcel of stamps in his hand and stood up too. He seemed to forget I was still in the room. Nobody answered me so I went to the door to leave.

"Howard, you shouldn'ta talked to Mrs. Cohen that way. I know you didn't mean it, but you shouldn'ta done it. They won't let us across their yard no more. Look at this." She put her hat down on the table.

"I didn't talk to her any kind of way. She bawled me out in front of all the neighbors. Yelling at me, 'Hey you,' loud enough for the whole block to hear. Saying I left the gate open."

"But ya told her to shut up, Howard."

"I told her to quiet down. That's what I said. I'm tired of them picking at me. Mr. Cohen embarrassing me when I go into the drug store to use the pay phone, telling everyone I don't have a job and you have to support me. Mrs. Cohen yelling at me on the street. I'm tired of it."

His voice wasn't loud. It was straight and even. I had my back against the door, watching them. I'd seen Howard's mother around, walking to the bus stop to go to her job at Eavenson's soap factory. She always kept to herself in her big dresses and coats. She reminded me of a bird. Flighty and edgy. Halfway to a nervous disorder.

"What's gotten into you, Howard? You don't even go to church anymore. Pastor Bauer's been asking. I can't even answer him. I don't know what to say."

"I just took some time off from it all. I'll go back. But I'm getting out of here now and going to Philadelphia." He stood up and walked into the living room and up the stairs. He banged hard on the common wall all the way up with his fist so the Cohens right on the other side would be sure to hear it.

"Where are you going in Philadelphia? What is it you do there every night? It's too late to be wandering around that city." His mother had moved to the bottom of the stairs and was yelling up at him. He didn't answer. "Talk to me. Tell me what you're doing in that city. Do you still have a room there? Is it drinking, or worse? Or is it a girl, Howard? Whatever it is, it's no good. We need to fix this by you coming back to church. You shouldn'ta broke it off with Maryanne. You'd be married by now. She's a good girl. She'll be at bible study…"

Howard was having none of it. He flew down the stairs past her, and me too, without a word, and out the door in his brown jacket. I left right after that and crossed the lot Mrs. Unruh had been through only a minute before. My sneaker sunk down in the mud good and I had to pull hard to take another step. I stood there looking at their yard and thought there was no solution. I only had to go through this muck when I delivered stamps. If the Cohens wouldn't let them use their yard, they had to walk across this lot every day. I felt a little sorry for Mrs. Unruh at that minute. She looked old to me, beaten down to still be working so hard and living alone with Howard like this.

Mr. Unruh, her husband, wasn't around much anymore—he'd taken a job working on a dredging ship, maybe to get away from her or maybe because it was the only work he could get. I knew from hearing my grandparents talk that things weren't good with jobs, that four years had passed since the end of the war, production was slowing down and they were afraid there was another depression coming. Some of the factories in Camden had laid people off and I saw more men walking the streets during the day than I could remember.

Mr. Unruh would appear every so often in town—I'd see him walking down the street with his hat on, heading towards the apartment. Howard told me they were still married—he was quick about that. I don't know if it bothered him that they weren't together, but I didn't see why it would. The war changed most families, with mothers going to work and fathers not coming home at all. But it seemed to me that since Mr. Unruh was still alive, he should help figure a way out of this problem.

I decided that the next time I saw Howard, I'd ask him about the Cohens. I was curious. But I never got around to bringing it up. It was clear now that Howard had come up with his own solution to his problem by putting in that gate at the very end of the yard and his father had helped him. He and his mother could just go through and get to 32nd Street without going anywhere near the Cohens' property. Pretty smart. But as soon as he put it up, somebody had smashed it down.

When he came back from the war, he enrolled in the Temple University Pharmacy program, but he only lasted some months. I'd seen him more times than I could count waiting at the bus stop on the corner in his brown suit and his combat boots for that number nine bus to take him over the bridge—all hours, but usually in the evening, probably meaning he was having a late night in town. I never asked and he never told, but later when I learned what he'd been doing all those nights, I swear I wish I never knew. It haunted me a little.

Chapter Four

Mitchell Cohen

The city attorney for Camden, New Jersey, was standing in his office in City Hall, staring out the window towards the waterfront. His eyes were fixed on the round, stained-glass window in the tower of the RCA building. *The little dog Nipper and the gramophone. His master's voice.* It was where Mitchell's eyes always went when he was thinking. The past few days since the shootings had been a whirlwind. He pinched the bridge of his nose and squeezed his eyes together tightly.

Mitchell Cohen was a fastidious man with a serious expression, dark hair and a smile that would consume his face from time to time. More than anything, he had a great appreciation for the city where he worked and lived. He'd been a city prosecutor for over a year, having served as a municipal court judge for seven years before that. He knew Camden, the population, the courts. Smart, ambitious, focused. That's what people thought when they heard his name, that and that he was known within his great circle of friends to be a worrier, consumed with detail.

Not even twelve hours before the murders he'd been at the shore, enjoying the last breaths of summer with his family, swimming, drinking. He'd returned to Camden late that holiday evening, rested, expecting a leisurely post-holiday morning. It all came to a halt at 9:27 a.m. when his home phone rang. The voice at the other end of the phone was muddled and confused, as was the city. He'd struggled to grasp what had happened.

Murder, gun violence, robbery were all part of city living. He'd prosecuted hundreds of cases like that as a lawyer and city attorney. This was different. Just the sound in Captain Carroll's voice on the phone—panicked, confused, horrified—made it different. At least ten dead, children too, the whole block chewed up with bullets. Mitchell Cohen struggled to picture it unfolding—a Mafia shootout, a domestic dispute exploding onto the streets?

But they were telling him there was no initial struggle, no fight in the street, no robbery, nothing. Just a quiet, peaceful sunny morning suddenly punctuated with gunfire. Bullets hitting children as an intended target, with no reason or purpose behind it. That had never happened before that he could remember. He'd reached the police headquarters in the basement of City Hall and rushed into the lobby.

"He's here," Captain Carroll said, grabbing his arm. "But listen. We made a little mistake."

"What? What mistake? This has to all be done right. From beginning to end. I can't have any of this screwed up by mistakes—"

"No, look." He pulled him further into the station room and pointed. A boy that looked to be about ten was slumped forward in a chair. Even from across the room Mitchell could see the kid was pale and trembling. A woman—probably a secretary—was squatting down near him having him take sips of water from a cup. "Charles Cohen. We're waiting for family from Philadelphia to pick him up."

"Oh, no."

"Whole family was killed. He's the only one who survived. They're just getting those bodies to the morgue now. He was in that upstairs apartment. Somehow missed being shot. The mistake was, we brought Howard Unruh through here without thinking—they saw each other. Looked at each other for a good two minutes before our boys pulled Unruh away. Poor kid."

"Good God," Mitchell muttered. "Charles knew Unruh, before this?"

Carroll nodded. "Next-door neighbor. Knew him well."

"Get Unruh to my office upstairs. I'll talk to him there. I want all the evidence, everything we have, on my desk. I can't wait to see this guy." He glanced over at the brown-haired child, sweating and limp, still sipping at the cup of water. "I'm putting him in the chair in less than a year for this."

"Right, boss."

Mitchell climbed the steps to street level and then circled the distinctive stone building to the main entrance. The City Hall building with the high round tower housed the city offices and the courts. The county jail was even tucked neatly inside on the sixth floor of the building, and sometimes if you were on the elevator just passing that floor the stench of human confinement was palpable.

He passed through the lobby office, and was suddenly flanked by three police officers. Once in the conference room, he dropped into a chair. A crude map of Cramer Hill had been outlined on the chalkboard with Xs clearly marked where the bodies had fallen. Mitchell stared at it and counted them. At least nine. With a circle around one X. That one must be clinging to life.

"He's here, Mitch. What do you want to do?" Captain Carroll asked.

"Bring him in. Let me talk to him first before we get this recorded." He closed his eyes and took a big breath. He was hoping when he opened them that he would see a burly man with a craggy face, someone unkempt, inarticulate—that would play well for him in front of a jury, give him a fast pass to conviction.

The tall thin man dropped into a chair at the table, still wearing a striped bow tie and a white shirt. His wiry brown hair was twisted in curls on top of his head. His wrists were neatly cuffed together. He wasn't struggling against them. He wasn't struggling at all in fact. His face was long and angled, his eyes were slightly clouded, but not confused at all, Mitchell thought. Not what he was expecting.

"I'm City Attorney Cohen, Mr. Unruh. I'm going to ask you some questions about what happened today. We're going to get a few more officers in here and get this conversation recorded on paper but I wanted to talk to you first."

The man nodded. That was all. He didn't rush in and interrupt to tell his side of things; he wasn't emotional or angry. He just sat. Mitchell watched him. Unruh wasn't looking around the room, studying the police officers or even looking at the chalkboard with all the markings on it. If anything, he seemed to be looking inside himself, unaware anything was happening around him.

"Yes," Howard said.

"Now Howard, at the present time you are under arrest charged with killing some eight or nine people, maybe more. Tell me what happened. What started this?"

Howard tilted his head slightly. "I deserve everything I get so I will tell you everything I did and I will tell you the truth."

Mitchell Cohen was sitting back observing him. It had taken a whole police force with tommy guns and Smith and

Wessons to flush this man out of his apartment and bring him in. He'd killed with military precision, without hesitation. Mitchell had expected rage, resistance, or at least silence. He was dumbfounded. "What was it that caused you to conceive of this plan to kill these people?" he asked, taking considerable trouble to conceal his own agitation.

Howard was staring off into space. His eyes were black, the pupils huge. "It was building for two years or so but it was this morning when I came through the gate that I decided." The words were flat and soft.

"Decided what?"

"To get back at them. All of them."

Cohen glanced down at the names on the paper in front of him. "All of them meaning the Cohen family, including the older woman?" He looked for names of other confirmed kills. "Zegrino, Pilarchik, Hoover?"

He nodded. "All of them."

Cohen ran his hands over the papers in front of him and took a breath. "From my understanding, you told officers you wanted to kill all of these people over a gate? Is that right? Over a gate? So what did the children have to do with it?"

Unruh wasn't moved by Mitchell's anger. He didn't even seem to notice. He went on to tell him how he started with the cobbler and shot him in the head, then went into the barbershop filled with patrons and shot the barber in the chest. It was all matter of fact; no emotion registered on his face. He talked about Mrs. Cohen screaming in the closet and how he unloaded the contents of a clip into her head. Of stepping over James Hutton's body on the pharmacy steps, as if it was nothing. About shooting a woman in the dry-cleaning store while she was on her knees begging for her life.

He talked about where the bullets landed, how he watched the victims as they died. Mitchell let Unruh tell the story in his own time, knowing that the answers would be recorded by the stenographer when he started back at the beginning again. He wasn't concerned with the answers as much as he was in watching the nuances, the stutters, the expressions on Howard's face. Every so often Unruh would gaze off as if transfixed by something in the corner, and Mitchell would nudge him to bring him back into the conversation.

"So, you're saying you bought a machete, a big knife, because you intended to decapitate the family next door? Slice off all of their heads? That was your plan? And do what with their heads?"

Unruh nodded. "Yes, that was my plan, but I hadn't thought about doing anything with their heads."

Mitchell just stared. He was talking like he was crazy, but he wasn't. He wasn't delusional or rambling, he had rational answers, but none of it was rational. He knew where he was, what he'd done. "But just a few hours ago you decided to shoot them with your Luger instead?"

"Yes."

"How is it that you could obtain revenge against the person who broke down the gate if you didn't know who it was?" he asked. "Help me to understand."

"You didn't live there. Every one of those people bothered me every day. Pilarchik with his trash, calling me names, and the fact that he flooded my basement. Hoover was badgering me all the time, just picking at me. Zegrino was talking about me, making up stories. I decided one of them took it and they were going to pay."

"You weren't sure though. But you did realize at the time you were shooting these people that you were committing murder?"

"Yes sir."

"You knew what you were doing? That you killed children—a little boy in the window. People who had nothing to do with your gate."

"No sir. I didn't know I killed children. I didn't even see them. But yes sir, I meant to kill the others."

"How could you not know you'd killed children when you pointed your gun and fired at them?"

"I wasn't firing at them. I was firing at the people around them."

"And you don't feel sorry about any of it?"

"No. I felt glad. When I stepped over the bodies, I felt glad. They've been bothering me for years."

"But you didn't even know some of them. A man driving a car—a Mr. Day—"

Unruh was looking at his handcuffs and didn't answer right away. "Once I started killing, something happened... I wasn't thinking about the gate anymore. I was mad at everyone. I would have killed thousands if I'd had enough bullets."

Cohen listened to the rest of it; his head was throbbing. He was going to finish this, push the indictments through and see Unruh put to death. "I'm going to bring in three officers and a stenographer to get this down on paper. Understood?"

"Yes."

He stood up and opened the door and waved. "Let's go."

Three officers came in and sat around the table. A stenographer was poised in the corner to begin recording. "My name is Mitchell H. Cohen, prosecutor for the City of Camden. This is Captain Carroll of the City Detective Bureau, and this is Benjamin Simon of the City Detective Bureau, and this gentleman is Sargent Wright from the Camden City police department. I want to ask you some questions about how people met their deaths this morning, but before doing so I want to warn you that this must be of your own free will, voluntary, and whatever you say in response to questions may be used against you in a court of law."

Unruh went through it all again, answering every question in the same way. "And this statement was made of your own volition, without coercion? And you understand this can be used against you in a court of law?"

"Yes, I understand," Unruh said. Mitchell checked his watch. They'd wrapped up the interview within an hour. He stared at Howard in his bow tie and proper shirt and trousers. It was then that he looked down at the floor. There were spots on the tiles directly beneath where Unruh was sitting. He leaned down and examined them further. Blood.

"Stand up," he instructed the man.

Howard stood up. His slacks were soaked through the back, and blood had pooled in the recesses of the chair.

"You were shot?" he asked. "Nobody saw this man was shot?"

The three officers looked at each other and shrugged. "We didn't see it. It wasn't like this before."

"Get him over to Cooper now. He's got a bullet in him." Unruh's eyes were fixated on something in the corner but he wasn't moving. "Are you in pain? Does it hurt? Why didn't you say anything?" Cohen asked.

"It felt like a bee sting when I got hit. Small caliber. Doesn't hurt so I didn't think about it," he answered. "I'll be fine if you want to keep going. It's not bothering me."

"Damn it. Get him out of here."

Mitchell put his head down, swiped the papers in front of him onto the floor. "We just lost our confession. Inadmissible. He was wounded and bleeding the whole time."

Carroll lingered by the table. "They'll patch him up at Cooper and we'll do it again—"

"We can, but did you look at him? The whole time I was noticing there was something not right. He's in shock or something. I wanted him upstairs in jail tonight with murder indictments to follow. There's going to be pressure on this one. Now everything is going to be held up."

"We don't need his confession. A hundred witnesses saw him do it. Chief Doran's getting them now. He's going to the chair either way."

He raced to the door. "Call Cooper and get psychiatry on it. I want him cleared medically and psychiatrically. Then we're going to do this again."

That was three days ago. He turned away from the window. Unruh's buttocks had been tended to at the hospital, then he'd been promptly shipped off to Trenton Psychiatric Hospital for an evaluation. The tangled mess was just beginning.

Now he wished for the first time ever that he could change his last name. At least in regards to this case. While no relation at all to the family just killed in Cramer Hill, he was inextricably tied to it, wrapped up in his name and theirs, and the decisions he would make over the next few months would be entwined with the name of the victims forever. It didn't matter if he kept his eyes open or squeezed them shut, all he saw was Howard Unruh.

Howard's letter to Freda, January 1945

We've been on a train for days. The snow has been falling the whole way. Moving towards Lauterbauch. Villages are empty, filled with starving. Some dead along the way. So cold, Ma. Sgt. Koehn said I was the steadiest to man the machine gun. The most stable. I don't mind and don't worry because I'm good at it.

Chapter Five

Raymond

I was huddled under my covers with my grandfather's Eveready flashlight I'd taken from a hook in the basement. Milton was sleeping in his bed a few feet away and I didn't want to wake him up. That newspaper was keeping me up. The faces of all those dead people were bothering me, and I was thinking about Charles Cohen. I had gotten my hands on as many papers as I could and just kept reading them; the pictures seemed like a jigsaw puzzle, the pieces all out of order.

Mrs. Cohen was on the floor, having spilled out of the closet where she'd been hiding when Howard shot her. She was on her back, her white shirt soaked with blood around the collar. Mr. Cohen was sprawled, face down, in the gutter. I shut the paper and tried to picture them from before, when everything was normal and I was just going in to get a Coke.

The store was always dark. The pharmacy counter was along the back wall, the shelves behind it filled with all kinds of jars and ointments. Mr. Cohen's big head would pop in and out from the back, while he was mixing his potions. Mrs. Cohen cleaned and ran the little six-stool ice-cream counter and register. They had so much stuff for sale in there: school supplies, aspirin, things for a sore throat, cough medicine, and any kind of snack you might want. Not to mention the three tall telephone booths that took up one whole side of the store. They used every part of that space to sell their stuff; it was like a really crowded flea market. There wasn't much room to walk.

Mrs. Cohen was the louder of the two, if that's the right word. She wanted everything right, but it wasn't going to be right because there wasn't enough room. I wouldn't say she was mean exactly, but her voice was sharp when there were too many kids crowded around after school digging their hands in the candy jar or the cookie bin or whatnot.

One hot afternoon, me and Bobby Shaw were there, just trying to shove some potato chips from this big wooden box near the register into a paper bag, and she didn't like it. Our fingers must have been grimy; the dirt from Farragut's boat club down off North 25th Street was still under our nails. We'd been hanging out in the water and mud all day.

"Out, hands off. Out." With that, she hoisted both of us through the door by our shirt collars and deposited us on the concrete steps out front.

Though the Cohens had a reputation among us kids, and some adults too, of being unfriendly, after what happened to them, the neighborhood was in a state of shock the likes of which I had never seen before. It was as if a nuclear bomb like the one they dropped on Hiroshima went off just down the street. All the stores and schools were closed. There were a bunch of reporters from all over the country hanging around letting people repeat their stories for the hundredth time. My grandparents told me not to talk to anyone, and wouldn't let me see my friends. It left me with this lump in my throat that didn't leave. For the first time in my life, I felt completely alone—as if the world was gone.

Even downtown Camden was closed up since it happened, as if the whole city was in a state of mourning, closed up tight, which made it harder because I couldn't get any proper funeral clothes. My only good black pants were getting a little bit short, climbing up to my ankle bones. I would have been happy not to go to any of the services at all but my grandparents thought it was necessary to pay our respects, at least to show up, given that I'd been spared and all. My grandmother let out the hem of my trousers and ironed them. They looked a little ragged around the edges but they would have to do.

Going to the funerals wasn't going to be all bad. I knew Charles's seventeen-year-old brother Leonard was coming home from the Air Force where he'd been stationed in Japan—he'd been given leave to attend his parents' and grandmother's funeral. That would be interesting because Leonard had always been, from what I knew, a bundle of trouble of a different sort. I wasn't sure how he'd behave in the middle of all the tragedy. But mostly I was hoping I'd see Charles again, if only for a minute, if only to look him in the eye so I could see what was left inside him.

*

It was a circus. The sun was shining through parted clouds that September morning. The heat had finally lifted enough that the almost one thousand people who showed up for the Cohens' funeral were spared the uncomfortable humidity of the day of the killings less than a week before. We walked the two blocks from the Columbia Avenue subway stop to the front of the building with ornate carvings drawn into the stone surface. I knew it was the right place even before I saw the sign for Levin & Sons Funeral Home, because three hearses lined the street in front, awaiting their burdens. The sight almost stopped me in my tracks.

I always knew the Cohens were different. There were a lot of Jewish people in Camden, but the Cramer Hill section of the city was filled with mostly Italians, Irish, English and a few Poles, but mostly Germans. And mostly Catholic, but not all. They would walk down the streets, in a sort of procession on Sunday mornings, heading down River Road to St. Anthony of Padua. We were Methodists, and us Protestants all walked to church in the other direction. If you were watching our community on Sunday, we were like the parting of the Red Sea, all splitting apart and going different ways. And there in the middle, going nowhere, were the Cohens.

I never saw anyone bothering them because they were Jewish, or calling them any kind of names. That didn't happen, but it was whispered that maybe they were just in Cramer Hill to take Cramer Hill money. Not that there was much of it, but their little pharmacy seemed to be doing pretty well. And people who were out of work, or scraping together coins at the end of the day to buy basic things, might have resented it a little. After this whole killing thing happened, after the three Cohens had taken bullets alongside all the other shopkeepers, you might think they would have been seen as one of us Cramer Hillers, but I'm not so sure that's the truth.

What I do know is that the people milling about outside that morning in front of the funeral home who didn't have the white invitation card for admittance seemed angry and restless. The mystery, the disbelief of the shootings, was churning them up to something—exactly what I didn't know. Howard and his bullets had made his victims into celebrities. That's what I was thinking as I squeezed through the door with my grandparents and took a seat at the very back of the room.

It was crowded and muggy, as if everyone had exhaled hot breath at the same time. I glanced around looking for familiar faces, Leonard's and Charles's in particular. I'd seen a picture in the newspaper of Leonard stepping off the airplane in some Air Force base in California, saluting. He looked the same as I remembered him—sort of like his father, solid but short with dark hair, stooped posture—except that Leonard had this funny look in his eye most of the time. Excitable. That was the word for him. He was the kind of kid who couldn't pass a full trash can without setting it on fire, always in trouble, stealing, lying. Not so much fighting—he was more of a passive kind of troublemaker. He was only seventeen when he went into the service. Now both his parents were dead and he still wouldn't turn eighteen for another month.

"Ado-nay Hu na-chalatah, v'tanu-ach b'shalom al mishkavah. V'nomar: Amayn." Rabbi Weine finally said his last words. It was over. I just wanted to get out of the door, to find a place to breathe, when I bumped right into Leonard. He stared at me for a second, fists clenched. I had heard his parents had sent him off to the military to straighten him out after years of turmoil, but he wasn't gone long enough for any straightening to take place, I don't think. It was hard to read the look in his eye, but he seemed as crooked as ever.

He put his head down, found a spot near the corner of the building and started muttering to himself. I realized later that his parents' deaths left him in a kind of situation, more than just grieving their loss. All the people at the service had separated themselves into two groups, as they do at a wedding. The groom's family was on one side of the room, the bride's on the other, with Leonard and Charles just smack dab in the middle. There was this sort of tension already building and if you were paying any attention at all that day, you would have noticed it in the wide berth the respective families gave one another when they congregated on the slab of concrete in front of the building after the service.

"Charles," I said, when I finally saw him in his dark suit and white shirt buttoned up so tight his neck spilled out over the collar. He was standing with his brother and seemed to be taking in the throngs held at bay across Broad Street.

He stopped and nodded at me; his face was red and puffy, streaked from crying, but he was really pale at the same time, as if there was no blood left in his body.

"I'm sorry… for everything." I twisted my head around to keep an eye on my grandparents, making sure they didn't leave without me, but they had found a few other Cramer Hillers and were settling in for a chat.

"Okay," he said. I saw the water building in the corners of his eyes and watched one tear plop out onto his cheek. He wiped it away with the back of his hand.

"Are you coming back? To the store, to your apartment?" I had so many things I wanted to ask him—but not here. There wasn't enough time and it didn't feel right.

"I don't think so. I'm with my aunt and uncle now, here in Philadelphia. I couldn't live in that house by myself."

I took a step back. "Oh. I thought maybe Leonard or a relative would stay with you…" Leonard was a few feet away but didn't give any hint he was paying attention to our conversation.

"No. My aunt asked me if I wanted to go back and get clothes, but I don't want to see my room. He killed my mother in my bedroom. I don't want to even see that place again. I hate Cramer Hill."

I nodded. I felt a little bit the same. "Charles, do you know what set Howard off? Did something happen between him and your parents the day before? Did they have some kind of fight?"

He shook his head. "No, my parents weren't even home on Monday. I was there with my grandmother. Nothing happened."

"Something with the gate?"

Charles looked stunned, that was the only word I could think of to describe his blank stare. "I saw him and his father putting a new gate in in the back end of their yard. I watched them from my bedroom window. And Mr. Pinner was there too, helping. But my parents didn't say anything about it, if that's what you mean."

"Someone ripped it out. Monday night. A few hours after he finished putting it up. Did you see them? Do you know who did it?"

He tilted his head a little bit, as if he was thinking hard about it, and for the first time I wondered if Charles had some part in it, maybe as a prank, or maybe just to get back at Howard for the all the misery of living next to him, and as a result his whole family had been gunned down. "You think whoever took his stupid new gate—it's their fault?" he asked. "Or maybe it was my bugle playing that made him do it, or because I fussed at him one day when he was in the yard." He was upset now; his face was red and splotched. "Do you think that was it? Because I've been thinking about it—"

"No, no." I waved my hands a little bit, trying to calm him down. I didn't want any adults coming over to see what the fuss was. "It's Howard's fault and he's going to pay for this. They're going to fry him, Charles."

Leonard walked the two paces to where we were standing and jumped in. "No, they're not. He's going to the crazy house. They won't kill him because he wasn't in his right mind. He's going to get away with it. My uncle told me. He killed them all, shot our grandmother right in front of Charles, and he's going to get away with it."

I hadn't even considered any other alternative but that he'd be strapped into the wooden chair, the wet sponge on top of his shaved head, the metal hat in place. I even pictured them putting the hood down over his brown eyes. I thought about it for about two seconds before saying anything else. "When he was shooting Mr. Hoover, I was right there. He didn't look crazy. He looked sort of... like nothing. He pointed the gun right at me but didn't kill me."

"Like nothing," Charles repeated. "He didn't kill you because you were his friend."

I shook my head. "Why do you think that? We weren't friends."

"You visited him all the time," Charles said. Leonard just stared at me hard in the eye and didn't break the gaze until I did.

"Just dropping off stamps. And he didn't kill you either." I wanted to take it back as soon as I'd said it but it was too late.

Charles opened his mouth to say something, but I'll never know what it was because just then a man appeared in front of us. "Charles, Leonard, say your goodbyes. It's time." He had a soft, wet look in his eye.

"We weren't friends," I whispered. "And it wasn't your fault, Charles. Not the gate or the bugle playing."

"Let's go, boys," the man said.

Charles gave a small wave. "Bye, Ray."

I looked into his eyes and found one answer I was looking for: what was left inside of him—practically nothing. He was glazed and sealed like nothing would ever get inside him again. Shock. He was in shock.

As I lay in bed that night, reading comic books with Milton, I wasn't even paying attention to the pictures or the words. I kept seeing Charles buttoned up in that funeral suit, all sweaty and sad. And then for some reason this memory from third grade popped into my head. Dodgeball. People kept beaming him in the head with the ball, even after he was out. Bam, bam, bam. The gym teacher didn't even stop it. He finally went and sat on the floor, his back against the wall. Nobody knew he was crying, but I did. I saw him. He kept his face in his hands and pretended he was looking at the floor of the gym. But every few minutes he'd wipe at his face with the back of his hand.

Later, when we were changing, I asked him if he was okay. He just pretended he didn't know what I was talking about, even though his cheeks were all red and splotchy. That was Charles.

I didn't see Charles again after that day. In fact, his face was fading from my memory as the years went by until one day, thirty-one years later, out of nowhere he popped up again, not in person, not in Cramer Hill, but in the newspapers. He was bigger, with darker hair than I remembered, but all those years hadn't taken that sealed look of shock from his eyes. It hadn't dimmed one little bit.

Chapter Six

Freda

She could hear them outside her bedroom window even in her sleep. The two of them were playing; the chatter was like a seesaw—James's strident voice, then Howard's softer tones would break in, back and forth. She listened harder, waiting for it to reach a crescendo, preparing to jump in and intervene. Howard, though the older of the two, was never really up to the task of defending himself, not ever. He didn't even try. Candy from a baby. They were both her sons but Howard needed her more.

Their noise grew louder, the annoying pre-pubescent pitch in James's voice grew higher and more insistent, then the softer, pleading muffled wails of Howard broke through. The sound of skin on skin, a slap maybe. "No. Give it to me." Howard's limp plea.

"James. Inside. Now," she called to them.

She didn't look out at them because she didn't want to see the red mark on Howard's cheek from James's hand, or the tears of frustration on his cheeks. It was always the same. He was so passive, it was a wonder he'd made it to this point in life. There had been something different about Howard from the time he was born, though the thought didn't dawn on her until James came along, howling, emboldened, ready to battle the world.

Her husband, Sam, always said Howard was just like her and James took after him, but she didn't see it. Howard was just meek, she thought. Blessed are the meek, for they shall inherit the earth—that's what Pastor Bauer said. And Howard would, she'd been sure of it. He just needed time.

"Big baby." James's voice came to her. "Go tell Mommy." Another smacking sound.

That was it. She opened her eyes and charged to the window and put her head out but it was dark outside, the window cracked enough that a breeze came through, billowing the edges of the curtain. No one was there. She checked the clock on her bed stand: 5 a.m. A dream, though she hadn't slept in six days.

It had been four days since Howard loaded his gun and shot thirteen people. But in these dreams, she saw him how he'd been, how he really was, despite what had happened—fragile, picked on, needy. For the past four years, the cadence of her life had been lived out under the roof of that small two-floor apartment with her adult son. Sam had taken a job as a cook on the dredging ship, and James had married and moved a few towns away, leaving her to stew in her own anxiety and fear.

She stood by the window now, looking out into the darkness, appreciating the quiet anonymity. People knew she was here, hiding at her sister's house, and would come by and yell things occasionally. The thunder of disapproval and stagnant anger reached her even through closed windows. Her sister had married Robert Wonsetler, the fire chief for the city of Camden, so his position allowed her a bit of protection. But the protection she really needed was from her own thoughts, her own guilt and utter despair that not only had she not stopped the rampage when she'd had the chance, but she'd contributed to it by doing nothing.

He'd come down the stairs in a white t-shirt and brown pants that morning, his hair askew as the curls would allow, and she knew there was something wrong, just by the look in his eye, an empty hollowness.

"They took my gate." The first words out of his mouth. His clothes were wrinkled, hanging off his lanky frame.

"Which gate, Howard?" She hadn't been out into the yard, hadn't noticed.

"Look. Just look." He pointed to the very back of the yard and she could make out the hole in the fence line. It was never-ending with the people in the neighborhood.

She'd hoped the Army would help him socialize, that having such a responsible position as a tank gunner would make him fit in, make people in the neighborhood respect him, but it didn't seem to help at all. He came back worse than ever. Distant, aloof, quieter, paranoid. He seemed to take every interaction with the people around him and eviscerate it, pulling out the entrails and then drawing a whole different picture from it than what had really happened.

Mr. Horner, the grocer at the American Store, had short changed him once, an accident, an oversight probably, but by the end of the day Howard was convinced it was on purpose. He came back to the apartment, flushed and angry, and dropped the bag of groceries onto the table.

"Do you see what he was trying to do to me? Steal from me? I liked him until now. I think the Cohens poisoned him against me."

It took ten minutes for Freda to understand what had happened.

"It mighta been an accident, Howard. A mistake. It's not that people don't like ya, they just don't understand ya." But she knew that what he was saying was true. People didn't like him. And for all his anger at Mr. Horner, he didn't have it in him to confront the man. Howard hadn't said a word to him. He saved it all up and dumped it on her.

The list of slights from the people around him, some imagined, many real, played over and over in Howard's mind and he couldn't let them go. So, he wrote them down in his diary, to count them, to keep track, to pore over them so he'd never forget.

Freda knew that instead of the war making him better, it had made him so much worse. Something inside him had died along with the Germans he'd killed. Though he'd written letters when he was overseas, he wouldn't ever talk to her in person about what had happened during the Battle of the Bulge, but he did come back talking about God and how he'd never be the same in eyes of the Lord. And sometimes at night, she'd hear him screaming in his dreams. Something in him had changed, just not for the better.

His back was to her that morning; he was just staring out of the window at the mangled wires where the wooden fence had been. They'd spent the whole day before measuring and framing it and setting it in place just right—Sam had, and Mr. Pinner, too. All three of them together. It had made her heart sing to see Howard involved in something, with his father and a family friend.

"Who took it, do you think?" he asked her.

She went over to the refrigerator to get milk for their cereal. "I have'ta get to work," she said. Hours on her feet packing soap into boxes at Eavenson's, slumped over the conveyor belt, in dim lighting, her hand motions so robotic by now that she didn't even notice when her fingers started to bleed. That's what she had to look forward to that morning. But it paid the twenty-six dollars a month in rent to keep a roof over their heads, and enough food to keep them from starving, though she didn't need much these days.

Howard was at the table, pouring his Post Toasties into the bowl and sprinkling sugar over the top, before carefully adding his milk. "It was Mr. Cohen. I know it. Can you make me some eggs?"

She took the frying pan from the shelf and set it on the stove. Mr. Cohen was a solid man, large, hulking, with one of those faces that was always scowling even when he wasn't. He wasn't always pleasant to her when she went into the store, and he was downright bad-mannered when he came to talk to her about his most recent complaint about Howard. "I didn't see or hear anybody out last night, Howard." She cracked two eggs into the pan and watched them sizzle.

"How could you?" he spat. "Your room is in the front of the house."

"Well, anyway, I don't see why the Cohens would do it. That gate solved the problem—you didn't have ta use their yard no more. No more fights. I'd think they would like the gate."

"Then who, Ma? Who took it? And why? Why can't they leave me alone?"

He was wired, restless when she put the plate of eggs in front of him. "Eat."

"It was their kid then, Charles," he went on. "I am so sick of him always sitting in that back window watching me. Or maybe it was Sorg. He was out last night, always hanging around in front of the store, bothering everyone that comes by. Probably thinking of going down in our basement again—"

"Oh Howard, stop." She pulled out a chair and sat down. "That was a few years ago when he was down the basement using our electricity for his Christmas trees—"

Howard's one fist clenched around his spoon. "Don't tell me that. He's always in that empty store." He pointed towards the adjoining wall in the living room. "Up to something. He calls me names every time I go outside. Him and that group of friends of his. Every time, and I don't say anything to him."

She took a sip of her coffee. She should have known then, looking at him tense up, angry, his jaw muscles pulled so tight he could barely chew his cereal. The vein in his forehead was popped out, and his eyes were just dead. She should have known he had finally broken. She should have stopped him, maybe offered to help find out who took the gate. Or promised to talk to the Cohens, even though it would have been as useless as the times before. And it was probably already too late for that.

She couldn't know that in just an hour and a half the room where they were sitting would be filled with tear gas, smoke and shell casings. And the street would be littered with dead bodies. How could she know? "Why'd ya leave me the note to wake you up, Howard?" She held the white paper he'd left on the table in her hand. "Are ya looking for a job?" It hadn't occurred to her that Howard had planned his rampage in the wee hours of the morning and then lay down to take a nap, leaving the note so he didn't miss the shops' busiest hours.

"Or the shoemaker. The shoemaker might have done it, to pay me back for breaking up his lumber. Him and the barber. The two of them might have ripped out my gate."

She said nothing. The rant about the neighbors was a nightly companion at dinner time. First, Hoover, the barber, started some renovations to his shop, then, next door, the cobbler, Pilarchik, joined him, piling up dirt and debris, causing water to run from the back lot into the basement. Both of them were at fault for the water problems. And it was true. Howard had broken up their lumber as payback.

She'd also seen them making fun of Howard when he walked by—especially the barber, imitating the way Howard walked so straight and rigid, getting in front of him and mocking the fact that he carried a bible under his arm. Hoover had even thrown mud at him once. A short, smart-mouthed man, Freda wondered how he stayed in business. He was always scrapping and fighting with someone. She could hear the noises from his shop through her bedroom window.

"I hate them all. And I'm not taking anymore." Howard pushed his plate to the middle of the table and stood up. For a split second, she'd been scared. His movements were quick and unpredictable. He stared down at her and went through the living room to the basement. Two minutes later he came back up with a wrench. Not a small little socket wrench; he was holding the heavy pipe wrench. He was swinging it between his hands and then up over his shoulder. His back was to her and she couldn't read him, but everything inside her told her to move.

She did. In the wrong direction. "What's the matter, Howard? What's wrong?" she asked, going to his side.

He didn't say a word, but when he turned to her, she saw it all on his face. She knew what he was going to do. He raised the wrench high as if he was going to hit her with it. He held it just above her head. His face was lightly coated in sweat, his eyes piercing. She could see that whatever he was thinking, it was consuming him. The house could have exploded under his feet and he wouldn't have noticed.

"Why would you want to do a thing like that, Howard? Why would you want to do a thing like that?" she said, all the while backing up towards the outside door. When she reached it, her back against it, she found the handle behind her and turned it, keeping her eyes on her son. He was still in the same spot, the wrench above his head, his eyes locked on hers. Then she opened the door, stepped out and ran.

Ten minutes later she'd heard the shots. And she knew. "What'd they make you do, Howard?" she'd muttered before passing out.

*

Now a hint of light was coming in through the window. She saw shadows of people on the street, starting their day. It took another half hour for Freda to make out the form of a woman across the street, just standing, arms folded in front of her, not moving. It took another ten minutes for her to recognize it was Catherine Smith. The woman's eyes were peeled on the front door of the house.

A week ago, she only knew her name and her face, no more. Now she knew so much more. Howard had killed her six-year-old son in the barbershop either by accident or on purpose while he sat on the hobby horse getting his hair cut. The woman had come here for something. Maybe looking for answers Freda couldn't give. They'd both lost a child just days ago.

Chapter Seven

Raymond

My father and grandparents were a little worried about me in the days after the funerals, as if they were waiting for me to fall apart, or talk to them about Howard. Every time I looked up, one of them was staring at me. When I caught them, they'd just mutter and look away. I kept thinking they were fussing over nothing. I didn't see anything wrong with the way my mind was working. I was back to hanging out with my friends, riding my bike to the river, or going to the boating club, or the train tracks, talking to the engineers. The start of school was still delayed so we all had time on our hands. Nobody asked me about the shootings and I didn't want to talk about it, but Howard was inside my head even when I didn't want him to be.

Little things would pop up when I didn't expect it. Like how he took that Luger out once when I was visiting and cleaned it in front of me, showing me how to take the chamber apart and how to alternate the bullets—some with steel jackets, some with lead—so the gun didn't jam when you pulled the trigger. I didn't touch the gun, though he wanted me to. I just watched his slim white fingers work over it as if he were fixing a clock, tinkering. He got so involved with that weapon, he almost forgot I was there and seemed surprised when I called his name.

I kept thinking about how he'd cradled it as if it were the most important thing in the world to him. He had a shooting range in the basement. Nothing extravagant. He'd just set up a stand and stacked a whole pile of old newspapers behind a target to catch stray pieces of lead. He was firing against the back wall of the house and when a bullet slipped through and hit the old cinder block wall, it would make this blasting sound, like the concrete was going to split apart. Sometimes when you were walking by, or in the pharmacy, you could hear it. It'd almost make you jump out of your shoes.

Nobody seemed concerned about Howard shooting away in his basement. He was just a veteran keeping up his skills. Those years right after the war ended, we were proud of all the men who'd served. We were proud of the women who served too, as nurses or whatnot, but mostly we honored the men. Howard had been in the 342nd Armored Artillery Unit, 7th Army Division. I didn't know what that meant until my grandfather explained the Battle of the Bulge to me. One of the last battles of the war, it was fought against the Germans in the dead of freezing winter in Belgium and northern France. I know the allied forces were caught off guard; it was fierce and terrible and the Americans had suffered, and many had died. Howard was a tank gunner during the battle and survived. That made him a little special.

He perched on the edge of his chair, telling me his stories one day. "We were in Switzerland near this town called Schaffhausen at the border of Germany. Trees everywhere. It was so cold, Ray. Snow up to your waist. Sometimes when the winter sets in here, it brings it all back and I feel the frozen aching in my bones." He hesitated. "It was quiet though, peaceful. That snow was like a blanket on the ground, muffling the sounds. Then we heard this clicking, clanking in the distance. The commanders started screaming. You could see the steam from their breath from half a mile away. That clanking was German Tiger tanks in the distance. Winding their way to us. We hadn't eaten good in three days. Not one hot meal. I had some frostbite on my left foot. We didn't even know what we were in for. Most of us were too stupid to be scared. Those Tigers could take out a Sherman tank in one shot. Jerrys called our tanks Ronsons. You know, like the Ronson cigarette lighters? Because one click of their guns on us and there'd be just flames shooting up into the sky. Burnt body parts everywhere. We were sitting ducks."

I was mesmerized.

"We had just a little air cover and no reconnaissance because of the storms. The sky was a solid dark gray as far as you could see, the color of a dirty nickel. They caught us by surprise. Then we got the word we were moving on. But we had a problem. This pack of boys—young teenagers—kept lobbing stuff at us. We were bogged down in the snow and we had to move. We had no choice. I need you to know we had no choice."

I'd moved to the end of my chair, my hands squeezed between my knees, holding on to every word. "So, what'd ya do, Howard?"

"Well, we waited it out, figuring they'd give up. Couldn'ta been more than fourteen." He stopped talking, just clicking the gun chamber open and then shutting it. Over and over. "This one Jerry, he looked even younger, your age. I think they'd run out of men and were using mostly kids. Looked a little like you too, light brown hair, baby face. He came out holding a Panzerfaust. A handheld anti-tank weapon." He held his arms up as if he was holding one. "He was staring us down, at all the bodies falling around him. I was thinking he would let it go, put it down, but he held steady. I prayed to God, Ray, but he was going to fire. Those things could take out an M7. I had no choice but to shoot him. I saw the look on his face right before he fell. And all the time the snow was coming down. Pine trees everywhere. If you could have taken out the bodies and blood, it could have been a Christmas card."

"Who shot him? They made you shoot him? The boy?"

His lips curled up a little bit. "We were trenched down in mud, starving, wet from head to foot, shrapnel aimed at us every two minutes. Seeing a tank in front of you blow up, body parts—"

"So you shot that Kraut? You shot him, Howard?"

He put the gun down on his desk. "I shot lots of them. You don't want to know about that."

"No, I wanna know. The one kid with the Panzerfaust, what'd he look like? You said you saw his face as he fell."

He stared at me, or through me for a long time without answering. "Like he was waiting for God to save him. That's what he looked like. But God never showed up. And I don't know why. Though he was fighting for the wrong side and all."

I looked down. I didn't want to catch his eyes. I was going on about killing Germans and forgot about his religion. "I don't know why either."

"I raised my rifle to him, and I kept thinking of Exodus 21:12. *He who strikes a man so that he dies shall surely be put to death.* That kept going over and over in my head. I prayed for something to save him, to take it out of my hands. I squeezed that trigger, aiming for his legs. Thinking he would just fall. God should have made sure that bullet didn't kill him. Instead my aim was too good and it caught him right in the side of his head. Right here." He put his index finger on the left side of his head right above his ear. "And the side of his face flew off." His voice had lowered to an almost whisper. "And his blood splattered this whole trail across that pure white snow for at least two feet. Two feet of just brains, blood and some bone."

Neither of us said anything for the longest time. I could hear his breaths going in and out fast. His eyes were moving back and forth as if he were seeing pictures in front of him; his face got a little sweaty, but as the seconds passed, he sort of came back to himself.

"I wanted to get his tags, but couldn't. But I named him Joachim. J-o-a-c-h-i-m. Werner. How many Werners do you know from around here? I can think of a few. So what's the difference between that Werner, and a Werner down on 27th street?"

I shrugged. "One was in the German army, one is American. One was firing on you." It was all I could think of to say.

"The Wehrmacht—that's what the German army was called. So, one died in some woods, the other gets to go downtown to the Towers Theatre on Saturday night to see some left-over Vaudeville act?"

"I guess it doesn't make sense," I muttered.

"But I wrote it all down, so I wouldn't forget. I wouldn't forget, and I could pray on it later. I figured it would all make sense later. I didn't know I didn't need to write it down, that their faces would be right there." He jabbed at his eyes with his fingertips. "Right there all the time."

"But you won. You won the battle. You got medals and everything." I pointed to the wall. They were there hanging against the faded flowered wallpaper, along with the ribbons and war mementos.

"Did I?" he asked, but he was staring at the wall lost in his own thoughts.

My fascination with this story was over. It was for Howard too. He put down his gun and turned his attention to the journal he was always jotting stuff in, in his quick slanted scrawl. That's how our conversations usually went. Howard was there, vivid in his telling and talking, and then he wasn't. He'd just tune out and I knew it was time to leave.

What I didn't know was that all that time he was feeding me his story and I was feasting on his every word, right in the closet behind where I was sitting was a machete. He'd bought it by mail order weeks before from the LL Bean Company, specifically to decapitate the Cohens. That was his original plan before someone ripped out his gate.

Crazy was rolling through his head when I was there, looking up to him, worshipping him. He was only worshipping his anger towards his god and the Cohens. I can only imagine what poor Charles would have done if he'd come home from school one day to find his parents and grandmother headless.

Chapter Eight

Raymond

The back door was open. I wasn't looking for it but couldn't miss it when I rode by on my bike. It was getting dark and I was peddling as fast as I could to get home for dinner. I knew my grandmother was making sausage and potatoes that night. I'd seen the potatoes and the wrapped meat from Miller's butcher shop out on the kitchen table that morning, and the only thing on my mind was my rumbling stomach and the smell of that sausage when it came out of the pan.

I might not have stopped if I hadn't seen the flashing lights. They blinked so bright in the sky, it made me jump off my bike and push it by the handlebars back to the Cohens'. The police car was parked out in front of the pharmacy, the lights still spinning and flashing, a lone officer sat in the front seat, talking into his radio. It gave me the chills, standing there, because if you looked really hard you could still see a bit of a blood stain on the concrete steps of the pharmacy where the insurance man Hutton had died. I saw sudden flashes of Hoover dead, Orris Smith's blood dripping down the plastic pony onto his feet.

Engel, who owned the bar across the street, came outside, curious, and walked towards us. He was a sort of loud man in his thirties with a big brown mustache that almost took over his face.

"Officer, is something wrong?" he asked. He'd been so proud since the shootings, convinced that it was his bullet lodged in Howard's backside. He'd told the story so many times, about grabbing his p-38 pistol and taking aim from his second-story window as Howard retreated through the alley that day. And how Howard sort of dropped to one knee when hit, but then kept moving. After that, he'd sort of made himself the honorary block captain, though there wasn't much to captain because most members of the block were dead.

The officer got out of his car. I didn't recognize his face. They'd sent someone new from downtown. "Someone called in a break-in, in the pharmacy," he answered. "Have you seen anyone around, anyone you don't know?" He reached in through the window and pulled out his night stick and a flashlight.

I looked up at the second-story windows, and for a half second I thought I saw a shadow in Howard's window and that maybe they'd let him out of the crazy hospital on some sort of day pass to get his marksman medals from the Army and the rest of his belongings or something. I moved closer to the cop.

"The back door to the Cohens' is wide open," I said. "I saw it when I was riding my bike by."

The cop came around to us. "Let's go look. Son, you might want to go home now," he said, putting a hand on my back.

"I won't be in the way," I answered. I didn't want to go anywhere.

They ignored me and climbed the two concrete steps to the pharmacy door, peering through the glass. The flashlight illuminated the store, the racks still crammed with sale goods. But even I could see things had been tossed around. The cash register drawer had been pulled out and was lying on the floor, a few quarters scattered close by.

"Break-in," the officer said. "I'm going around the back."

All three of us trudged around the corner to the apartments and went through the gate from 32nd Street as if we were all in this together. The Cohens' back door was still wide open. We all hesitated. The cop looked at me and Engel. "Stay here." His hand wrapped tighter around his night stick as he went through the door into the kitchen.

"What do you think happened, Mr. Engel? Do you think someone robbed the Cohens because they knew the place was empty?"

"I don't know, son, but I feel like I need to go get my gun."

"Do you think it's Howard? Maybe they let him come home to get something. Maybe he didn't have something he needed." My eyes shifted over to the Unruh yard a few feet away. The street lights were reflecting off the bits of broken glass from his windows, still scattered across his patio. The whole back of the house was pitted with bullets holes. I shifted from foot to foot.

"They'd never let that crazy son-of-a-bitch out of the hospital alone. You'd find him strung up on one of these telephone poles if they did."

"Like Mussolini?" I asked. I remembered seeing a picture of the Italian leader hanging from a pole at the end the war.

Engel gave a half smile. "Worse than Mussolini. They killed him first before hanging him. Unruh wouldn't be so lucky. He might even get an old-fashioned crucifixion."

I could see the beam from the flashlight bouncing off the walls inside the apartment, then everything went black. I didn't hear a sound. Engel noticed it too, and took a tentative step inside the house. I followed behind him, holding my breath. There's something about death that makes all the hairs stand on end, and I could feel it now down to the base of my neck. Three people had died in here.

I wanted to grab Engel's arm but I was supposed to be mostly on my way to being an adult, so I kept my arms by my sides, my fingers clenched into fists. The kitchen was a mirror image of the Unruh's on the other side. Sort of. This one was a little bigger and had more room for a table, but all the appliances were in the same place.

Engel moved forward, and his feet crunched on something. When I leaned down to inspect it, I saw it was shards of ceramic. "Somebody broke something," I said. The kitchen cabinets were open; a ceramic cookie jar was smashed on the floor.

We kept going through to the living room. It was small, filled with a couch and a few chairs. Pristine, as if someone was coming home. We could hear footsteps above us. "Hey, is everything all right up there?" Engel shouted but got no response. Pitch black, quiet.

The stairs to the second floor were right there in front of us, but Engel kept going to a door on the right that led to the pharmacy in front. We slipped through and stood in the middle of chaos. "If you want to stay in here, don't touch a thing, boy. Do you hear me?" he said.

"Yes sir," I answered fast. This was too interesting to get thrown out now.

I put my hands to my sides and moved behind him. The street lights lit up the front part of the shop and we could see the outlines of a mess. Then Engel flicked the light switch and I was blinded for a half second.

"Should you do that?" I asked.

"Why not? As long as we don't touch nothing. The cop's already here."

Someone had ripped out the cash register tray, emptied the money from it and threw it to the floor. I saw the quarters next to it that I'd seen earlier when peering through the window. The drawers behind the pharmacy counter were all opened, rifled through. Bottles were tipped on their sides, the powdered contents spilled across the counter and floor. The racks of sale items had been tipped over. Whoever did this was in a hurry.

Engel wrapped his finger in the edge of his shirt and turned the lights off. "Wonder what's taking that cop so long. Let's go upstairs and find him."

I said yes, but my head was shaking no. When we walked back to the living room, I could see my bike through the open back door, just leaning there against the edge of the garage where I'd left it. I wanted to keep going straight and ride home to those warm potatoes, but I found myself following Engel up those stairs. And all I kept thinking was that Mr. and Mrs. Cohen ran up these very stairs to get away from Unruh not that long ago and whatever was on that second floor now, it might be just as bad.

The door to Charles's room was right at the top of the steps. The door was open; there was no sign of the cop. Even with just the bits of light that came through Charles's back window, the big stain on the carpet in front of the closet was plain to see. The door had at least three jagged holes in it, the wood splintered all around it. Mrs. Cohen was shot right there, in that closet, surrounded by Charles's cleats, khaki shorts and school shirts.

"Come on," Engel said.

We heard the voices. Whispers was more like it, coming from the front bedroom. We passed the bathroom with a jade-green toilet and then the grandmother's bedroom. I stopped in my tracks, though Engel kept going. The bed was against the common wall with the bathroom, and the small bedstand was in the corner with the telephone set on it. What stopped me was the pool of blood, a circle about a foot across spread on the pillow and bedcover. Howard had shot Charles's grandmother when she was calling the police on that phone. She must have fallen onto the bed.

The grandmother's closet was ajar and her purses were pulled from the shelf, unzipped, open like big startled mouths. I started to shake and the big white puffy-looking flowers that covered the wallpaper started spinning. My legs got weak and shaky and I thought I might throw up.

"Come on, son. It's okay." I heard the voice and I thought it was directed at me, but it wasn't. "Whatever you were doing in here, it doesn't matter. Do you hear me? Let's go downstairs."

I saw the shadows coming down the hallway, past where I was standing. Engel went by first, then a smaller man, then the cop. They forgot I was here, surrounded by death. I heard the footsteps on the stairs and the shuffle of them moving through the living room. A door slammed below and I was alone.

I was in the doorway of the bedroom, not sure which way to turn. I had spent so many days trying to picture Charles in this apartment that day, needing to know what happened. Now I just wanted to get out of here and never think about it again. I raced down the stairs and out of the back door to see all three of them clear in the light. Mr. Engel, the cop and Leonard Cohen, standing by the gate to 32nd Street. Leonard had a look of shame on his face, as if he'd been caught doing something terribly wrong. A couple of bills were sticking out of his one pocket and he didn't seem to notice. He was just talking real low, keeping his eyes on the ground.

It took me a couple of minutes to put it all together—Leonard had come back to the pharmacy looking for money, but he didn't just use his key, take a few bills and leave. That would have been one thing. Instead, he ripped through the cash register drawers and threw them aside, tipped over pharmacy bottles, took his mother's and grandmother's purses, pulled out the contents and left them open, violated, almost as if he were desecrating their graves, ignoring the fact that if you looked, you could see the path Howard had taken that morning, and the bloodbath he'd left behind in those upstairs rooms only weeks ago.

In all of this, something else caught my attention. When I turned my head to look at my bike, so I could get on it and ride out of there, I saw the bits of metal reflecting the light in the very back of the yard. The stolen gate. Not attached by its hinges or anything, but it was back, just resting against the fence line, partially covering the gaping hole where it had once been. Whoever had taken it had propped it up in the flower bed. An act of ultimate guilt and sorrow.

I looked up at Leonard, still talking to Engel and the cop. He showed up and the gate suddenly reappeared, but it didn't make sense. He was in Japan when it was stolen. Unless he was returning it for someone else. His brother Charles maybe? But where had it been all this time? Without another word, I hopped on my bike and peddled down 32nd Street and over to Beideman. My porch light was on and I knew I was in for a cold dinner and a scolding from my grandmother, coming home so late. But I didn't care. I had a mystery to solve.

Chapter Nine

Freda

She had her bible open in her lap but couldn't even concentrate. This was the first time it couldn't provide her with any solace. Howard was going to the electric chair. There was no other possible outcome she could figure. He'd killed thirteen people, three of them children. She tried to remember those last words they'd spoken that morning before it happened, but it was shuffled inside her brain, all out of order. She wanted it to be something that would make sense of everything that happened afterwards, something that would help her defend him, make everyone see it wasn't his fault, but mostly to give her some peace. But his words fell short. "I'm not going to take anymore." Maybe that was what he'd said.

Every day, the newspapers came out with new photographs, new stories. Mitchell Cohen, the city attorney for Camden, held news conferences talking about what was going to happen next. There was a cry for blood. And with each day that passed, that cry redoubled, and found new ways of expression. People came with cameras and took pictures of what might have been a speckle of blood on the pavement; they peered into the windows of the pharmacy, and gaped at the hole in the Hamilton's front window where the bullet had passed through, finding a home in Tommy Hamilton's head.

Freda's eyes slid over to the boxes stacked in the corner of the bedroom in her sister's house in East Camden on Pleasant Avenue—the bedroom where she'd hunkered down for the past fourteen days, in the little attic room her sister had tried to make nice for her. Those boxes were the sum total of what was left of her life at 3202 River Road. Maybe it was all that was left of her life, completely.

The day before, Freda had showered, changed into a long, faded dress, one that hung like a sack over her thin shape and would make her feel invisible—that's what she was hoping for—and made her way back to her old apartment. Not alone. She'd had her sister, Louise, her brother-in-law Bob, and some people from the church to give her courage.

Bob had handed her the letter from the landlord, which demanded that all her personal items be removed from the premises by the end of day on the 19th. That's what the letter said. People had offered to go and pack up her things for her, but she had to be there. It would be her last chance to make sense of any of it, and to say goodbye to the place where she'd lived for the past seven years.

In the early hours of the morning, they'd crept back to Cramer Hill and entered the backyard of 3202 River Road, observing the destruction. She'd seen photographs in the newspaper, but wasn't prepared for the reality of it all. The stucco at the back of the house was a tapestry of bullet holes,; the upstairs windows in both apartments were shattered, glass scattered about. Her eyes lingered on her son's room, imagining him barricaded inside.

Just beyond the garage was the spot where Maurice Cohen had been splayed after being shot from the roof. She was frozen, thinking that just a month before, Howard had tended to her morning glory garden not even a foot or two from where she was standing. She'd watched him from the kitchen window, the sun beating down on his head. He'd stripped off his gardening gloves and laid them by the front door. She turned her head. They were there, by the trellis, as if nothing had happened since.

Freda felt her sister's hand on her shoulder pushing her through the front door. Walking into the house was like looking at a snapshot of time, as if she had just wandered back in and picked up where her life had left off.

The breakfast dishes—Howard's empty cereal bowl and plate—were still on the table, his spoon tipped so the curved edges just touched the bowl. Dried remnants of the fried egg were still on his plate. His empty glass of milk was cloudy with residue. It was all the same, but different. Her things had been pawed through; the trunk in the living room where Howard kept some of his belongings was open, papers scattered across the living room floor.

Freda walked past it all in a daze and climbed the steps to the second floor. She packed her clothing and personal items into some boxes and then wandered into Howard's back bedroom. It was where his last stand with police had taken place. The white t-shirt he'd used to signal surrender was lying on the floor, just below the broken windows. She scanned the floor around her, looking for empty cartridges, anything that would indicate he had fought back against the police siege, but there was nothing. Nothing but pockmarks in the walls from the hail of gunfire and some empty tear gas canisters.

Her fingers found a hole in the plaster at eye level near the closet door where a bullet had nestled. She dug in, trying to find it, her fingertip resting at its smooth metal edge. She closed her eyes, trying to imagine Howard's moments in here alone, the view of the backyard plain to see, and she was sure that the missing gate had ignited his resolve and anger. This bullet she was feeling had missed her son's head. She took a breath and a moment to revel in the miracle that he'd survived.

His bed was rumpled, the blankets tossed to the side. She went over and ran her hand across his pillowcase. If only she'd been able to get to him when he'd last lifted his head from it, things would have been different. She turned and exited the room abruptly when she saw people at the edge of property line, staring up at the house, taking pictures.

"I'm just going to get my photo albums. I don't want anything else. They can take it all as far as I'm concerned," she said to her brother-in-law.

He nodded. "But what about the furniture? I know John at work has a shed he wouldn't mind letting you use for storage for a few months until you figure out where you're going."

Where I'm going? She heard him but hadn't given it any thought before now. She wanted to stay with her family, at least until Howard was transferred to prison. Then she'd decide, depending on where it was, so she could visit. She didn't have many options. Her job, her only source of income, was gone. Samuel had gone back to the dredging ship, burying his head in his duty away from the scandal of the thing. She was alone. And now Bob was hinting at a time in the next few months when she'd be moving on with her furniture. To where, she had no idea.

"Okay, fine. I will take the storage." She didn't think to thank him, because underneath her roomy dress, her body was starting to shake. She just kept going and went down the steps to the first floor and out of the door to the backyard. This trip had exhausted her. She shouldn't have come here.

"He killed three children. What kind of a mother are you? Why didn't you stop him?"

The voice came from the edge of the yard near the broken fence. A thickset woman in a blue checked dress was standing there, alone. Freda knew her face, maybe her name; if she studied her long enough, she'd figure it out. She just couldn't bring herself to look the woman in the eye. She hung her head, waiting for someone, anyone, to come out of the house.

Then it came to her. Madeline Harrie. Her left arm was bandaged to her shoulder in white gauze. Her face was hollow and pale, her dark hair brushed straight back severely from her face. The Harrie home had been Howard's last stop on his shooting spree. This woman lived there with her three teenage sons: Armand, Leroy and Wilson.

"He came into our home," she spat in Freda's direction. "Wearing that suit of his like he was going to church, with sweat all over his face. We were eating breakfast, Armand and I. I thought he wanted something. To borrow something. Can you imagine? I thought you'd sent him over for coffee or sugar."

"Oh… I didn't—" Freda responded.

"Then I saw the look on his face and his gun." Freda started to back up. "No," Madeline went on. "You're going to listen to this. He raised his gun and fired at me. Hit my arm." She touched her bandage. "I was scared out of my mind, and all I was thinking was that I needed to get out before we all died."

"I'm sorry," Freda stammered.

"You're sorry? You're sorry? I threw a chair at him, thinking we could get out of the back, but he shot at Armand. Hit him in the arm too." Madeline walked right through the hole in the fence but stopped a few feet in. "He's only sixteen. Your son put him against the wall and put that thing to his head and pulled the trigger again. Did you know that?" Freda glanced behind her towards the apartment door, thinking of taking refuge. "Him running out of bullets is the only reason my son is alive. Wilson was hiding at the corner store with the canned goods and Leroy was under his bed upstairs, hiding for hours—wouldn't come out. Are you listening to me?"

Freda nodded. Her lips were trembling. Those three boys had tormented Howard in one way or another. She'd seen it herself. Unruly, no discipline, they'd called him retarded and stupid. Made fun of his combat boots and his bible. Followed the lead of the adults around them. This woman hadn't seemed concerned about that at the time. She'd turned a blind eye.

"They say it was all over your stupid gate?" Madeline reached for the gate resting against the fence line and shoved it so it toppled over.

Freda stared at the wire framed in wood. They'd brought it back. Whoever had taken it had brought it back.

Freda folded her arms in front of her and walked to where the woman was standing. It was warm, the humidity starting to pick up again, and she saw the sweat collecting along Madeline's hairline. "Who took it? The gate, do you know?"

Madeline backed up a few steps as she approached. "Pfft. That's the only question on your mind? What about, is Armand okay? He was in the hospital. How about, how am I? How about, is there anything you can do for us? How about, you're sorry?"

Freda reached out her hand and then pulled it back. "I said I was sorry. It's the sorriest I've ever been about a thing in my life."

"A thing? Well, I'm going to tell you this. When they stick your son in that electric chair, I'm going to be there. I have that right. I'm going to watch them plug in that machine and I'm going to watch him sizzle. I'm going to have my three sons there with me. We're all going to watch, all of us in this neighborhood that are left. We're going to be there and you're going to hear us celebrating, so you think about that." She started to turn away.

"I don't know why Howard chose your house. The detective told me that Howard had a list. Of people he wanted to hurt. You weren't on the list, so I don't know why he chose your house."

Madeline turned back to face her. "A list? He had a list?"

She nodded. "That's what the detective said, yes. I didn't know about it. Howard said people were bothering him. He told me that. All the time. Those boys that hang around on the corner. And some others. But he never said anything about you or your sons that I remember. So, I don't know—"

A look came over her face that startled Freda. Guilt, fear. Understanding. Maybe all of them combined. Then she leaned down and put the gate back upright, resting it against the fence near the gaping hole where it had been. "I'd get out of here, if I were you. There's nothing left for you here."

Freda watched her walk slowly towards the back of her own home. Instead of feeling guilty or that she'd failed as a mother, there was a little bubble of anger in her gut. She wanted to scream after this woman in the checked dress and bandaged arm, tell her that Howard knew everything about that gun of his. He'd loaded and unloaded it in front of her, told her about how many bullets the clip would hold, about alternating steel and lead jackets so the gun was weighted right and wouldn't jam. She wanted to tell her that if Howard had hit them both in the arm, he'd meant to. If he really had put Armand up against a wall with the gun to his head and pulled the trigger, it wasn't an accident the clip was empty. He'd have counted. He told her he counted. Automatically. Always.

At some point, she'd be able to talk to Howard, ask him why he'd made the choices he did, figure out what was happening with him that morning. He started out just wanting to hurt specific people. Then he lost all control, shooting anyone he came across. But at the end, he seemed to be pulling it all back together again. Wounding, not killing, on purpose. From what they'd told her, he'd never fired a bullet after he'd ducked back inside their apartment. Not even when he was under a hail of gunfire from the police. Even though he had access to ammunition, and tear gas. It was over for him by that point.

Madeline Harrie was inside her house, staring through the window at her. Freda stared back. This woman didn't have the presence of mind to be grateful that her life was spared. Or grateful that her son's lives—all three of them—were spared. She muttered to herself and turned back towards her apartment. Her mind had latched onto one thing and she wasn't going to let go. Someone had taken the gate and they'd brought it back.

Chapter Ten

Raymond

Those days between the shootings and when school started back up again seemed to stretch on longer than the whole of summer. The days blended together and every day brought something new. It was either a different news outlet on the corner interviewing, or a new dispatch of detectives from downtown combing the streets looking for information. I think they thought there was some tidbit out there that hadn't been found, a new angle, something that would piece this whole puzzle together for them. I don't think they ever found it.

It was during this time I first heard the words "mass shooting" put together to fully describe what Howard had done—the shooting of massive amounts of people. That's what I took it to mean. And though I heard ladies standing in front of Miller's talking about how this was the first time something like this had happened, I knew it wasn't true.

I was on my bed, staring at the ceiling, wondering how I was going to pass the day. The Rio was showing a matinee, and if I could get my grandmother to give me a dime, I could walk down to 27th Street and maybe sit through it a few times just to chip away at the afternoon. As soon as I got that thought in my head, my bedroom door opened and my grandmother walked in. She still had on her breakfast apron, hands on her hips.

"Ray, time to do some chores. The basement could use some straightening and I need you to run an errand for me. It's no good, you lying around like this."

I sat up and put my feet on the floor. "Grandma, why do they keep saying that this is the first time so many people were shot like this? It's not true."

"Talk about something else other than killings. Come on." She motioned for me to follow her.

"What about Melvin Collins, last year, in Chester? He killed eight people." It was in all the papers at the time and for a least a week it was all anyone talked about.

Chester, Pennsylvania, was just a float down the Delaware River past Philadelphia, and was like Camden in a lot of ways. Chester was a big hub of industry with Scott Paper and oil refineries. The town grew up around that industry and then spread outwards towards Philadelphia. I'd only been to Chester once. It wasn't really a destination—more of a pass-through if you had to. Dirty. And, like my grandmother said, not a bit gentil.

"Melvin Collins killed eight people but he was a convict. Wanted by the police for stabbing his own brother. Melvin Collins was a colored man, a negro. It's not the same as what Howard did," she said.

We walked down the stairs to the first floor. "But he shot eight people in the street from his bedroom window." I wasn't going to let it rest. "Just people walking by."

"Not people just walking by. No. He shot eight colored people from the room in his boarding house. After a fight. He had a fight with someone in the street and killed that man first. Then he went to his room. And he only started shooting at the police when they came to capture him, in a standoff. Not just random people. A standoff with police. Why are you talking about this?"

"He shot seven colored people and one white person." I knew I was flirting around the edges of her tolerance but I needed some answers. "I don't see much difference between the two things."

We'd reached the basement steps. "The difference is that Melvin Collins was dangerous and violent. He'd been in prison. The police were looking for him, had a warrant out for him when it happened. And it happened in a busy part of the city, not where people lived—"

"But Melvin lived there—"

"Over a restaurant or something." Her voice was going up.

"But I still don't see—"

I pushed it too far. A little color came into her cheeks. "It was completely different, Ray. Melvin Collins only killed people who were coming for him. He was holding them off with his gun. And it was in Chester for god's sake. Howard was just Howard. He hadn't hurt a flea in his whole life before this. Nobody saw this coming." She stopped talking, her eyes crawling all over my face. "Are you trying to tell me you saw this coming, that Howard was violent in some way?"

My head was moving back and forth before she'd finished her sentence. "No. I was just wondering because I heard Mrs. Bruestle and Mrs. Rice saying this was the first time this had ever happened, and I thought it wasn't. Then I thought maybe it was the first time this had happened when the killer survived. Melvin put a bullet in his own brain—"

"Enough about bullets and killings, Ray. It's just so morbid. I don't think I want you to know when Howard goes to the chair.

I think it's just too much. Sweep down there." She pointed to the bottom of the steps. "Then I want you to take some things over to Mrs. Hamilton for me. Help her out."

"Mrs. Hamilton?" I would have rather scrubbed the basement on my knees for days than go to the Hamilton house. Howard shot her two-year-old son, Tommy, and the last time I walked by, I couldn't look. The bullet hole was still there in the glass. The thought of actually going in and sitting there, looking at Mrs. Hamilton, made my heart hurt. She was going to have a baby soon.

"She's having a terrible time. I made her a chicken dinner and a pie. Take it over and ask if you can watch the younger children for her."

"She has little Joe—"

"Joe is only nine years old. We have to be good neighbors." She put her hand on my shoulder and guided me down the basement stairs.

Instead of the Rio and the matinee, instead of more talk about death and bullets and brains, she sent me to the Hamiltons' steps, a place worse than any violent movie, worse than any talk about Melvin Collins. Death had played out on this street and in this apartment in a real and horrible way.

The Hamiltons rented the bottom of what was a long, narrow, three-story building. It was connected to the dry cleaners on one side, then there was a little alley that Howard used to go through to his apartment, then the cobblers shop. Death row, it was.

Mrs. Hamilton opened the door. Her face was so colorless I thought someone might have sucked the blood out of her. There was pain etched in all that blankness. Her dark hair was a little tangled; her stomach protruded so far out that her house dress was straining all along the front.

"My grandmother sent me over with some food. And to see if you needed any help." She just stared at me as if she hadn't heard me. My eyes bounced off that bullet hole, still there in the front glass window. "I'm Ray Havens. Willie May Havens's grandson? My father—"

"Yes, yes." She backed up and let me through into her apartment.

Inside was worse. The playpen where Tommy had died was pushed up against the window. There was blood on the carpet, a blood stain anyway, that had been scrubbed but not completely erased. And you could see the bullet hole through the curtain without straining your eyes. The apartment smelled of cigarette smoke.

"Can I put these in the kitchen for you?" Anything to get out of this room.

"Yes. Thank your grandmother for me." She walked down a narrow hallway to the back of the house.

The kitchen was as basic as a kitchen could be. The big utility sink was filled with dishes. The table was littered with even more. There was a refrigerator against one wall that looked like it had been put there before the First World War. I moved some things out of the way and put my grandmother's food down. "How is little Joe doing?" I asked. He was younger than me by three years—Milton's age.

"He's fine," she answered. She was distracted. As if she was somewhere else.

"Do you need any help? Need me to do anything while I'm here?"

Her hand touched her stomach briefly. "No. Thank you."

"Do you need help with the dishes? I don't mind." Sometimes I did the dishes for my grandmother on Saturday mornings. I washed, she dried. I liked the hot soapy water.

"That's very nice, but I can do them," she said. But she stood where she was, not moving.

"Is anyone helping you, Mrs. Hamilton?"

"People stop by. And Mrs. Rice."

Mrs. Rice was a nervous little sliver of a woman who lived in the apartment just above the Hamiltons. Howard shot at her that day but missed. I never did get a full account of where that happened but she was admitted to Cooper Hospital with hysteria. I imagined she was almost as much a basket case as Mrs. Hamilton.

She turned and walked back through the apartment and I followed her. I was feeling kind of stupid and helpless. She stopped in front of the playpen and just stared.

"He was three yesterday. He didn't get to see it. But he was three." My arms were at my sides, my head down. "Why'd he do it? I keep asking myself that. Why'd he shoot Tommy? Tommy never did anything. Never said a word to Howard."

"I don't know, Mrs. Hamilton."

Her head jerked up; her eyes met mine. "You do know, I think. All those days you went through that alley to see him. You knew him better than most. I saw you, out in the yard with him, going in and out of his door. Tell me. Was it big Joe? Did he do something to Howard?"

My mind froze. Howard did talk about Joe Hamilton, but not by specific name. He called him the guy in the apartment. The guy who yelled at him, made cracks at him when he walked by. I'd heard Joe Hamilton myself telling Howard he should be arrested. A squabble over Howard breaking up lumber the cobbler was using to build something. Howard was angry that Hamilton was getting into the middle of it when it didn't concern him. "I don't think he wanted to shoot Tommy. I don't think he meant to. I can't guess what was going through his mind. He talked about the war so much. I think he was back there again maybe, shooting Germans, and he got it all mixed up in his head."

"No. That's not right, Ray. That's not right. He knew what he was doing. He had a list. Mrs. Rice told me he had a list, so he wasn't shooting Germans. He was shooting Mr. Pilarchik, and Mr. Hoover and the Cohens. And the Zegrinos. Why was my Tommy on his list? That's what I need to know. Tell me."

"I think it's both. He had a list maybe and he thought he was in a war. So innocent people got hurt." It was the best I could do. I was maybe the most uncomfortable I had ever been in my life and thought I was going to cry.

"None of them deserved this. What exactly did he say to you when you were sitting there with him all those days? Did he tell you he was going to do this?"

"No." I felt my insides rumble. She was blaming me in a sideways way. "He just talked about the stars. And about God. He talked about stamps and war stories and about trying to find a job—"

"About God, did he? Carrying his bible. How do you think God likes him now?" she spat. She wasn't waiting for an answer so I didn't give her one. "I am not sure you're being truthful. He talked about us. About the people on this street."

My back was to the door and I wanted to turn around and run. "Some. His quarrels with the Cohens. He did. He said they were bothering him, or trying to annoy him. Little things not big things." I noticed just then that she was barefoot and her one big toe was touching what was left of Tommy's blood. "I think I blame them for this partially. That maybe they set this off. But that's probably wrong."

"Someone ripped out his gate, Mrs. Hamilton. He'd just put up that gate so he wouldn't have to cross the Cohens' yard. That Labor Day Monday he built it with his father and someone ripped it out that very night."

"Who took his gate?"

"I thought maybe you knew. That you were out that night in the yard. That maybe you saw something?"

"No…" It was a whisper. Then silence. "I was getting things ready for Tommy's party. We'd gotten him a cowboy suit. Little hat. Do you want to see it?'

"Okay." She seemed to think this was important right at this minute.

She disappeared and came back with a hat in one hand and the brown suit in the other. There was a little holster and a plastic gun attached. It didn't seem to bother her. "That day, I was in the back. I heard the shots. I heard people screaming. Mr. Granville told me to get my children inside and lock the doors. I got Joe Jr. and Jimmy and told them to stay there." She pointed to the hallway. "In the middle of the house, in case bullets came in. Then I realized Tommy was in his playpen. By the window. I told little Joe to go get him." Her fingers rolled along the hem of the brown cowboy pants. "He ran to get him and came back. He said Tommy had a hole in his head. That's what he said. A hole in his head. He was dead. I—"

"Should you be talking about this, Mrs. Hamilton?" I asked.

"I don't know why not. It happened. Right there." She looked at the window. "You were asking about Labor Day night. There was noise over there. I thought it was those boys. Always those boys. Joe chases them out from in front of the pharmacy all the time. What're their names?"

"Sorg?"

"Yes, yes. Sorg. They live down on 32nd Street. What's his first name?"

"Carl. Carl Sorg."

"Carl Sorg and his group of friends. That's who I thought it was. Trees in the way and I never really looked. But there was noise. You think they took the gate and that caused Tommy's death?"

I wasn't going to say that because I didn't know. The gate probably didn't cause the Cohens' deaths. Howard had a machete already earmarked for them. I couldn't say about the others. "No. It could have been somebody else." She nodded slowly. I took that lull of silence to get out. "Well, I'm going to go now. If you need anything, let us know." I turned the knob and was out the door before she could open her mouth to say anything else. I'd heard enough.

I was on the street, my insides shaking, when I saw Joseph Hamilton senior coming out of Engel's. He was walking straight, but his face was flushed from liquor. A tall man with light hair and a doughy face, he passed me with barely a glance and went in through his front door, letting it slam behind him. It was the sorriest sight I think I'd ever seen. They'd had three children—Joe Jr., James and little Tommy—and she was going to have her fourth any day now. The sadness and desperation inside that apartment was almost suffocating. They didn't even have it in them to repair the window. Somebody needed to do it for them.

I didn't go straight home that day. I walked down to the river and just watched the water for a while. The boats bobbed along, some coming and some going. Life was moving on, but nobody around here seemed to know exactly how to do that. I thought back to what my grandmother had said that morning. *It was completely different. Melvin Collins was a convict. He'd been in prison.*

I'd pondered that some and realized Melvin might have been different from Howard but he wasn't so different from any other man on that block of River Road. Most of the men who lived or had a business there had seen the inside of a jail cell in their lives. One had even seen years and years. It seemed the only man who hadn't was Howard Unruh.

Howard's letter to Freda, April 1945

Reached Salzburg. Lines of POWs everywhere. They thought they had a better chance with the Americans. Not sure about that from what I've seen. Collecting as many souvenirs—P-38s and Lugers—as I can.

Chapter Eleven

Freda

The dreams started after her visit to the bloodbath on River Road. But they weren't of gunfire or death. Instead, her mind was pushing her back further, back to when they lived at 27th and Westfield in the place with the little walkway down the alley to the front door. The two little bedrooms and kitchen had been enough back then, even after James was born. She could see the white walls and their blue tweed sofa, the window that looked out over the street. She could hear the noise of the cars below, and the shallow sounds of Samuel's breaths while he slept beside her.

At first, she thought these images were coming to her because she was desperate for a time when things were simple, when the boys were little, in hopes of fixing everything that had gone wrong. But now she knew it was something else. She was yearning for her husband, the way things were when they were first married, when the boys—Howard and James—were little. A time when she had some control.

Samuel had been a chauffeur, driving fancy people around Camden and Philadelphia. He'd come into their little apartment and leave his blue uniform and a hat on the armchair by the door knowing she'd always smooth out the wrinkles and hang it in the closet. Chauffeur, handyman, taxi driver, gas station attendant, auto mechanic—or assistant to the auto mechanic—he had any number of little jobs over the years, none of them sticking to him really well.

Money was tight. Money had always been tight in her family, so her husband's lack of income wasn't anything new or different for her. Even when the economy was good—before the stock market crash—she'd had to work hard. Scrimping and saving, stretching food, clothes and household items was second nature. She could have handled all of that. It was the other things she couldn't manage too well. Her sister Louise always said Samuel wasn't the type to cheat, to cavort with other women, and she'd been right. He was too plain. Too simple. He was, however, the type to just disappear, and disappear he did on and off until he left for good when Howard was around twelve years old.

It had been a hot August morning, the heat burning through the walls of the small apartment without even the benefit of a fan for relief. Samuel was driving a cab to make extra money that night. Freda was alone with the two boys, and, uncomfortable in the hotness and monotonousness of the day, she'd stripped down to just a thin nightgown and pushed the blankets aside. She was just drifting off when she felt weight on the end of the mattress as Howard crept into bed next to her. Her patience was wearing thin.

"Howard, go back to bed," she muttered. "Your father's going to be home soon." His attachment to her was worrisome. He was always by her side, wanting to breathe and sleep in the same room with her. Getting him even to leave to go to school was sometimes difficult, with her having to linger by the fence of the schoolyard and promise not to leave just to get him inside.

He stayed put on the bed, on his back, staring at the ceiling. "I can't sleep and I like it better in here." His leg was touching hers. She moved it away. He shifted closer.

"It's hard to sleep when it's hot. Get a cold cloth in the bathroom and strip to your underwear, it'll be cooler. What's James doing?"

"I got into bed with him to read a story and he told me to get out, to get off him. He's in there now, rolled in his blanket so I can't get near him."

Howard started removing his pajamas when Sam walked in. She bolted upright. She hadn't even heard the front door open. He stared at shirtless Howard and she braced herself for a fight. "I was held up. A gun in my face. They took my cab."

Freda jumped up. "Are you hurt?"

He was frazzled, his hair in disarray. A red bump was forming on his temple. "I didn't know if I was gonna be shot—I was waiting for the bullet. I took him from West Collingswood to Hilltop. Nice guy. Well dressed with a gray felt fedora and all. We get there and instead of giving me my fare, he jumps out and sticks his gun in my face. Took all my money and hit me a little." He slumped onto the bed. "Then he made me get out and took off in my cab. I was at the police station all this time. They're looking for my car now."

"Oh, Sam." She went to him and rubbed his shoulder. "I'm sorry. Can I get you anything?"

He seemed to really take notice of Howard for the first time. "What's he doing in here again? Get him out of here." Howard gathered his pajamas and scampered out of the room. "What's with that kid, Freda? Every time I'm late, he's right next to you in bed."

"He just couldn't sleep."

Sam was on his feet and started taking off his shirt; he was stiff, moving slowly. "It ain't natural." His face was drooping with fatigue and despair. "Why was he taking off his clothes? He's not a baby anymore, Freda. He was getting naked?" His voice was going up. "Something's not right with that, I'm telling you. And you let him, dressed in practically nothing yourself." He pulled at her nightgown. "Put an end to this, now. I mean it. We talked about this before. I'm not taking it anymore."

Freda recoiled. She got up and shut the window. "Shhh. The neighbors will hear. There is nothing unnatural about it, Sam. He's fine. He just needs me is all, you know that. I'll keep him out. I promise."

He pointed towards the next room. "It's not just him being in bed. He's just always next to you, talking to you. Doesn't he have any friends? Like James does? James is out with his friends all the time, not cooped up. It's like you only have one son, not two."

Howard had a hard time making friends, always had. "He's shy is all."

"Crawling next to his mother in bed isn't going to make him not shy. Next time I find him in here, I mean it. That's it. That's it. The twisted sickness is going to stop."

That was it for that night; she was able to calm him down by rubbing liniment oil into his shoulders and icing the knot on his head. But three days later he came home late to find his son lying next to her again, and he was true to his word. He said he was leaving because of work. He found a job as a cook on various ships going out to sea and it would pay well enough for a bigger apartment closer to her sister, better things for the boys. She knew it was because of Howard, that the arguments about him had pushed him away. She had no grounds to argue. She was heartsick over it.

He packed up his clothes in the tattered brown case, gathered his overcoat and hat, and headed for the door. She remembered the way the sun was coming in through the window, making a bright splash across the wall near the clock. He only looked back at her, Howard and James for a brief second, his eyes resting on Howard for maybe a bit longer. The boys watched him from the front window head down Westfield to the bus stop.

"He's not coming back." Howard's words were simple. He understood more than he ever said, always thinking. He spent the rest of that day in his room by himself.

James didn't seem to notice. He was out the door too, right after his father. Not to talk to him or to ask him when he was coming back. He was headed to play stickball on the corner with other boys. His eight-year-old mind was always propelling him forward to the next thing, while Howard was a tire stuck in mud spinning and brooding in the same place forever.

That first night without her husband was long and sleepless and empty. Howard didn't even creep in and take his hard-won spot next to her. She was just alone as the minutes ticked by, realizing it was all on her shoulders now. Raising the two boys, keeping a roof over their heads. Providing everything they needed. She wasn't strong enough. Her sobs were loud enough to make their way through the walls but Howard didn't so much as peek around the corner to see if she was okay.

Sam did return, for a night, a weekend, but he was never with them as family again. They signed a formal separation agreement a few years later and Samuel agreed to give her twenty-one dollars a week in spousal and child support, which was a huge amount of money. Guilt money, she thought. Enough to pay for the rent, food and clothes, with enough left over for a few extras. She knew then that she might not see much of it, but a promise from him was better than nothing. After a time and with income from the soap factory she had enough money to afford the three-bedroom place on River Road. There was enough room there for everyone to breathe. And a little garden for her morning glories too.

She sat at her kitchen table one morning several years later, drinking her coffee alone. James had got a job helping out at Frankford Arsenal. Howard was working for Printcraft. She was looking around at the peeling wallpaper and listening to the endless drip of the faucet behind her, when there was a knock at the door. She knew Sam's jacket and worn black hat before she saw his face. He'd aged in the eight years since they'd separated, the gray taking over his hair, his forehead wrinkled, his skin pale.

He turned the knob and came in without invitation. She noticed his trousers were worn and patched. "Freda. I was in the neighborhood—"

"No you weren't, Sam."

"Well, I came to give you money. I don't have twenty-one dollars this week. But it's something." He laid a ten and two ones next to her plate. "How long are you going to hold me to this? The boys are nearly grown."

"You left me, Sam. Not the other way around." She got up and poured coffee into a cup and gave it to him. "Here, for your time and trouble."

Sam pulled out a chair and sat down. "I had to get out, Freda. I had to. We weren't getting along. No money, scraping by, fighting about the boys all the time…"

She didn't answer. "Don't bring your unnatural thoughts about Howard into my house. Everyone suffered with you gone. You cheated all of us. The plans we had…"

"They wouldn't have happened anyway, with the depression. The whole world's suffering. You think you're special? And since you mentioned Howard, does he have a girlfriend? Is he doing anything normal?"

She put her cup in the sink. "He's working. Is that normal enough for you?"

He came up behind her and placed his hand on her shoulder. "He might be working, but is he normal? You need him as much as he needs you. Always have. More than you needed me. There was something between you two that left me and James out in the cold. That was the problem. You were too weak to set him straight because there was something wrong with you too. You know it's true."

She was staring the sink. She couldn't admit out loud that he might be right, so she just nodded. "Maybe you were never the father he needed. You ignored him. He was too quiet, not enough of a boy for you, so he turned to me."

He waved his hand at her. "No, no. I was gone making a living. And besides, James turned out just fine," he added.

"They both did," she responded.

He shrugged. "Kid was in your bedroom until he was around fourteen years old. Talk to Pastor Bauer about that." With that he opened the door and walked out. She watched him, slightly stooped as he rounded the corner and headed for the gate.

In those dreams that were coming to her now of their old apartment on Westfield with the dingy walls and the old blue sofa, there was some comfort of a time before that night when

Sam was robbed, before that night he'd come home to find Howard with her, when her husband slept in her bed and shared her life. When they'd stay awake cuddling, making plans for their life together of buying a house in Haddonfield where he'd been born, of having a garden, walking their children to school. He was going to start a trucking company. She was going to get a job in an office.

Now she was waking up and finding herself in the attic room at her sister's house, her son miles away in a psychiatric hospital, her husband hiding out on a dredging ship, ducking away from any responsibility for what had happened. It made her weep.

Chapter Twelve

Raymond

I heard on the radio that school would be starting in a few days. Veteran Memorial Jr. High School, that's where I was going. Seventh grade. Vets was a little over six blocks from my house so my friends and I had it all planned, how we'd all meet at 30th and Hayes and walk together on the first day—before all this shooting stuff happened, that is. Milton was still at Sharp School so we'd be separated and I was a little happy about that. I felt I had grown up, was ready to be with my own friends.

My grandmother had washed and pressed my three sets of school clothes and had them ready for me. My lunch box was sitting empty on the counter. Now, two weeks later, my clothes were still sitting there, folded in my dresser. My lunch box was still in the same spot in the kitchen. The hysteria, the aftermath, the community reconciliation and restoration were all too much for anyone to think about starting school sessions right now. They needed to make sure everyone was safe.

That idea of safe was all about being physically secure, not really mentally secure because the truth was that the mentally secure part might never come. Just that day, Jennie Marsh and Marie Deaner, girls around Milton's age, were heading north down 32nd Street ahead of me. They were too far away for me to know what they were saying, but I sure heard them when they got right around the Cohens' garage, near where Mr. Cohen died. The screaming that came from the two of them scared the dogs in the neighborhood. Everyone came running, including Mr. Engel and his gun.

When I got closer, I saw them shaking. Not just a little, but their whole bodies, just rattling, and they were shrieking like they were being bludgeoned through with a knife. After a minute, I saw what it was all about. A piece of gum. Gum that was a dark pink color that had maybe been not so hard when it was spat out onto the concrete, so that it splattered a little bit. They were convinced it was a blood clot. I couldn't make this up. It only took half a second and a good pair of eyes to know what it was, but Jennie and Marie had convinced themselves it was a piece of Mr. Cohen's innards.

I couldn't laugh out loud because it was all too serious with Mr. Engel and Mr. Fuller from next door, standing there with their foreheads all scrunched up and folded arms. Ronnie Dale came running down the street, a look of terror on his face, but when we locked eyes, we couldn't help but crack a smile. I don't know what either of those girls would have done if they'd seen that bloodbath in the upstairs of the Cohens' apartment. They needed a circle of support after seeing a reddish spot of gum on the sidewalk!

Ronnie was three years younger than me, so we didn't run in the same circles. I hadn't seen him at all since the day of the shootings, but I had thought about him some. Ronnie was one of the only other kids who had witnessed death up close that day. He actually saw it before anyone else because he was in the cobbler's shop when Unruh came in and fired his first shots.

I plopped down on the front steps of the Harries' house and moved over and gave him enough room to sit next to me. The two of us were staring over at the Unruh's backyard, just letting it all sink in. "It's hard walking past here every day," Ronnie mustered. He had his cleats tied around his neck, probably coming back from a game of ball at Sharp School.

I just nodded.

Ronnie shook his head. "I didn't even see him. My parents and the police kept asking me that over and over. I was there in the cobbler's shop but I didn't even see what happened."

"No?" I asked, thinking I wished I hadn't seen it.

"I was there, in the shop, reading my comic book, thinking I was gonna go next door to the barbershop when he walked by. I saw his boots go right past me."

I winced. "You didn't hear it? The gunfire?"

He shook his head again. "I don't remember it. If I did, I thought it was something else. But when I stood up, I saw the cobbler just lying there with this black hole in the middle of his head, and blood everywhere on the floor."

I was feeling a little sick about this conversation. I'd seen it too, after I'd circled the block and come back around. The back of Mr. Pilarchik's head had opened up where the bullet came out. The blood and bits had sprayed all over the polishing wheel where I'd sat a million times helping the cobbler finish a product.

"Remember when he built that shoe shop this summer?" he asked.

I nodded. It was hard to realize that he'd only been in business for a couple of months before the shooting. He, his two brothers and his father took that patch of dirt on River Road and built that little store over a period of three or four weeks just as the days were beginning to get hot. They'd be working, pouring cement or whatnot, laughing and talking. The ladies in the neighborhood lined up to drop off all the shoes they had lying at the back of the closet when he first opened. I just remember him standing behind the counter with his apron on that day, smiling.

"Why'd he do it, Ray? You know him better than most people," Ron asked.

I squinted into the sun and tried to think how to answer that. I don't know exactly how the problems started between Howard and the cobbler. It had something to do with Mr. Pilarchik piling dirt into the rough lot behind his shop during construction, which then blocked Howard's only exit and entrance into his apartment. Mr. Cohen had banned him from using the entrance to 32nd Street, and then the cobbler made it harder for Howard to use the side gate to get out to River Road.

One day on my way through the back to Howard's, I climbed through a pile of loose dirt and saw the lumber and what was left of some building project behind the cobbler's shop. It was a mess, and I was covered in dirt, almost ruined my shoes getting to the Unruh yard. But the real mess yet to be seen was inside the Unruh basement. The water that used to drain into the street was now draining into their basement. I'd stood on the third step from the bottom and surveyed the puddled water across the cellar floor. It wasn't completely submerged, but it was wet and smelled like mold.

"My mother's getting sick from this," he'd said, motioning for me to follow him back upstairs. "The constant moisture."

"I dunno," I said. It didn't help but I couldn't think of anything better. He was right about the water, but the construction was done. "Maybe ask Mr. Pilarchik to do something so the water drains better. Have you talked to him about it?"

"There's no point."

Howard would get so mad about something, thinking people were doing things to him on purpose, but wouldn't take the easiest way to a solution. "He's nice. If you showed him the basement, I bet he'd offer to help. Maybe your mother can tell him it's making her sick."

But Howard thought of a better way to get his point across. He went behind the cobbler's shop and started breaking up his lumber one morning. Just taking the two-by-fours and smashing them with a hammer, banging them and then taking this saw that was there and cutting them up. Everyone saw him—the barber, Thomas Zegrino, Mr. Hamilton. Pieces of broken wood were everywhere. So, they said something to Howard about it, like somebody ought to put him in jail for destroying property. And that was it. That was the only part of the whole thing that Howard latched on to.

I don't remember the cobbler doing anything specific to Howard on a regular basis, not outwardly, but when he was part of the circle of men, the shopkeepers, standing out front, he threw a few words—Nancy boy or queer—his way. There were a few taunts about how he looked, or where he was going, about how he walked. Maybe he just stood there with the other men and laughed, his soft little cackle approving of the harassment. And for Howard that was probably enough.

"I should be in jail, that's what they said to me, for protecting my mother from getting sicker. They've all been in jail, but I should be the one in jail for touching that lumber?" Howard's face was red; he was sweating.

"Do you want me to talk to Mr. Pilarchik for you? I can ask him about the water," I offered. "I can tell him why you broke his lumber. Try and fix it."

"No. I'm not explaining anything to them. That cobbler needs to go dry out in a cell."

I knew what he meant, though nobody ever talked about it. Mr. Pilarchik had a past. He'd served in the war, as a medic in the Pacific, and was decorated and all. He came home and had a hard time figuring out what to do next with his life. Sort of like Howard. So, he started to drink a lot. This was before he had the shoe service shop on River Road.

When his drinking had got bad enough, he was caught driving his car drunk, and it all came to a head. He plowed his car into something or someone, and spent some time in the county's City Hall sixth-floor jail cell, drying out. I don't know if it happened more than once. It might have. He had a rough time of it. When you live in a small town, everybody knows the bad things about you. It's like stored common knowledge people pull up when they need to. But Mr. Pilarchik never gave anybody a reason.

"I don't know why Howard shot Mr. Pilarchik," I said to Ronnie. "I don't know. I guess in his mind it made sense. It was a lot of things, and maybe he thought Mr. Pilarchik was making fun of him or that he stole his gate."

"My parents said he didn't."

I looked up at him so fast my neck bones cracked. "How do they know that? He mighta been mad that Howard broke his lumber."

"I heard my dad talking about it. He said it was the Cohens."

"Mr. and Mrs. Cohen?"

He shrugged. "That's what he said. He said that's what you get when you keep picking on a crazy man. My father said he heard Mrs. Cohen bawling Unruh out, right on the sidewalk on the side of the house when he walked by. He said no man should be talked to that way, let alone in public."

"Oh." I scuffed my shoes on the sidewalk.

Ron got up and walked towards the back of the Cohens' garage. He picked up a pebble and threw it towards Charles's window. It made a little pinging sound and fell onto the roof. "And Mr. Pilarchik didn't live here. Someone took the gate late at night," Ron went on. "He would'a had to walk or drive, break the gate in the dark and then go home."

"You think?" I asked.

He picked up another stone and tossed it towards Unruh's broken back window. It missed and hit the wooden frame. "I think whoever did it, they paid. My father thinks all the people that bothered Howard, every single one of them, paid in some way for what they did."

"Maybe," I answered. "Maybe they did."

He walked towards the sidewalk in search of another stone and stepped right on the splatted gum. He turned his foot over and inspected it. "The only one who isn't going to pay? Howard Unruh. He's going to sit in that hospital forever."

I was beginning to agree with him. We parted ways that day and hardly ever spoke again, though I thought about Ron Dale all the time. We'd see each other walking, or in the neighborhood and nod, like a secret handshake, and maybe that was enough. I felt as if there was more said in that quick dip of the chin than most people say to each other their whole lives. Just knowing he was there was good.

I remember John Pilarchik's funeral procession that went right down River Road in front of his shop, specifically at his family's request, the Friday after the shootings. The hearse rolled by, flowers and cars and cars. Everyone in the community was out on the sidewalk watching, still in shock over what had happened. I stood right by the Hamilton's apartment, watching it all, and I couldn't help but notice that those broken pieces of lumber were still lying by the side of the cobbler's shop as the cars went by. I thought it was odd that nobody had cleared them away.

The hobby horse in the barbershop with a ring of blood around the base, the hole in the Hamilton's front window, the broken lumber by the side of the cobbler's shop, the rickety broken gate just leaning up against the Unruh fence line—it was all a story that was being told as those funeral cars crawled by, but I'm not sure anyone was paying attention.

Chapter Thirteen

Freda

He was just a baby in the photograph, not more than four months old. She held the picture in her hand, letting her eyes wash over the graininess. The pastor had snapped that on a cold April morning after church. Howard's eyes were closed, his head was forward, and you could barely see his chubby features. Her mother had made the hat for him out of leftover yarn. You couldn't tell in black and white, but it had been a pale shade of gray-blue, which matched his eyes.

She remembered her sister telling her that all babies were born with blue eyes, that they'd change, and they did, taking on a brownish hue as he approached his toddler years. But that day his eyes were a deep slate, and the older women in church took turns holding him and cooing appropriately. Freda's eyes held fast onto the image, staring at the tiny curled hand just visible at the edge of the photo.

She pulled it closer and examined it. The thumb was exposed, the fingers folded underneath. Her mind flashed forward twenty-eight years to that same right hand holding a wrench above his head, ready to strike her dead. She dropped the picture onto the album and turned away. The look in his eye that morning was burned into her brain. He wasn't angry or vengeful. It wasn't a moment of passion or rage. What she saw was nothing. He was empty.

She grabbed her bible from the bedstand and walked down the stairs quietly, hoping not to see her sister. She needed to walk and think. Her timing was bad. When she got to the bottom of the stairs, she saw Louise, just at the edge of the foyer, talking to two men. Both were wearing dark trousers, and buttoned-up shirts, but just from the way they were standing, carrying themselves, she knew they were policemen.

"Oh, Freda," Louise said. "I'm glad you're up. These detectives are here to talk to you."

The younger one was wearing a white shirt; his light brown hair was cut close to his head. "Detective Mulligan, ma'am. We just have a few questions, if you don't mind."

She clutched her bible harder and nodded. She led them to the living room and sat down, Freda in the single chair, the two men on a sofa across from her.

"I'll make coffee?" Louise said and disappeared. From the look on her sister's face, it was clear she was uncomfortable. Her husband was the fire chief for the city. Having detectives come to the house on real business had ruffled her a little.

"Do I need to call Pastor Bauer? He's been with me since this happened. I'd like him to be here—"

"I'm Detective McLaughlin." The older one, with a flattened rough face, was speaking now. His shirt was wrinkled and he looked tired, almost bored. "No need for that, ma'am. This will be short, we promise. You haven't done anything wrong. We had a chance to look through your son's—"

"Howard's—"

"Howard's diary and papers. A few questions. Did you ever read his diary, or did he read it to you? Were you aware of it?"

Her eyes half closed. Of course she knew of it. He'd read parts of it to her at dinner sometimes. Filled with rambling thoughts. Things that had happened to him, about people in the neighborhood. "I never read it," she answered. That was the truth. "I knew he had it, but I never read it."

"Did he talk to you about it?" McLaughlin continued. "About the diary or the things he wrote in the diary?"

"Either one," the younger one chimed in.

"He told me some things. About how he felt about the people in the neighborhood."

"Anything else?"

She swallowed hard. She needed Pastor Bauer here to guide her. "Like what?"

"Anything at all."

Freda lifted her head and looked him in the eye—something that wasn't always easy for her. "He felt trapped in our apartment. Every time he left lately, someone was bothering him."

"So, the reason we're asking questions is because his diary is interesting. If you look at it really good, you can see this… this… escalation in the way your son was thinking, of taking revenge. And we wanted to know what you saw."

"What I saw was an escalation as you call it, in the way people treated my son. That's what I saw. The cobbler was throwing garbage at us. Well, maybe not at us, but dumping it over our fence. And—"

"We didn't come to rehash his problems in the neighborhood. He had a kill list, Mrs. Unruh. Eleven people were on it. Did you know that?"

She shook her head. "I don't believe it. You're saying things and he can't defend himself."

"Some he killed, some got away, like the rest of the Zegrinos, Latela the sandwich shop owner next to the dry cleaner, the Hamiltons, Carl Sorg, they escaped."

"Nobody escaped." It was a bit louder than a whisper. "Mr. Zegrino lost his wife. Latela probably lost his shop, the Hamiltons lost their son. Sorg, well, maybe he escaped," she said.

"What do you know about this Sorg?" McLaughlin asked.

Freda looked to the side and saw her sister enter with her little special tray, with the good cups and saucers that had belonged to their mother, a sugar bowl and creamer and a small plate of cookies, carefully placed. Louise put it down and scuttled off. The men didn't really even look at it.

"Sorg. What do you want to know? He used the empty store in front of our apartment as his second home. He was always in there. Him and his friends."

"Doing what?"

"Bunking, troublemaking. That's what."

"Such as?"

Freda shrugged. "He lives down 32nd Street across from Sharp School. His father died a few years back. Left the mother with a couple kids—three I think—to raise alone. What is he, eighteen, nineteen now? He's no good…"

"Why do you say that, Mrs. Unruh?"

"Always on the corner in front of the pharmacy, making wise cracks at everyone that goes by. Mean. Would call me a bird when I walked by. 'You old bird,' he'd say. Laugh when I had to cut through the alley across that lot to get home. He was in the store front and in our basement. All the time."

"In your basement? How'd he get into your basement?"

Freda was getting exasperated now. "From the store. There's a door in the store that lets you down to the basement. It made Howard so mad. It's our basement. He shouldn'ta been down there. A few years back he used our electricity for lights for the Christmas trees he was selling. Without asking."

"Can you tell us about the night before? About Labor Day. Everything you can remember from that night before."

She took a deep breath. The afternoon before had been filled with morning glory gardening, grass-cutting, iced tea and sandwiches. "Howard built the gate with his father and Mr. Pinner all day. You know that. They finished up and Howard cleaned up to go to Philadelphia—"

"Why was he going to Philadelphia?"

Her stomach tightened. "To go to the movies. To the Family Theatre, I think. To see a picture."

"Why didn't he just go down to the Rio five blocks away?"

"I don't know."

"He went there quite a bit. To Philadelphia?"

She nodded. "Number nine bus."

"Did you ask him why he was going all the time? It wasn't just to go to the pictures, was it?"

"He was in school—"

"But he wasn't in school, Mrs. Unruh. Not for over a year. Yet he went to Philadelphia at night four or five times a week, at least. What was he doing?"

Her stomach clenched harder. "Seeing friends, I suppose."

"What friends? Do you have names?"

Her fingers started playing along the closed pages of her bible. "No. He didn't tell me their names."

"And he'd been renting a room. On Clinton Street, across from Jefferson. It cost him thirty dollars a month to keep that room. He was paying that all the way up until last month."

Her mind was spinning. The rent on their apartment on River Road, for five rooms, was only twenty-six dollars a month. She paid that herself with money she made at the soap factory. She didn't really ask him for money much because he didn't have a job.

"For months he kept that room. And he wasn't in school. He was—" The younger officer had started to speak when McLaughlin put his hand on his arm and stopped him.

"Maybe he just needed privacy. He's grown," she said.

"The Luger wasn't a war souvenir. He bought it, the one he used in the killings, in a store in Philadelphia. For," McLaughlin flipped through some papers in his lap, "thirty-seven dollars and fifty cents. He also bought a tear gas pen and some cartridges. And he ordered a machete from the Bean Company and had it delivered to your house on River Road. Were you paying attention to any of this?"

She cleared her throat, her eyes landing on a photograph Louise had on a table across the room. Her daughter Roberta, son Robert, Howard and James on one Christmas, taken twenty years before. The cousins were all in row in front of the Christmas tree. Howard was smiling.

"He's not ten years old. He's a decorated war hero. He was allowed to buy a gun if he wanted one. None of that was illegal. Was it?" She shifted in her seat and her long dress stuck to her legs.

"Not illegal. No. But given what happened, we're just wondering if you noticed these things, questioned why he ordered a machete, saw the guns in the apartment—and apparently he had quite a few up until recently. Did you hear him shooting in the basement, read his diary where he said he wanted to decapitate your neighbors? Anything at all?"

Freda felt her face go red. Her fingers were running along her bible. She wanted these men to leave. "No. I did not. I did not notice. I did not know about the machete. I didn't read his diary. I did not."

The two glanced at each other and let the moment hang in the air until it was uncomfortable. "Hmmm. Okay," McLaughlin said. "Moving on. Back to the night before the incident, then."

"There was noise outside the night before," Freda jumped in. She didn't want to talk anymore about Howard's secret life. She had a sick feeling about it. "After everyone left, I was upstairs in my room in the front. Plenty going on at Engel's. The music. People were walking around. Sorg and two of his friends were out in their usual spot. They had some sort of firecrackers. I saw them from my window."

"Did you see out back at all?"

"I went down to get some milk, for my stomach, and I saw boys out in the back. Charles Cohen, I think. And the Harrie boys. Near the fence line. But I didn't pay much attention."

"When you say near the fence line—"

"Charles was over near his garage. Further that way. The Harrie boys were just leaning on the fence near him, talking. Or maybe not leaning on the fence at all. Maybe the Harrie boys were just talking to each other and were further away. I didn't pay it that close attention."

"Were they touching the fence? The gate? Any of them?"

"You think they ripped out Howard's new gate? I can't say I saw anything at all. I would've told Howard if I had."

"We don't know if they did. We're investigating its return. That's all. Did you get along with the Harries? Any reason those boys or Mrs. Harrie might want to take the gate?"

"I can't imagine any reason at all. I barely talked to them." She thought about Madeline Harrie by the property line, her right arm bandaged, a look of hatred on her face.

"Where are you going from here, Mrs. Unruh? Have you decided? Or are you staying on with Bob and Louise for a while?"

"That depends on how long all of this takes with Howard. When are they going to kill him, do you think? How long will it take? Months? Or years?"

The two men looked startled. "Less than a year, when things start moving forward like they should. He'll be transferred to Trenton State Prison when they are finished with their psychological evaluation. The execution would take place there." Freda was silent. "Most likely by electrocution."

Her eyes were filling up and she didn't want them to see. "Is that painful?"

The two men stood up together. "Depends how you look at it, Mrs. Unruh," the young one said. "No more painful than getting a bullet in the back and falling into the street like Cohen, but probably hurts less than getting a bullet in the neck and bleeding out over a whole night in the hospital like little John Wilson."

"If you remember anything about Howard, anything at all about his activities, call us?" McLaughlin said. "We'll be in touch."

There were no more words as they walked out the door and shut it behind them.

Chapter Fourteen

Mitchell Cohen

Mitchell Cohen sat in a conference room at City Hall. He could hear the noise from the street through the window. Most of it was general street noise but he could hear reporters too, camped out, waiting for word about Unruh's fate. "It's the blood and the machete. The blood and the machete. I have to keep reminding myself of that," he said. "I wish I could scream it from the rooftops to make everyone understand, because they don't."

Dr. Robert Garber sat across the table with a stack of papers in front of him. His eyes were an angry red, his shirt was wrinkled. "This has been the most stressful three weeks of my life, I have to say. I want to go through these reports with you. Give you a glimpse into who this guy really is, Mitch, before you make a decision about anything."

Four psychiatrists had been studying Unruh for weeks. Mitchell Cohen had been waiting for the reports. Three weeks now, just sitting on thirteen murder indictments, imagining the press as they brought Unruh into City Hall and up the elevator to the jail, hands cuffed behind his back.

After that first meeting with Unruh, Mitchell Cohen realized his murderer might be more fit for the psychiatric hospital than the electric chair. As much as he didn't want to admit it, he was going to have a hard time explaining the blood on Unruh's pants and the sharpened machete hidden away in the closet, to a jury. He had no doubt he could do it if he had to, but that dull expression on Unruh's face was always right there with him. It bothered him.

"So, we met with him on September eighth, that Thursday after the shooting. Me, Yaskin, Spradley and Bennett," Garber said. He was talking about the four most prominent, respected psychiatrists in the area. "We gave him hours to talk, no sodium amytal. So, Dr. Yaskin asked him if he thought the death penalty was a just punishment for stealing a gate." He looked up. "This gate seems to be the crux of the whole thing. He kept coming back to it over and over, and no matter how much we circled around it, he wouldn't let it go." Garber pointed his finger up towards the ceiling. "This is important. He said their actions against him had been escalating, so he had to escalate too."

Mitchell folded his hands in front of him. "Good Lord. They never hit the man, physically attacked him. Nothing."

"Exactly, but then he deteriorated into this skewed logic, paranoid thought process about people giving him the wrong change on purpose, about disparaging his character. Name-calling. He was so afraid of these people knowing something about him, learning his secrets, that he became fixated on it in every interaction with them."

"Go on. Then he bought the knife."

"At the Bean Company. Mail order. This machete, he had it for over a year, just sitting in his closet. He can't fully explain what he was thinking, but he talked at length about cutting off the Cohens' heads. Now he doesn't mention the boy, Charles, in any of this so I don't know if he intended Charles to keep his." He chuckled at the bizarreness.

Mitchell was getting fidgety. He stood up and started to pace. "Garber, do you think he's feigning any of this? That he just wanted to kill people and now he's just acting like he's crazy so he won't go to jail or be prosecuted? Is that possible? Did you get the interviews with any of those neighbors?"

Garber shifted his papers and pulled out another file. "We did get the interviews conducted by the police. They were exhaustive. They interviewed anyone who was willing. I'm going to say this. Cramer Hill is a crowded working-class neighborhood. The average person there has an eighth-grade education. They work in trades, or in factories. They line the floors of RCA and Campbell's. They drive trucks and open small businesses, if they're lucky."

Mitchell nodded. "You're describing most of Camden. Nothing wrong with that. What's your point?"

"My point is that the people interviewed were worried about their next meal or making the next rent payment. They knew Unruh was odd. But they didn't stop to examine his oddness. It was the same commentary over and over. Weird, kept to himself, quiet. They didn't have much corroborative information to lend to this evaluation because Unruh didn't cause any commotion, no drama at all. And they were too busy to care."

"That's what bothers me. There was no escalation. It was just an explosion out of nowhere. No sign, no hint anywhere. No call for help from his mother. No red flags, nothing in his military record. Nothing."

"Exactly."

"And his mother?" Mitchell asked.

"I'd love to do a Wechsler[1] on her. Get an IQ. She absolutely has a nervous disorder. She admitted she was sometimes afraid to leave the house. She felt the neighbors were looking at her, judging her for various reasons."

Mitchell ran his hand over his face. "Sounds familiar. Apple didn't roll far from the tree."

Garber shook his head back and forth, contemplating his next words. "Yes and no. Freda Unruh has no psychotic processes in her thinking that I could see. She's just anxious. And so enmeshed with her son. Neurotic, absolutely. There's a bit of an incestuous feeling to their relationship, I must say."

"Meaning?"

"Well, under sodium amytal he speaks of touching his mother intimately, of sleeping in her bed, of wanting to have sex with her. But of hating her at the same time."

"He was having sex with his mother?" He was flabbergasted.

Garber flipped some pages. "No. I wouldn't say that. And I'm not sure how much is his imagination. There were blurred lines, I am quite certain of that. How blurred, I don't really know."

"Oh god, is there more?"

"He had these moments of rage towards her, very conflicted. He needed her to survive. He had little else. But his rage towards her was palpable. He blames her for his father abandoning them, though he admits that it was his father's choice to leave."

"And his father?"

---

1 The Wechsler-Bellevue Intelligence Scale was created by psychologist David Wechsler in 1939 as an alternative to other standardized IQ tests at the time. Another version of the test is still used today.

Garber shrugged. "He feels towards his father like some patients feel towards a dead parent. Frozen in time. Revered. Untouchable. His father is on a shelf because he abandoned them. He wasn't around. It's his mother that he focuses on, blaming her for everything, smothering him, babying him."

"So what else do we have?"

"The diary. We have his psyche in this book he's kept for over ten years. All his thoughts. All his feelings." He tossed it to Mitchell. "It's more than we need really. Erase his assessments, the opinions of neighbors. All of it. Everything we need to know about Unruh is in this book."

Mitchell flipped through the pages. Symbols, letters, a code with some full sentences scattered in between. "Did you decipher this?"

"Working on it. It's not a code exactly, we just don't have the exact references for some of it. He was in the Battle of the Bulge. Not the worst of it, but from what he wrote in there, he saw enough—"

"Shell shocked? Is that what you're saying?" Mitchell Cohen asked.

"I'm saying he was definitely affected. You see a change in the content as it goes on. Consumed with killing and blood, bodies. He tries to make some peace with it, in terms of his religion, but can't. The notations about killing aren't remarkable in and of themselves, but the amount of detail changes as he progresses. It becomes more morbid. Killing prisoners of war, killing teenagers in battle. The grimness of it all. He starts to really describe it. It plagued him."

"So, is he feigning? Do you think?" he asked again.

Garber stared across the table at him, hesitating, choosing his words. "He's smart. That's all I'm going to say. He may not want to go to the electric chair. But he can't reproduce facts from six years ago. He didn't back-date diary entries. He bought the damned machete."

'So, where are we going? What are we going to do? Jail or the hospital for further evaluation?"

"If you were to ask me if he knew what he was doing, the answer is yes. He knew. He knew it was murder, he knew it was wrong. He did it purposefully, knowing there were consequences. The choices are, one—send him to jail. Let his lawyer file a motion for further psychiatric evaluation and competency—state of mind—at the time of the crime. Go from there. If you do this you need to plan to fight for conviction. They're going to go for insanity. Two—commit him ongoing to the hospital. Let him sign himself in. Hold the indictments against him should he be sane at some point in the future. Let us continue to work with him. The flatness, the lack of emotion, the inability to emote at all is fascinating. I haven't seen anyone exactly like this before."

"I know which way you're leaning." Mitchell started to pace again. Whatever decision he made all eyes were on him.

"He has dementia praecox, mixed type, with pronounced catatonic and paranoid coloring. That's our official diagnosis. All of us agreed," Garber said.

"Under the laws of this state an insane person cannot be tried," Mitchell said.

Garber held up his hands. "I'm not a lawyer but it seems like a legal wormhole to me. Plenty of insane people are prosecuted.

Committing him to the hospital is really skirting the system but it does get him where he needs to be faster—"

"Or maybe he needs to be in jail?"

Garber stood up. "I don't know if you'll get a conviction. Weigh it out."

"The calls from the victims' families are unsettling. They come in daily. The Cohens lost three people in this. I can't forget that little boy sitting in the police station. I think about my own son. And committing him removes due process. It just puts him off to the side, in some unspecified category. Not released, not imprisoned. Can I legally do that? Is it within my rights? I'm just thinking out loud here."

"You have latitude in this. Is it legal? I don't know. It removes due process. It fast tracks a not guilty by reason of insanity. It puts him there without the benefit of a judge or jury to put their stamp of approval on it. But does he need more time in the hospital? Right now, does he need more time? Do we need more time to figure this out?" Garber stood up. "I'm leaving the reports. Look them over and make up your mind. We'll talk tomorrow."

Mitchell patted Garber's back. "It's in the blood and the machete," he said.

Garber looked back over his shoulder. "And the fact that he killed three children—without a thought about it—no sane person would do that," Garber added.

Chapter Fifteen

Raymond

One morning my grandmother popped her head into my room and said classes were resuming the next day. And just like that I was off to Vets for middle school, with barely any notice. It wasn't exactly just like that, because it wasn't the same as any first day of school that I can remember. The teachers did the same thing as usual, told us about themselves and the subjects we'd be studying, but all the while there was this feeling hovering overhead that everybody felt. In fact, at one point, Mrs. Smith got all choked up and started to cry for no reason. She tried to hide it at first but couldn't. Then Mary Wells started, and Louise Uhler and Jenny Jones. It was a mess. I just put my head down and hoped it would pass. I couldn't cry anymore.

Nobody talked about the fact that Charles wasn't there. They didn't leave his seat empty, or have a moment of silence. They didn't honor him at all. I think they were afraid if they mentioned anything about Howard, everyone would be bawling and we wouldn't get through the day. I noticed the big space between John Coburn and Isabelle Cone, though. There was no actual space really, but that's where Charles would have sat. It punched me in the gut a little and I wondered what classroom he was sitting in at that moment.

Though they dismissed us at noon, it was one of the longest days I can remember. It was that day that I realized nobody was really in charge. This kind of thing had never happened before so they were just going through the motions without any real idea of what to do. We always expected adults to have answers and they didn't this time. There was no roadmap or policy. For some reason, it made me think of 1942 and the blackout drills.

I was only five when those sirens sounded. They were so loud they bounced off my eardrums; the shrieking drowned out every other noise. People scattered, running as if we were being bombed. My grandparents told us to prepare for it, that no matter where we were when the sirens started, we needed to come home, put our heads down, that everything was going dark. And it was. All at once, the entire cities of Camden and Philadelphia went completely black. It was a drill for air raids, to blacken everything so the German pilots wouldn't know where to strike. Those sirens sounded for a whole thirty minutes, while we held our breaths, afraid to whisper till the lights came back on. There was a drill for that, but not for what happened with Howard. So, we all felt a little undone. Unprepared.

I walked down 32nd Street after school let us out, to Sharp School to wait for Milton. For some reason, I didn't want to be alone that afternoon. The elementary school dismissed twenty minutes before the middle school so I parked myself and my bike on the Purnell's front steps right across the street to wait. I had this pit in my stomach when I looked at that building, as if I'd left my childhood there.

Last June, those doors had flown open and Bob Bowers, Ed Brestle and I had come running out, heading to Cohen's for some chips and soda, and then to the river to start our summer throwing rocks and looking for tadpoles. Who would've thought so much would change in three short months? I was staring across the street when I saw movement at the house next door. Sorg and two of his friends came out of the front door and onto the steps. I kept looking straight. I hadn't seen him since the incident and I knew he was full of opinions.

"Look, it's little Ray."

I didn't answer.

"Hey Ray, I'm talking to you." His friends turned towards River Road and he came over to where I was sitting, alone. "What're you doing? Not waiting for Hoover, are you?" He gave a little chuckle.

That was a bad joke. Clark Hoover had been renting a room from the Purnells as a boarder for more than a year. We'd see him coming and going down the exact steps where I was sitting on our way to school. "Waiting for Milton," I answered. Carl Sorg scared me a little. He was a pack animal, always with two or three friends; he was loud, hooting and hollering as people walked past him. It was best to just duck your head and ignore him.

"You were there, weren't you? When Howard went off? That's what I heard."

"I was there."

He sat down on the step next to me and lit a cigarette. "I wasn't. I was sleeping. I got home from work, working half the night, and went to bed. But then Merrill came and got me." Merrill was his younger brother, sixteen years old, and just like him. "Said a dog got hit by a car at the corner or something." He drew hard on his cigarette. "I wandered up there, just looking at all the excitement, the cop cars. Police everywhere carrying submachine guns. Saw Cohen with his face in the dirt. Couldn't believe it."

I looked at him, skinny, his light brown hair combed to the side, always dressed neatly. He had a hard story, but maybe no harder than anyone else around Cramer Hill. His story was just more well known. His father, also a Carl or sometimes Charles F—always an F in there—had been some sort of city political big-wig. A republican. So, he had connections. He was sort of prominent. But my grandfather told me the whole city was rotten with corruption at that time, so you can take that for what you will.

I never met the man. He got sick one night in 1936 when he was down at Long Beach Island, managed to get home, but was dead before midnight. Complications. That's what they said he died from. Carl Jr. was only eight at the time, and his mother was left with three kids, none over the age of eleven, to raise during the worst of the depression. Carl was a good eight years older than me, but I remember him when he was barely a teen, in his ratty coat and shoes stuffed with newspaper to keep the wet out, walking the streets looking for any scraps of work he could find.

The whole Sorg household was cut from a basic hard-working German Catholic stock. The mother too. And they were able to hold on to their house at 925 N 32nd Street through it all. But it left Carl weathered and a bit hardened. With an edge.

I prayed for the school bell to ring to end this conversation. "I was in the barbershop."

Sorg swung his head and looked at me. "You saw it then. Old Hoover took a bullet?"

"Yes."

"What was it like? Tell me."

I gripped the handlebars of my bike harder. "It was fast. He came in and just raised his gun and shot—"

"And what was Hoover doing? What'd he do? Did he try and run out the back?"

I shook my head. "Not really. He wouldn't have made it. Howard had the gun on him. He ducked behind the hobby horse, is what he did." I saw flashes of it in front of me. Of Hoover's face losing all color, his hands starting to shake, the brush he had in hand quivering, knowing what was to come. I swallowed hard and closed my eyes.

"He tried to hide behind the kid?"

"I don't know, Carl."

"Huh. Old Clarkie. I bet he did. I bet he ducked down and let that kid get it right in the side of head."

"He got hit in the neck. Orris did. Not the head."

"You won't say it, and I don't blame you, but Hoover was a coward to the end, wasn't he? Would've hid behind his own mother." He motioned behind him, towards the room Hoover had been renting. "All his crap finally caught up to him."

My mind was zig-zagging. One thing I was certain of was that Howard wasn't aiming for Orris. Orris wasn't his target. And I wasn't going to say it, but maybe Sorg was a little bit right about Hoover. He was alone after going through two wives. He had two children by his first wife, but I'd never seen them in my whole life. Ronald and William, I think were their names. My grandmother whispered that he had abandoned them, just left them to fend for themselves so he could be with another woman. I don't know how close he was to his children, but he had some secrets he was trying to bury, that was for sure. He used to come out of his house and throw pennies at any kids he came upon. He wasn't mean to us in any way, but I'd heard my grandparents whisper about him. "Bad news," they'd say, "just bad news."

"It caught up to everyone, I think," I mustered.

He gave me a sideways look. "You talking about me?"

My lips were pressed together tight. I might have had a handful of conversations with Carl in my whole life. I wrestled a little in my brain about saying nothing and telling him what I really thought. "I don't think you were nice to him."

He rubbed the end of his cigarette against the concrete, watching until the embers died. "You were his little buddy, bringing him your old man's stamps, listening to him, weren't ya?"

"I brought him stamps." I felt that little squiggly worm-like feeling in my stomach. I wasn't sure whether to deny I talked to Howard or ignore Sorg. "And I talked to him some."

"He never talked to anyone else. Just you and his mother. Nobody. Just real quiet. Like creepy quiet. Did you ever notice his eyes, all sort of glazed over, black, like? Always had a weird look on his face."

I thought about it for a second. "I don't know if he was creepy. I think his eyes were just turned inside out, always looking inside himself, just running over his own thoughts all the time; he didn't have enough energy left to see anyone else. Or to try and figure anyone else out, I'd say."

"He was a Nancy boy. I don't know if anybody's told you about them yet, but your old man should sit you down and spell it out. He was the kind that don't like women—prefer the company of men. Surprised they let you go in there with him alone." He elbowed me in the ribs. "Maybe you're a Nancy boy too, huh Ray? Is that it? Is that your secret?" He laughed.

"Whatever you think, Carl." Carl was all mouth—I'd never seen or heard him actually fight anyone, or hurt anyone. The best weapon was to just ignore him. He wanted attention. "I gotta ask you something, though. Do you know anything about the missing gate?" This look came over his face that I'd never seen on him before. He was a little afraid. "Because somebody brought it back. Whole. They took it that night before and then put it back last week."

"It wasn't me." The way he said it, all straightforward, no dancing around it, no wise come-back. He was scared.

"That night, though. You were out front, on the corner. You know who took it?"

"I was out front. The police already asked me this. I was out front, not in the back."

"But Carl, you know everything that happened on that corner. Every single thing. You practically live in that store in front of the Unruhs'. How could you not know?" I glanced over at his house. It was long, and set all the way back on the lot, but there was a little shed there. Perfect for stashing a gate.

"I didn't take it. I had to go to work, ya know. I wasn't hanging out there all night." That was true. Carl was working doing odds and ends for a carpenter, Clarence Dunkelberger, further up on 32nd Street. "I saw nothing."

He hadn't answered the question and we both knew it. "If people had just left him alone, this wouldn't have happened. He wasn't really bothering anyone."

He stood up and put his hands on his hips. "How do you know it wouldn'ta happened? How do you know that? You can blame me, but it wasn't my fault. He wasn't right in the head. You should know that better than anyone. Walking back and forth with that bible under his arm and his combat boots on, all straight like he shoulda been wearing German jack boots, marching in Poland. What about the Cohens? Did ya blame them?"

"They're dead," I said, staring hard at those school doors across the street.

"They're dead, but you know it was them. Everyone knows it was them. Ask anyone around here. Go house to house and ask. Mrs. Cohen was an arrogant person. She probably threw you outta her store at least once, didn't she? Her and her husband and that yard of theirs—"

"I know." I didn't want to hear him go on.

"Nobody hurt him, Ray. Nobody hit him. Nobody forced him into a fight. We razzed him, is all. He just took it wrong."

I lived in this neighborhood, passed by that corner all the time. I knew what Sorg and his friends had done. I'd witnessed it myself. Not just to Howard, but to everyone who walked by. He and his pals Bill and Paul liked to comment on people—men, women, children, it didn't matter. They liked to provoke, they razzed, but Howard had by far got the worst of it.

"Took it wrong? Everybody razzed him all day long. Every day. Throwing stuff at him—" The bell sounded loudly and the doors of the school opened; kids poured out the front door. I felt my stomach unclench and my whole body relax. "Have you been back over at the Unruh's since this happened?" I'd seen him in the empty storefront the other day. There was a door in the back of the store that led down into the Unruh basement.

His eyes shifted towards me. "Maybe. Just looking around. Nut had ammunition molds down near his shooting range. He was sitting in there making bullets, had this old black pot he was using to melt down the metal. We all thought he was in there reading the bible but he was preparing to take us all out."

"Bullet molds?" I hadn't seen any, but then I wouldn't know what they looked like.

He nodded. "These big cast iron things." He held his hands up about a foot apart. "Police left all his stuff down there. I don't know why. His target and calendar were still there too." He rubbed his face. All of this was bothering him though he would probably never admit it. "Target had at least twenty-five holes in it. It was like looking at hell, after everything that happened."

"I'd stay away from that place. And if you took the gate, the police'll find out. Sooner or later."

"I didn't take it. I told you that already. Don't try and blame me. And the police probably already know who took it but nothing's going to come of it. Mark my words. I know. Cops aren't looking to blame anyone around here for what happened. It'll all be forgotten."

I felt a little sick. "You think? The police don't care at all about what set this off?"

His jaw clenched and unclenched. "Yeah, I do think that. How were any of us supposed to know he was gonna go off? How were we supposed to know he couldn't take a little teasing? Last person in the world—" he said. I'd had enough of this conversation. I stood up and grabbed my bicycle handlebars, ready to cross the street. "Ray?" I turned and looked at him. "You oughta stay quiet about all of this," he called. "Stop talking about it, or maybe people'll start wondering why you're so interested, if maybe you're a Nancy boy too. Might start throwing garbage at you too. How'd you like that, Little Ray?"

I crossed the street and didn't look back. That was Carl Sorg.

Chapter Sixteen

Freda

"It was a sight, Louise, that's all I can say. It chokes me up a little to even talk about it. That woman was on her back. Her legs were bent and I swear she was on her knees begging for her life when that son-of-a-bitch shot her," Robert Wonsetler said.

Freda was in the hallway on her way out the door when their voices stopped her. If Howard was a son-of-a-bitch, then she was the bitch. She reached for the doorknob and then stopped.

"Tom took David that morning to get an extractor for one of his machines. An extractor saved his life. He comes back to see his new wife dead in the back, blood seeping out of her head. The cops had to pull him off of her, wailing like an animal, I tell you. I can't get it out of my mind."

He was talking about the Zegrinos: Thomas, Thomas's son, David, and Thomas's new wife, Helga. She couldn't get away from this. Sam was out on the water away from prying eyes, and James was hunkering down in Runnemede with a friend, refusing all contact. She was right in Camden, not even a ten-minute walk across the train tracks from where it had all happened. She was visible, vulnerable, no matter how much she tried to hide.

"That kid David was on his hands and knees wiping up his step-mother's blood. Tom couldn't bring himself to do it.

Can you imagine? I saw it, Louise, pieces of her brain were splattered—"

"That's enough, Bob. What if she hears you?"

Freda opened the door and scampered down the front steps. She'd take a quick walk down Pleasant Street, circle the block and come back. Her shoulders relaxed as she moved. St. Paul's Evangelical Lutheran Church was only a few minutes away by foot. She wanted to go to the chapel and pray, or sit for a minute. Instead, her legs took her to the Pavonia Yard. She stared across the train tracks to the other side.

Five or six stretches of rusted train cars squatted on the tracks, waiting to be switched over to another engine and moved. Most people opted to walk to 36th Street and take the bridge over the tracks, but this yard was always filled with kids of all ages, playing along the sides, putting pennies or pieces of metal down to watch them get squashed by the weight of the locomotives. People walked across them all the time as a quick cut-through to Cramer Hill.

Freda moved fast, head down, ignoring the engineers and train handlers that were walking back and forth, inspecting. She alighted on the other side at Beideman, only a block over and up from her River Road apartment. She wasn't headed there, that wasn't her intention. For days, she'd been in turmoil thinking about Cramer Hill and the people who'd lived there beside her.

Newspaper reporters, neighbors, Pastor Bauer, even her own sister and brother-in-law were picking over the minefield of Howard's mind, trying to figure out what had happened, how they'd missed all the signs that he was crazy, that he could kill children. With all their figuring, they never came close to hitting on the truth, because they were only looking at her son, not the other people involved. That's what she thought. And the real truth about what happened could be found in that stretch of road from Cohen's drug store down to Latela's luncheonette.

Four Psychiatrists Find Unruh Insane, the newspaper article had said. There was a picture of the tailor, Thomas Zegrino, in the center of the page, his hands on the counter in his shop, leaning forward. "I come home to nothing but four walls," he'd said.

She went home to four walls too, in a small bedroom under the roofline at the hospitality of a weary sister and a not always pleasant brother-in-law. And she'd done nothing wrong at all that she could see. Nothing except witness those people push her son until he lost control. It was all of them. The Cohens, Hoover, Zegrino, Pilarchik and Latela. When she thought about it, her mind lingered on Thomas Zegrino because he was the one Howard was fixed on before the shooting.

The small man, not taller than Freda, had a long sharp face, dark curly hair and black eyes. He'd been in that busy shop at 3416 River Road from the day she moved into the neighborhood. His store and the apartment above were sandwiched in between Latela's cafe and the apartment house where the Hamiltons lived.

Mob man, that's what they called him. She'd heard Mrs. Cohen or Mrs. Rice say it, she couldn't remember which. Running numbers from that little dry-cleaning store, and it must have been a lot of numbers because he was hauled out in handcuffs in 1947, in front of his first wife and children. He spent some months in the jail on the sixth floor of City Hall. People whispered that he had a high bail, that he had some ranking in organized crime. But he paid his bail, had a trial and came right back to Tom's cleaners, minus his wife and daughter, Diane, and picked up right where he left off.

Zegrino had been divorced and remarried not even a month before Howard started shooting. Freda would see his new wife on the street; pretty, with light brown hair and a wide smile, she seemed nice enough, though Freda never uttered so much as a hello in her direction. Now she couldn't get her face out of her mind.

"Zegrino was telling stories about me," Howard said one night, only weeks ago, while they were eating dinner. He was tense, leaning into the table.

"What kind of stories?" she asked, though the litany of offenses perpetrated against Howard was growing longer and longer, and these conversations were wearing her out.

"Him and his son, they were standing in front of their shop and said it to me when I walked by today."

"What'd they say, Howard?" she asked. She ran her fork across her food, waiting to hear about his latest wounding.

"I don't want to tell you, Ma. It was disparaging of my character."

She dropped her fork and looked at him. "Then why'd you bring it up? Why are you talking about it, Howard? Put your plate in the sink if you're done."

"He said I wasn't a man, Ma. Then his son started laughing. That's what he said."

"You're a decorated war hero, Howard. Why would they say you aren't a man? What does that even mean?"

"In a certain kind of way, I'm not a man."

Freda was confused. She thought they were picking on him again because he wasn't working, because she was supporting him with her wages at the factory and the little bits of money Sam gave her. "So get a job, Howard. Doing anything. See if

Horner needs someone to deliver groceries. I heard him talking about it the other day. Go ask him."

Howard made a sound out of his mouth like she understood nothing. "David said he knew all about me and my perversions. Said he was going to tell everyone in the neighborhood he saw me in an alley with another man, doing things…" Howard's fists were balled up. "It's not true, Ma. They never saw me doing anything at all, other than walking to church or waiting for the bus. Why can't they leave me alone? If he tells everyone that, how can I defend myself?"

Freda chewed her last mouthful of potatoes and pushed her plate away. She didn't want to look at Howard when he was talking about these things. She'd heard the names they called him: Nancy boy, Mary, girly. It was constant. They took his manhood from him every time he went outside. "We'll bring Maryanne over for supper after church on Sunday. Hold onto her hand real tight and just look 'em dead in the eye, Howard."

This seemed to enrage him. "For the last time, I'm not getting back together with Maryanne. I'm sorry I even mentioned this," he yelled. He got up and disappeared into the basement. Ten minutes later she heard the sound of gunfire hitting his target.

She walked to the basement door. The sounds were deafening. She cracked open the door and tiptoed down the steps, one at a time. The light bulb hung from a string down into the middle of the room. She smelled the smoke, gunpowder, metal. Her old banged-up cooking pot was on the floor. She picked it up and ran a finger over it. It was ruined by a heavy dark substance stuck to the bottom. Howard fired off another round. She picked up a metal contraption, ten inches long by six. Deep oval holes an inch wide pitted both ends. It weighed at least ten pounds.

"Are you doing some kind of experiments down here, Howard? More of your science stuff? It smells terrible. What is this?"

He whipped around, dropped a handgun onto the floor and jumped to his feet. "Leave it alone, Ma. Leave it alone. Get out of here."

She looked at the cooking pot and the thing in her hands. "Jesus help me. You're making bullets. You're making bullets, melting metal in my old pan, using this mold." She felt she had violated some secret underworld that was dark and dangerous. She looked into her son's eyes that day and didn't completely recognize him. She dropped the mold and started back up the steps. They never talked about it again. That was only a week or so ago.

Now Freda found herself at River Road and Bergen. The end of the block. She saw Latela's sign, the awning for the dry-cleaning shop, and the corner where the sign for River Road Pharmacy stuck out from the building. They deserved it. All of them in some way. They had tormented her son so much that he wept at night, so much that he struggled to even open the door to go out into his own backyard.

She stumbled forward, pulling her hat down a little further over her face. Everything was closed up tight except for Zegrinos. She saw the door slightly ajar, movement inside the shop. She was going to keep going, circle back to Beideman and then cut across the train tracks again. That was the plan, but the red striped tie in the window of the dry cleaners caught her eye. She stopped full in her tracks and leaned against the plate-glass window to get a better look.

David Zegrino came to the door and she took a step back. He looked terrible. His complexion was a waxy gray, as if he hadn't slept in months. He'd lost weight and that smart-guy look he always had on his face was gone.

"What are you looking at? Can I help you?" he asked. He didn't recognize her.

"Why do you have these ties and slacks hanging in the window?" she asked.

Something registered and his whole face dropped. "You want them?" he asked.

"No, no." She started backing up. "I was just wondering."

"Dad? Come 'ere, quick."

"I don't want them." She waved her hand and started walking away.

Thomas Zegrino was suddenly there, standing behind David. His black hair was off his face, and the two of them at that minute looked so much alike it was hard to tell them apart. Both needed a good bath and a hair wash.

"Howard left them to be cleaned. Dropped them off that Saturday… Was supposed to pick them up Tuesday… that Tuesday," he said.

She saw the little tags fluttering at the end of the strings. There was a clear HU marked on each one.

"You can't have them back, Mrs. Unruh. They're staying in this window until your son feels a zillion jolts of electricity go through him. I'll take them down when he's buried," he spat.

She was frozen for a second, finding it hard to move her feet. She raised her hand and started to say something but her throat closed. She took a step and stumbled on the uneven pavement, catching herself before she hit the ground. "I'm sorry," she muttered.

"Get out of here before I do something that's gonna make things worse. Get out of here," he screamed.

She heard his voice as she hurried all the way down 32nd Street. She found a ledge of concrete near the train tracks, dropped down onto it and sobbed into her hands. She was utterly trapped. Madeline Harrie's words rang in her ears: "There's nothing left here for you."

Chapter Seventeen

Raymond

The sun rose and set over Cramer Hill a dozen more times and even if things weren't exactly the same as before, they were getting predictable. School was pretty much back to normal, with teachers actually expecting us to show up on time with our homework done, and nobody cried unless they fell and skinned their knee. My father and grandparents got us into the routine of chores, dinner, homework, bed. It had a sort of rhythm that was comforting. The newspaper men were gone, and a whole two days could go by without some reminder of what had happened. For the most part.

We were heading into early October, and though it was still warm enough during the day, Milton and I would wake up to a cold room in the morning, cold enough that we wrapped up in our blankets and took a few extra minutes to get out of bed.

"Boys. Now. Breakfast," my grandmother called down one morning. "Or you're going to be eating cereal on your walk to school."

We raced down the stairs with our books and pulled a chair up to the table. My father was there too and we were crowded, elbow to elbow. "It should be any day now," he said, already in the middle of a conversation.

"Maybe we should just eat in peace, Ray." My grandfather was talking to my father.

"It'll be this week, anyway. They said it would be this week. Mark my words. It's been a whole month. How much talking can they do to the man before they decide it?" My father glanced at me and I just knew they were talking about Howard. They always gave me that look when the subject came up, just to make sure I wasn't going to have some kind of nervous breakdown.

"I read in the paper the prosecutor is just waiting for the psychiatrists. I don't think there's going to be a trial. I can't see there being a trial," my grandmother added. "Everyone knows what happened. Plain as day."

"I think it depends, Marie. It all depends. If he pleads guilty, then no trial."

"Dear Lord," my grandfather said. "How can the man plead not guilty? That doesn't make any sense."

"What if he says he's guilty but wasn't in his right mind at the time? Or if he says he was pushed to it?" I asked. They were talking around me, so I figured I'd jump in.

All eyes in the room were on me. "Pushed to it? To kill children?" my father asked.

"I think he's going to plead to it and that's that. Then we'll see it all stirred up again when they move him from the hospital to prison. Reporters on the street and all that, but it'll be done, and we'll all be better for it." My grandmother put another pancake on my plate. "Boys, eat fast, and get on to school. And make sure you come right home. I have things for you to do this afternoon."

I chewed the last of my breakfast and grabbed my books. "But it's Friday. It's the weekend."

"Home," she said.

As it turned out, home was the only place I wanted to go that day after school. The news hit sometime in the afternoon. A press conference was held by the city district attorney downtown. We heard bits of it but I didn't believe it was true until I saw the groups of women and men gathered together in little clusters walking home. It wasn't coincidental. They were talking with a purpose, an angry buzz rising from the center like a cloud.

I opened our door and saw my grandmother's face first, her arms folded, just waiting for me. "You heard, Ray?" she asked.

"Is it true?"

She nodded. "I heard it on the radio myself. Howard is going to be committed to Trenton Psychiatric Hospital, ongoing. They can't charge him, because they say he isn't in his right mind."

I was circling all the facts and kept coming back to a center place where none of this made sense. "Ever? They can't charge him ever?"

"No, no. They didn't say ever. They said right now. He's not going to prison for now. They aren't going to execute him now. Those psychiatrists are going to work on him, is all. Tinker with his brain a little."

"How long are they allowed to tinker with his brain before they have to charge him?" I asked.

My grandmother sat back and looked at me. "You should be a lawyer, Ray, because that's the best question I've heard all day. I have no idea."

I thought back to Leonard at the Cohens' funeral. How he said they'd never fry Howard because he was crazy. He was right. Crazy knew crazy. For the past month, people had been sitting on their hands waiting for some justice so they could make peace with the thirteen people being dead, but there wasn't going to be any. It was a hard lump to swallow.

"Did you know Mrs. Hamilton had her baby? A little girl. Named her Maryanne. She's at Cooper right now." Mrs. Hamilton and her enormous stomach, the little cowboy suit she had for Tommy, and her death crib came to mind. She'd have another baby to put in it now. "Something good to talk about," she continued. "I'm going to make up some food and take it over there early next week when she gets home. Try to make her as comfortable as I can."

Her words were a buzz in the background of my thoughts. All I kept thinking about was Howard. I'd brought him some Columbian Issue stamps from my father and we'd chatted for almost a half hour not even a month ago. He wasn't deranged then, though maybe I wasn't the one to judge. But he was talking normally. He even smiled a few times. He told me a small story about losing his last ferry token, of it falling out of his pocket, of how he was down at Ferry Terminal and realized it was gone. He had to use the money he had on him for another one, and was forced to walk the bridge home from Philadelphia. It had all made sense to me. He wasn't a madman. But the machete in the closet, the planning to decapitate the Cohens, that made me realize that the brain can break up into different parts, one part normal, the other insane. And the insane part of Howard's mind might have just saved his life.

"I'm sure Howard's mother is happy," I said.

"Mrs. Unruh's been hiding out at her sister's long enough. People are getting a little antsy having her so close. I think the fire chief is getting a little heat having her there." She chuckled at her joke.

"It wasn't her fault," I said. My grandmother put a glass of milk in front of me and I took a long drink. "Do you think she'll be moving on soon?" I wanted to talk to her before she left. I had to keep an eye on things.

"I have no way of knowing what that woman might do. Mrs. Unruh has another sister, Carrie, and a brother Fred, and grown nieces and nephews. She also has James." Howard's younger brother hadn't reared his head since the incident, that was for sure. He had been hiding out there in Runnemede, a town about twenty minutes southeast of Camden, without a peep. "But I doubt she'll be moving in with him."

James was a funny one. I had only faint memories of him, living in that apartment with his mother and Howard. He went off to the war, came home briefly and was gone, hardly ever came around to help out. But what I do remember is that he was different. Different from Howard and his mother, that is. He was younger than Howard by a few years but seemed independent from the start. He got a job at Frankford Arsenal in Philadelphia maybe before he even graduated from high school, and enlisted in the Army as soon as he could, maybe just to get out of that house.

I couldn't blame him for not wanting any part of his brother's mess. He was separating himself from his mother and Cramer Hill way before this happened. It was as if he took a wife, moved two towns over and didn't look back. In all my visits to Howard, I had not once seen him around the place. In fact, I'd never seen any of her family around the place either. A church person here and there maybe. And Mrs. Pinner. That was it. Howard's mother was really completely alone in this world, unless you counted God. And maybe for her, God was all she needed.

I went to my room straight away and flopped down onto my bed, staring at the ceiling. I let myself think about something I'd pushed away for a long time. I thought about what Howard was doing. I thought about him sitting in that hospital with a bunch of doctors standing over him, poking at him, trying to figure out what made him tick. I wondered if he was happy with himself, what he did, or if he was sorrowful, wanting to take it back. I wondered if he missed his apartment at 3202 River Road, tending to his mother's flowers, or taking his trips to Philadelphia, or collecting his rare stamps, reading his astronomy books and looking at the stars.

I couldn't even guess. But the one thing I knew about Howard was that he was smart. Cagey smart. Curious smart. He played the chess game five moves ahead of everyone else. He could take a bunch of information and just absorb it through his pores. People never looked hard enough at him to know that. They had talked to him, and about him, as if he was retarded, because he was quiet and sometimes answered slowly. But I knew the truth. I'd seen it when he was taking his pharmacy classes last year at Temple University. He just jumped into it when he got back from the war.

One day, when I was at his apartment, I watched him build these three-dimensional molecules out of wire and wooden balls. He was reading a book, talking to me at the same time, and building. Then he'd stop building and start scribbling something on a piece of paper really fast, then he'd go back to building. For at least half an hour, he was building and talking to me, and writing.

"What're you doing, Howard?" I finally asked.

"I figured these compounds are easier to see in three dimensions. So, I'm building them with wire. Each piece of wood represents an atom."

The book was open on the table and I lifted the front to see the cover. *Organic Reactions, Volume 2.* "Is this your textbook?" I asked. "For school?"

He shook his head. "No, this one from the library is better."

I don't know how it happened that he went from a man interested in science and math, literature and music, to being obsessed with guns and knives, tear gas and killing. People said it was the war, and they might have been partly right. The rest of it was something else. Something I'd never be able to put my finger on, something that would plague me until the day I died.

My window was open, letting the air, working its way to a winter chill, flow over me. And I was listening to the sounds outside. The cars, the trains going by in the distance, the really faraway sounds of the boat horns blowing from the Delaware River. But mostly the sounds of people on the street, gathered together right on the sidewalk below, digesting what had happened today. I couldn't hear it all, only snippets.

"… What are we going to do?"

"I don't know. How is Joe going to tell Mary about this? A gift from God she didn't lose the baby she was carrying…"

"… I saw Mr. Zegrino in his store an hour ago. Poor man. Standing at the counter. He's lost without his wife. Lost. Now this…"

"Maybe we should go to City Hall. Tell them what we think. They can't ignore all of us. We have rights…"

"Psychiatrists. They don't know nothing. He's a cold-blooded killer…"

"We need to go to Trenton and hang the son-of-a-bitch ourselves. Nobody would blame us."

I listened to it all, the broken and torn voices. And then the picture of Howard and his molecules popped into my head again. "You can take anything, Ray, anything it all, and make it into one of these." He held up his crazy contraption, all wires and wooden knobs. "There wouldn't be enough room in the world to hold them all, but it's amazing. I'll teach you if you want. What each wooden piece represents. It's such a clear representation of the universe. Once you understand it, everything makes sense. It's like talking to God. Let me show you." He'd been wearing his white buttoned-up shirt; his curly hair was like a little mop on his head. His eyes were alive, jumping, happy that day.

It was all a mishmash in my brain and I didn't realize that I had hot tears streaming from my eyes until Milton came in and stood over me with a concerned look on his face.

Howard's letter to Freda, January 1945

The worst part of it when a tank blows up is the smoke and the smell. And the body parts. They are everywhere. If there's time we gather what we can, but mostly we leave them there. Pray for cold, Ma. It's the bitter temperatures that make it easier. Leaving all these dead bodies in the heat would do us all in.

Chapter Eighteen

Freda

She was in prison herself and she knew it. The room at her sister's on Pleasant Avenue had become her cell, her sister and brother-in-law her jailers, though she knew they were doing the best they could in terrible circumstances. It was a waiting game. She'd figure out some other arrangements when Howard was transferred to Trenton State Prison. That's where he'd be going eventually. It housed the worst criminals in the state: murderers, rapists, arsonists. It was the home of death row.

The last execution to take place in New Jersey had been only months before. A man named Ralph Cordasco was sent to the electric chair for killing his wife, Rose, on the street in Newark in December 1947. It only took a year and a half from his arrest days after the crime until his execution on June 27, 1949. It was short and sweet. Governor Alfred Driscoll refused a reprieve and he died in the chair at eight o'clock that night, without a footnote.

The case interested her not only because the execution was so recent, but because Ralph Cordasco had been in a psychiatric hospital before, was treated in a mental hygiene clinic in 1930, and had had outbursts and emotional problems ever since. The state supreme court heard the case because he wanted to get life in prison on the grounds of insanity. From what she'd read of the case it came down to one thing. One standard. She'd had Bob write it down for her.

The simple question to be decided is whether the accused at the time of doing the act was conscious that it was an act which he ought not to do. If he was conscious of this, he cannot be excused on the score of insanity. He is then amenable to the law.

Freda read the words and wrestled with them. Howard knew what he was doing that day, and planned it out. He knew it was wrong and didn't care. The time from Howard's eventual arrest to his death would be cut from a year and a half to maybe eight months, she figured. Everybody was watching the case. There wasn't going to be any arguing about it, no back and forth, no supreme court of New Jersey intervening. It would just be fast and quick. This latest wrinkle of committing him to the psychiatric hospital only made things worse, not better. It just meant it was all going to be slower and more painful.

"Freda, are you ready?" Louise was in the doorway, looking anxious. She had her coat on, purse in hand. It was time to go.

Now that Howard was officially committed, papers signed, with Samuel agreeing, after some hesitation, to pay fifteen dollars a month towards Howard's keep, Freda would be allowed to see her son. Bob wanted nothing to do with any of it. He was getting enough flack for just keeping her in his house, so Louise agreed to drive her to Trenton. Every inch of her face showed distaste at what lay ahead.

The hospital was so enormous Freda caught a glimpse of the dark brick building with small windows set high, then lost sight of it behind some trees, only to have a different wing appear again moments further down the road. She had a tissue balled up in her fist, twisted and tangled; she squeezed it tighter as they approached the car park. Louise had been quiet during the hour-and-a-half drive, doing what was expected of her, but removed from the situation in all other ways.

"I'm not going in with you, Freda," she said, turning off the engine. "I don't want to see Howard. Bob doesn't want me to go in either. You'll be fine." Her eyes were glued to the dashboard when she said it.

Freda smoothed her long gray coat and straightened the black wool felt fascinator on her head. It had beading all along one side, and was only worn for weddings or formal occasions. Louise had suggested she wear another hat, or none at all, but she wanted to appear her best. She gathered her purse and opened the car door. "I have an hour. You're going to sit in the car for an hour?" she asked.

"I might take a drive. Get a cup of coffee."

Freda got out and looked back in at her sister. "Do you want me to give Howard a message for you?"

"No," she responded. "I'm sorry. You go on. I'll see you back here in a bit."

Freda felt her sister's eyes on her all the way across the parking lot until she passed through the glass doors into the lobby of the building. The smell of bleach and disinfectant was so strong that she put the tissue against her nose to block it. It only took a few minutes to be directed to a small waiting room with four chairs arranged in a circle. It wasn't comfortable looking or inviting in any way. The single light above flickered every few minutes, making Freda dizzy.

"Dr. Garber will be right with you," the woman said.

"I thought I was here to see my son." Freda was still standing, hesitating to sink into the brown chair.

"He wanted to meet with you first. He has some questions, I believe." With that she turned and disappeared.

Freda stood clutching her purse with both hands, waiting. She considered leaving but wasn't sure exactly how to get her coat back without making a fuss. It had been taken from her and she didn't know where they'd put it. A large man with dark hair carrying a file in his hand found her before she could figure out what to do.

"Mrs. Unruh, please have a seat. I'm Dr. Garber." He motioned towards the chairs and took a seat himself. "I've met with your son several times and I wanted the opportunity to speak with you." Then he leaned forward, his eyes on hers. "How are you? This is a difficult thing, I'm sure."

Her hand clenched and unclenched around the tissue balled up in her right hand. "Very. I wasn't told we'd be meeting. I would have made my husband come along. He can answer questions better than I can." She felt a nervous twist in her stomach.

"It's actually you I wanted to speak with. I had the opportunity to read your son's confession and I met him when he was in Cooper, right after the shootings."

Freda stared at him and blinked a few times. "What do you need to know?"

"I want you to tell me about your son, if you could. What is he like? So I can get a better understanding."

"What's he like? I'm his mother."

"Then as his mother, what's he like?"

She cleared her throat. She'd never had to answer anything like this and she was having trouble finding the words. "He's a quiet boy. Always looking around him to see what's going on. Curious. Smart. On the lookout—"

"On the lookout for what?"

"For how people treated him. He didn't like to confront people but he didn't forget just because he didn't say anything. And they treated him wrong. He did what Jesus told him. He turned the other cheek." Then she realized he really didn't. He'd just retaliated in the worst way. "Before this, I mean," she added.

"So, let me ask you this. All his milestones—his walking, talking, toilet training—it was all on time, no problems? No problems as a child? At all?"

"No. He was stubborn for toilet training, but he was fine. He started school right on time."

"No issues in school? In high school?"

"He didn't smoke or drink or go out with girls like other boys probably did. He went to church and studied the bible." She felt proud saying that.

"Because he wanted to?" he asked.

"Yes, he wanted to," she shot back.

"So, did anything happen that changed that? Any trauma? Anything between the two of you—"

Her purse was in her lap and she sat it upright, a divider between the two of them. "Things were different after the war. He was quieter in some ways. Kept more to himself, I guess. I know it was the killing he did that got to him."

"He told you that?"

"He didn't like to talk about it, but yes. And he wrote to me during the war. Lately things seemed to be getting harder. He couldn't find a job. Had people trying to help him and all. Officer Ferry was looking into it for him. Nothing was panning out. He tried to go to pharmacy school… I don't know where his life was going. He stopped going to church regularly."

"When did he stop?" He started writing in his file as she was talking.

"About a year ago, maybe a little longer. Didn't want to go to bible study, then stopped going to Sunday service too."

"Did he say why?"

"Just had no more interest. We fought about it a bit. He'd been a good boy all along—"

"And he started going to Philadelphia?" He glanced up only long enough to know she'd heard the question. "What was he doing there?"

She squeezed the tissue in her hand tighter. This question again. "The police asked me the same thing. He had a room there, they said. I didn't know." She stopped talking and thought for a second. "I mean, I did know he had a room when he was in pharmacy school, but he hadn't gone since last year. Almost a year. And I didn't think about the fact that he kept the room. I expect he was seeing friends, going out. Maybe drinking. Things he didn't want me to know about." The light above started to flicker again and she closed her eyes. "Why are they asking about this room over and over? Does it have something to do with the killings?"

"It has more to do with who Howard was and what was happening with him before all of this," he responded.

"The police said he was buying weapons. Is that what he used the room for? To hold his weapons?"

"He probably was buying weapons, but he was using the room to entertain."

"To entertain friends, then? He was going out with friends?" She was struggling to understand the importance of this. That was normal and a part of her was relieved that he had someone to entertain. "Then that's good."

"You could say that he was entertaining friends. But it was more than that, Mrs. Unruh. He was entertaining men in his room."

Her fist was squeezed so tight she could feel her nails digging into her palm. "So, he had some male friends. School friends? And they would go to the pictures? Or parties?"

"Mrs. Unruh, I think he was using the room just to entertain men. In a sexual way."

She felt as if someone had smacked her in the face. She could even feel the sting, feel her face redden. "I'm not even sure what that means. Where'd you get that from? I'm not sure why you're saying that. Did you get that from the police?"

He looked up quickly and caught her eye. "I didn't get that from the police. I got that from talking to your son. He has been engaging in homosexual relationships in Philadelphia only. He was very worried about people in your neighborhood finding out. I think those fears were feeding his paranoia—"

"He may have had that room, Doctor, and he may have had some friends coming and going. He may have been doing things he shouldn't have. Things that sin again God. But I think you've been talking to the neighbors. They only say those things to bother Howard. That's all. Because they know it'll upset him. You've got it all mixed up."

"Mrs. Unruh—"

Her eyes were glazing over, making it hard to see. Her hand holding the tissue started to shake a little. "Don't say that again. Don't say that about my son. It's not true. He's a Christian. They want to take everything away from him. Everything. Leave him with nothing. He's in this hospital, will never come home. He had no job, no way to fill his days, he lost his girlfriend—"

"I think—"

"This is what they want you to think. Don't you understand? All of them. They bothered him—those neighbors—all day long. They threw mud at him, called him those horrible names, got in his way when he was just walking down the street, and now this."

"I'm sure that was difficult for him. For you—"

"They took his gate, now they want to take his manhood too? Leave him with nothing. And leave me with nothing. Leave me with nothing!"

He was watching her, everything about her. "That isn't my intention. But tell me about this gate. It seems to have significance for him. Why is that?"

"He wanted to fit in, that's why. Be left alone, to come and go, just get along. The way the yard was, what with the Cohens not letting us cross their patio to get to the street, the gate at the end of our yard was the answer. He said to me that it was finally done, all this squabbling. He only got to use it once. One time and they ripped it out. Took it. I think he realized it was never going to end."

Dr. Garber seemed to be deep in thought for a few seconds. "I see. This may be too much for one meeting, but Howard has been holding many things in. His anger towards the neighbors and the shame of these other secret… shall we say… sexual liaisons are partly what drove him to this place of feeling he had to lash out. He has been indulging in these perversions with other men for several years now."

She wiped at her nose with the shredded tissue. "They're only saying that to put more charges on him—of…" she waved her hand around, "of being with other men. To add more to what he's facing. That's all."

For the first time since sitting down, Dr. Garber smiled, though it faded fast and he put a hand up to his face to try and hide it. "They don't need to add more charges. Homosexuality, though illegal, and maybe reprehensible to most people, is not often prosecuted. Howard killed thirteen people. He killed five women, five men and three children. They don't need to add sodomy to that to get a conviction."

"Don't you use the word sodomy in front of me. And especially when you are talking about my son. Don't you dare." She felt the rage moving through her body. She'd never talked to anyone like this before. She only wished Pastor Bauer were with her to guide her through this.

He shut the file and kept it in his lap. "Mrs. Unruh, I am sorry. For telling you this. I'm sure it adds to your burden. We've been giving him sodium amytal during some sessions to help relax him and get him to tell us how all of this happened. He's got moments of confusion. He's talked about growing up, about you. He has a very shallow emotional range." Her eyebrows went up questioningly. "He doesn't show much emotion about anything, and almost no emotions about what happened. He doesn't react to things, good or bad. He's very flat."

"How long will he be here? Before you send him off to prison?" She was steeling herself for his answer. Once he hit prison, the countdown would begin.

"We have no plans for that right now. He can't be sent to prison until he's deemed sane. And right now, he's not."

"So, how are you going to make him sane?"

"We're going to work with him. Do some more narcosynthesis sessions. Sedate him as necessary. The police turned all of his writings over to us—"

She waved a hand. "I know."

"Pages of notes about his neighbors. Some of it's in code. Initials or notations. We'd like your help deciphering it, if you could? I've copied some pages. Not now, but when you go home, if you could look at them? Would you mind? See what you can make of it. It would be helpful. Howard's explanations are lacking."

She didn't want to help them sort out anything. The quicker it was sorted, the quicker he was going to Trenton State Prison. She nodded. "I'll look at them. I'll have my husband help me. I have one more question for you."

"Of course."

"Was he really going to kill me with that wrench that morning?" She needed to know. "It looked like he was."

"He'd made up his mind that he was going to seek revenge against those people and he didn't want you to see it. His fear of upsetting you, of you going through exactly this—"

"It would have been easier for him to kill me than to see me upset? Is that what you're saying?"

The man sat back as far as he could in the chair. "That's a difficult way of putting it. He was too conflicted to carry through with it. He didn't kill you. And I believe if he had, it might have created such discord within him that he wouldn't have been able to carry out the rest of his plan."

"The rest of his plan? You mean thirteen people would be alive if he'd hit me with the wrench?" Freda didn't like this man. But his words were making her so ill she placed one hand on her stomach. It wasn't enough she carried the guilt of her son's actions, now he was telling her she could have traded her own life for theirs if she had known.

He nodded. "There isn't any way to really know that absolutely. Though he's very attached to you. You have to know that. He's more attached to you than anyone else in the world. He loves you and he resents you. You're part of him, but separate. He chose not to kill you."

She'd had enough of his babbling. He knew nothing about her son. "Can I see him now?"

"Yes, absolutely." He took her through a maze of hallways that emptied into a large room. Howard was there, dressed in black trousers and a long-sleeved white shirt she'd never seen before, sitting at a table with his hands folded in front of him.

He saw her but his expression didn't change. "Howard?" She sat next to him, clutched his arm and bit her lip. The tears fell down her cheeks and she let them. "Are you okay? Are they treating you okay?"

He nodded. "Yes." His eyes were completely glazed and she knew they'd been giving him medication. He wasn't the Howard she knew.

"What did they make you do, Howard?"

His movements were slow as he lifted his head in her direction. "I don't remember all of it, Ma. I don't remember killing Mr. Cohen. He climbed out the bedroom window onto the roof. They say he was dead in the street, but I don't know how he got there. I don't remember shooting the kid in the barbershop either. I wasn't trying to kill him, or any of the kids. But the rest of them, I did it. I'd had enough. I couldn't take one more day of it."

"The psychiatrist told me some things, Howard. Things that can't be true." She glanced at her son. He had no reaction. "Terrible things. About what you were doing in that room in Philadelphia."

His head was down. "I'm sorry, Ma."

"I think they're just making it up. Making it up to make you look worse. Saying things to take your manhood."

"I told them the truth. It doesn't matter anymore. I was using that room to be with other men, in a place where nobody would know."

She put her index finger to her lips. "Sssshhh. Don't say that. I don't want to hear that, Howard. Don't talk about that anymore."

He shrugged. "They wanted to know about that night before. About what happened. Every bit. They kept picking at me, again and again. And they gave me these drugs, to get me to talk. I don't have control, when they put that needle in my arm."

She grabbed his forearm. "Tell me then, Howard. Tell me all of it. From the beginning. Everything. I don't want to hear about my son from strangers." He nodded but didn't say anything. "Go on then, I'm listening. I'll be here with you no matter what happens. I won't let them destroy you, I won't. I'll fight for you this time. I should have fought for you before and I didn't. I'll be sorry about that for the rest of my life."

He looked at her, his mouth slack, his eyes showing no reaction. "You want me to start from the beginning. Where is the beginning?"

She nodded. "From when you first got the thought of killing them."

Chapter Nineteen

Raymond

Camden wasn't Philadelphia. It didn't even want to be Philadelphia. We were sort of like Brooklyn, across the river within eye view of the greatness, but trying to make our own way. We were much smaller but better in the ways that mattered. We thought so anyway. Philadelphia had Benjamin Franklin, Thomas Jefferson and the like, the Liberty Bell. But we had Walt Whitman. And all through grammar school we had his poems shoved into every class in some way—didn't matter if it was math or social studies or physical education, Whitman was in there with his old *Leaves of Grass*.

I remember Mrs. Smith making us sort through the *Calamus Poems*, all about adhesive love and comradeship, she said. I hated it until John Borton whispered to me one day at recess that the poems were really about men loving each other. I didn't know what he meant exactly until he explained it to me in detail. That wasn't something that was ever talked about. But Walt Whitman was way ahead of his time, I guess. We went into fits of giggles after that in class, wondering if Mrs. Smith knew about Walt Whitman liking men, or if it was our secret.

Yes, Whitman was the most famous resident who ever lived in Camden, and he said somewhere that those were the happiest days of his life. He didn't live near Cramer Hill. His house, a little two-story rowhome, was downtown on Mickle Street, a few blocks from the piers. I don't think anyone lived in it after he died, but every time we drove by, there was a light on in the little foyer, as if his house was sitting there waiting for him to come back. I'm not sure he ever really left.

I couldn't help but think of those *Calamus* Poems after Howard told me what the Zegrinos yelled to him when he was just walking by. It happened all the time, people calling him a Nancy boy, a Mary, fairy, pansy, and not just the Zegrinos or Sorg. I even heard Mrs. Cohen call him something one day when he left the pharmacy. He'd been asking for change to use the pay phone, and Mrs. Cohen whispered "It's the queer" to her husband on the other side of the counter. Howard heard it and his face went red.

It was the thing about Howard that hung in the air. It was blatantly said, but never really discussed. Those sorts of things never were. Living in Cramer Hill, going to school, it wasn't even a half second of a thought that there was any other kind of lifestyle than the one I lived. But after the shootings, something shifted a little. The whispers were louder or maybe the whispers were now coming from people who never whispered or muttered before at all. It was just rumors, or grist for the mill—something else to be thrown at Howard.

That's what I thought until my father asked me to take a walk with him one Saturday morning. I pulled on my jacket and headed outside after him, not knowing where we were going, and I don't think he did either. We ambled up Beideman to River Road and turned left. My father was silent most of the way, his hands in his pockets, walking slowly, then speeding up a little. This went on for over five minutes.

"Are we going to the print shop? Did you forget something?" I asked. I thought he'd left something at work.

"No, we're going to take a walk, maybe stop by the shop later if you want. Get a soda or something to eat. Are you hungry?" he asked.

"No." We'd finished breakfast not that long ago.

We got to 27th Street, where the Rio was, and a cluster of stores, and for a second I thought he was taking me to the pictures, though he would have said so when we left the house.

"The matinee already started," I said.

"No movie today, son. I wanted to talk to you away from the ears of your brother and grandmother."

"Okay," I responded. He had never done this before and at first I thought I'd done something terribly wrong.

"There are different kinds of men in the world, Raymond. All kinds of men."

"Like with different kinds of jobs they do?" I asked.

He half nodded. "The jobs they do, the way they live, the way they keep themselves busy."

I saw the Read's Pharmacy sign, with the little ice-cream cone in the corner, and suddenly wanted one. "Can I get a vanilla cone, Dad? Is it too early?"

He pulled a dime out of his pocket and handed it to me. "You go in. I'll wait here," he said. I tilted my head a little and looked at him. He was acting funny. He was dressed in his usual Saturday clothes, tan pants and long-sleeved flannel shirt, and everything about him looked right, but something was wrong.

"So, Ray," he said when I returned and handed him his change. "There are men that don't follow the rules. The rules that we all live by. I don't know why they don't. Nobody knows why they don't. But they don't."

"Like criminals?" I ventured.

"Like criminals. But in other ways too."

"Like what?" We'd got down as far as 24th Street and if we kept going, we'd no longer be in Cramer Hill but on a long stretch where the trains from Pavonia Yard crossed River Road.

"Like they don't get married, they don't have families. They don't have an interest in those things at all. They don't have any interest in setting up a house like me or your grandfather did."

It suddenly came to me all at once what he was getting at. "Are you talking about Howard?"

"Well, yes. Maybe. Maybe like Howard. People have been saying things about him since the shootings. Things I was afraid you'd hear. And I wanted to talk to you about it."

"What about it?" The ice-cream was making my hands colder but I had to finish my cone before it melted.

"Things have been, I guess, leaked, if that's the word, from the police or from people who were around when he was interviewed after he was arrested. I don't know how much is true. Maybe it's all just stories."

"They always called him names, Nancy mostly. Or Mary, like he was a girl. Is that what you mean?"

"But that was just name-calling. These stories are supposedly coming from him. Things he said himself. And it worried me for a couple of reasons. I didn't know how you'd take it because you spent so much time with him." I didn't say anything. I had my head down, just walking with him, feeling guilty but I didn't know why. "And I was wondering if he ever talked to you about it?"

"Talked to me about what?"

"About, well, about spending time with other men."

I shook my head. "No. He never talked about anything like that."

"Because if it's true what people are saying, that would mean… it would mean, Ray, that Howard was… well, he was interested in men, the way that men are interested in women. Doing things with other men that married people do with each other, if you know what that means."

"I think I do." Bill Shaw had told me where babies came from. I had an idea of what he was talking about, but I wasn't asking any questions. This conversation was bad enough.

"And men like that—they usually hang around together in groups. It's not looked on highly. It's not something someone your age should even be thinking about. But it worried me because I was wondering if Howard ever talked to you about men, or what he did with them or anything at all."

It had taken him half an hour to get to his real question. "No, he didn't. Not ever." We'd walked to where Federal Street and River Road connected and in another few minutes we'd be very close to City Hall. "Is that what he was doing in Philadelphia? Meeting men? He went there at night."

"I think so."

We were almost at 10th and Market and I saw my father flinch a little. You wouldn't have noticed it maybe, but I knew what it was. The Hollingshead fire. He'd been working at the plant right there back in 1940 when it happened. I didn't remember it at all, but he'd told me about it so many times, the stories felt like memories. Hollingshead was big industrial plant that manufactured floor wax, furniture polish and cigarette lighter fluid.

After a week of really hot weather, one of the vats exploded and caught fire. One man was blown backwards through the window and landed in a barbershop across the street. One explosion set off another, like a chain reaction. Ten people were killed. Hundreds more were hurt. The whole city was filled with heavy smoke and ash. Fire trucks from Philadelphia were dispatched, the whole city shut down. It took almost a week to put out the flames. My father wasn't in the big plant at the time of the fire, but he could have been. He still reacted to it when the name came up. His eyes were moving back and forth, looking at the empty lot.

"Is that why Howard broke up with his girlfriend? Because he wanted to go to Philadelphia?" I had to distract him. The fire was part of Camden's history, but I wanted to talk about something else.

"What?" he asked.

"Is that why he broke up with his girlfriend?"

"Yes. Maybe."

"So, that's where men like that go? That's where they hang around together? In Philadelphia." I thought about all the times I'd taken the bus with my grandmother to Philadelphia to the Mummer's parade, and to Wanamakers to see the Christmas display, or to shop at the Lit Brothers.

He half laughed. "Well, Philadelphia is a big city. The more people, the more chance of finding men like that. Philadelphia isn't just filled with people like that. Those people are probably everywhere."

"Oh," I said. I didn't really completely understand what he was saying. But it made me think of what Thomas Zegrino had said about Howard being with another man in an alley right in Cramer Hill.

"I also want to know if he ever touched you in any way or tried to tell you it was okay. You can tell me now. It's important. It's just us."

I stopped walking. "No, Dad. He never touched me at all or talked to me about what he was doing in Philadelphia. Nothing like that at all. I didn't even think it was true, what they said about him. He'd get real mad about it—"

He put his hand on my back. "I don't like people putting your name into things with that man. I didn't know any of this. I never woulda had you over there. I never woulda had anything to do with the man. So, do me a favor?"

"What's that?" I asked. We were walking past Cooper Hospital, headed up Mickle to the Delaware River, towards the Ferry Terminal.

"If people ask you about Howard, ask them to come talk to me. Other than the police, I mean. And even then, I need to know."

"Okay. I will. He knew an awful lot about stamps, Dad. Are you going to miss him?"

He frowned at me. "No. I am not. There's nothing to miss."

"I miss how things were before. I wouldn't tell anyone else, but I will miss him. He had interesting things in his apartment. War souvenirs. Books about all kinds of things. Stories. He had all kinds of stories about the war. And models. He built trains from little pieces of metal. And he liked chemistry. People—"

He put his hand hard on my shoulder and we stopped walking. "He could've killed you, at any time. He almost did.

And he was doing things… in private… I would never want you near."

I didn't know what to say. He was right and he was wrong. Howard wasn't on the edge of his chair ready to kill all the time. He was getting angrier as time went on and I saw it, but I was never afraid of him. It was never directed at me. He could have killed me that day, and didn't raise his gun. He didn't want to. I didn't miss Howard the killer. I missed the Howard I knew before all of this. "I just miss some of the stuff about him," I mustered.

He dropped his hand and we started walking again. "You can tell me that. When we're alone. Don't tell anyone else that. Ever. Not even your grandparents or your brother. I mean it. Understand?"

"I understand." But my father didn't. I didn't know what to think about Howard maybe liking men. It didn't make any sense to me, but what I did know was that those times I spent in his apartment or in his backyard with him, I learned more than I did in a whole year of school. He knew more than anyone I'd ever met about a little bit of everything, and I never knew what the topic would be.

It wasn't until that walk with my father that I could put into actual words how I'd been feeling. Sad that he killed all those people and he couldn't tell me he was going to do it, so I could have stopped him. Sad that people lost their lives. Sad that he gave up everything because he was angry. Sad that I'd never ever really got to say goodbye.

"Hey, Ray. We're not too far from the ferry. You want to catch it to Philadelphia and walk the bridge home?"

"That's a long walk home," I said.

"Not too long for us," he responded. I realized at that point that we were passing right by Walt Whitman's house, near the Chinese Wall for the railroad. "And if it is, we'll catch the bus. O Captain, my Captain, our fearful trip is done…" he yelled.

"The ship has weathered every rack, the prize we sought is won," I finished. "No more Whitman!" He knew I had to memorize that for English last year.

"All of this will be forgotten by next year, Ray. You'll see."

Chapter Twenty

Freda

She was standing outside the building, just looking. Clinton was a narrow street that ran one block north of Pine, between 9th and 11th Streets in Philadelphia. She'd written the address carefully on a piece of paper, folding it and putting it in her purse. Asking the police for it was the hardest part; in the end she couldn't do it, and had Louise call and get the information for her. She had to come and see for herself where her son had been spending his evenings.

It was an ordinary building, a rowhome attached on both sides, brick, with five cement steps leading up to the front door. A rooming house. She'd counted twenty-two people coming and going within the past hour, mostly men. It wasn't drab, dingy or seedy like she'd imagined. It wasn't marked in any particular way that would cause anyone to look twice.

A Jefferson Medical School building was across the street, an anatomy building of some sort, and young men in white coats or scrubs streamed in and out. Only one passed her and went through the doors of 1022 Clinton Street. She felt conspicuous, just clutching her purse, lingering on the sidewalk, looking around. A middle-aged colored woman in a plain light blue dress came down the steps; Freda caught a glimpse of the darkened foyer as the door closed behind her. The woman started for 11th Street.

"Excuse me," Freda called to her. The woman hesitated and then stopped. "What is that building, do you know what kind of building it is?"

"A regular rooming house. Rents single rooms, but there's a bigger apartment on the bottom floor," she answered. Her face looked worn and tired. The beginnings of gray hairs showed around her temples.

Freda clutched her coat tighter. "Is it for men?"

"For men. Students mostly, at the school." She tilted her head to the anatomy building across the street.

"But just men?"

The woman's face settled into a concentrated scowl. "Just men. You looking for a place to live? Coles House is up the street, just one block." She pointed further up Clinton Street. "It's for working women."

"No, my son lived in this building, rented there last year, and I wanted to know if it was reputable."

"Reputable? I know it's clean. Each week I clean a different floor. There's a bed, dresser. Common bathroom."

Freda ran her eyes up the building and did the math. Each room got cleaned once a month. "A place for decent Christian men, then?"

She shrugged. "Decent enough, I suppose." Freda watched a gaggle of men leave together through the front door. She couldn't help but notice how close they were to one another. One had his hand on another's shoulder. They were laughing.

Freda turned away and hurried to a small park just across the street, dropped onto a bench and hugged herself. That building was full of demons. She could just see darkness around it. The police told her they'd interviewed a maid at the rooming house.

It might have been the woman she'd just spoken to; she couldn't be sure and had been afraid to ask. This maid remembered Howard. She said he'd had men coming and going from his room all day long. That he wasn't rude to her in person, but had written the word *nigger* in the dust on the dresser knowing she'd be cleaning later that day and would see it.

The maid she'd spoken to was at the bus stop now, still within her sights. She could go back and ask her, ask her if she knew Howard. Ask her if it was true. Freda could feel herself trembling and couldn't stop. The person the maid had described to the police wasn't the son she'd raised. Howard would have never have written a word like that in dust. He didn't think about people that way. There was something dreadfully wrong.

She pulled the mimeographed papers from her purse and unfolded them. His diary. Pages and pages of his diary, which the psychiatrists had given her. She'd torn through Howard's things looking for the little brown book, hoping it would make sense of what happened. Now she had it, not the whole thing, just these select pages they wanted her to see. It was the missing pages that intrigued her more.

They'd given her a dozen sheets at most, all of it written in code. Single letters, sometimes letters combined; short sentences followed that didn't make sense. Psychiatrists thought she could help to decipher it. She looked up and watched the maid get onto a bus. The police didn't know that the aging colored woman knew her son better than she did.

She looked at two letters that appeared together many times on the pages. Howard had a slant to his scrawl but it looked like an O and a K. Or an O and an H. After it was written, *Lots of racket. Mostly him.* She pulled the pages closer to her eyes and tried to make it out. Maybe it was a C and an H. Charles Cohen. He was writing about Charles Cohen and his noise.

Multiple entries about Charles, down one whole page. Charles had cursed at him one day in the yard. Charles had banged on their common bedroom walls to annoy Howard. Charles had played his trumpet all day long. Charles had made fun of him outside in front of other people. Despite all of this, Howard hadn't killed Charles. He certainly could have if he'd wanted to. The police told her Charles was never on Howard's list.

The next entries had to do with a person named M. Maurice Cohen. Next to the M was, *Wish he would drop dead in his tracks*, and *Hope his hayfever gets him good.* There was no date, and the pages had been copied randomly. She had no idea if this was written last week or three years before. There was a C and an L and a T. And notations after each letter, on and on down the page. After some entries, there was the word *retal*. Retaliate. She dropped the sheets into her lap. She'd heard it all before, either from their mouths or from her son.

Queer, why don't you die? Hope your hayfever kills you. Walk through that mud, Nancy boy. Your mother must be ashamed she ever gave birth to you. What are you, a Nazi? Why are you walking so straight? Hear you shooting in that basement, Unruh. We're gonna give you a reason to use those guns one day. You're not a man, letting Mommy support you. What the hell is wrong with you? Did Mommy tuck you into bed in Belgium, you sissy? Saw you in an alley with another man, Unruh. Whad'ya have to say about that? Can't use the gate, queer? Gotta crawl through the weeds to get to your door?

The sun was slipping west, and she knew she needed to get back to Market Street and catch the number nine bus to her sister's house. There were no answers at the boarding home or in the diary. She crossed over and started to walk down Clinton again. The boarding home door was propped open with a book. Somebody was moving in or out and didn't want it to lock. She pulled the handle and stepped into the foyer. It had very tall ceilings, dimly lit, a tiled floor, dark wood wainscoting. The staircase to the upper floors was directly to the right. No elevator here.

She stood at the bottom and looked up, imagining her son going up and down the stairs, or him leaving their apartment in his brown jacket saying he was catching the bus to go to Philadelphia. He was a man. Part of her was glad he was getting out of the house, the neighborhood, but the other part knew that whatever he was doing, it would turn her stomach. She'd imagined sex with women, drinking. Hanging out in smokey bars, carousing all night. Not this.

Two men came down the stairs and brushed past her. She needed to leave. She meandered down Clinton Street, and then over a few blocks heading towards the Family Theatre. All she could think about was her son sitting at that cold metal table in the hospital, his hands folded calmly in his lap, telling her about his decision that morning to kill the neighbors. His eyes were clouded over and he'd drifted off mid-sentence into a silent stare, and she'd had to touch him to bring him back into focus.

In stops and starts, he had told her about that whole span of time, from the night of the 4th of September all the way through to that morning of the 6th when he pulled out his Luger. The words had come out of his mouth as if it wasn't his mother he was talking to, like she was a police detective, a stranger. He didn't look at her once, and his voice never wavered, flat, emotionless, as he described those hours to her in detail.

When she made her way out of that visiting room on shaky legs, she knew she had to go to the boarding home in Philadelphia and to the Family Theatre where he'd spent that last evening. That's where the missing pieces were hidden.

That north-east side of Market Street from City Hall down to 12th Street was seedy, filled with crowded, cheap stores, clutter and garbage. Wanamakers, just across Market, seemed a world away. Wanamakers was a fairly high-end department store, like Macy's or Gimbels, and its huge display windows were filled with expensive fashion. How the bowling alley, the cheap greasy spoon filled with mice and the Family Theatre ended up just a stone's throw away across four lanes of traffic made no sense.

The Family Theatre wasn't for families at all. Nobody would even think of dragging their children through those grimy dark doors. Situated in the middle of the block, the little round ticket booth with the dim yellow bubble lights overhead was an enthusiastic advertisement for what it was—a grind house playing cut-rate double features all night long. It closed for fourteen hours on Sundays to clean god-knows-what off the seats; otherwise, it was a revolving door for people who had nowhere else to go. Mostly just men. Though nobody said out loud what happened inside, the theatre's reputation was so bad that the Shore Patrol had declared it off limits for naval personnel.

"What were you doin' there, Howard? Why'd you go to that theatre that night? Tell me." They'd been sitting at the cold metal table in the hospital. She was talking about that night of cement. September 5. The night before the murders.

His whole body was still. His hands didn't bend or move at all in his lap. He didn't even seem uncomfortable. "I was meeting someone. Van. But when I got there, he wasn't there. I was late. The bus was late."

"Meeting him for what?" she'd asked.

His eyes were fogged over and it took him time to get his thoughts together. "We'd been together, for three weeks we'd been together. But he was moving, going away. We were supposed to be together that night. But I was late and he left me."

"Together?" Howard wasn't even trying to hide it but she wanted him to say it out loud.

He nodded. "I'd go to the theatre and sit in the middle, if I could. And then I'd wait. If someone sat next to me, I'd slide my foot over and touch his. If he didn't move it, it meant he was interested. I met Van that way. We got along really well. I really liked him. But I missed my chance that night. He was gone."

Freda felt sick at his words but she had to keep going. "I don't understand any of this. You had a good day. Labor Day was good with me and your father. But then you had to go to Philadelphia to meet this fellow? Is that why you left right after supper? Right after your father finished building the gate?"

He nodded. "I should've left earlier. I wouldn't have missed him."

"And then you sat in that dirty theatre for hours after you realized your friend was gone? Why, Howard? Why didn't you come home? Maybe none of this woulda happened if you'd justa come home."

He clenched his right fist. It was the first movement he'd made. "It would've happened. They would've ripped out my gate whether I was in Philadelphia or not. I sat there in the theatre thinking. I was just thinking. I had no way to reach Van. No way to ever talk to him again."

"From seven thirty at night until two in the morning you just sat there thinking? About what?" It didn't occur to her until later that he was trying to tell her he was broken-hearted.

He pressed his lips together. "About things. I didn't even act on it when someone else came over to me and tried to touch me. I just wanted to be alone. I finally got up and left, came home, and saw they'd ripped out the gate. Why'd they do that to me, Ma? Why couldn't they just leave me alone?"

Freda stared at the marquee as she approached the theatre from City Hall. The sun was going down and the little bubble lights in the entryway had come on. There was a time-worn man seated in the booth, waiting to collect money. She pulled her purse strap higher up on her arm. Howard's life was divided between River Road, the constant torment from the neighbors, no job, no way to fill his days, and the squalor of Philadelphia, of performing lewd acts in dirty theatres, and a single bed in a rooming house. Freda suddenly knew why he'd done it. As she hurried past the Family Theatre marquee, it came to her, clearly.

He had no other way out. Revenge was the only door left open to him. She bowed her head and walked faster. He'd failed in every way a man could fail. He couldn't hold a job, had been unemployed for almost a year with the recession bearing down on them, almost as bad as it had been in the early 1930s. He'd suffered the humiliation of flunking out of pharmacy school and had exhausted his GI Bill money. He was never going to marry and have children or a stable life because his perversions had taken him down a different path. A path of lonely rooms and dirty hideouts, which would never be accepted or forgiven. An unchristian life she'd never understand.

What was left for him? His diary, and a plan to not only kill the people who were making his days unlivable, but also end his own existence at the same time. The death penalty or the hospital, it didn't matter. Nothing would ever be expected of him again.

She'd talked to Pastor Bauer for hours after that visit to the hospital, trying to make sense of it all. He'd asked her one question she couldn't answer—was she more angry he'd killed thirteen people, or that he'd admitted to carnal acts with other men? In the end, she didn't say anything because the answer changed depending on the hour.

She made a vow as she waited for the bus to take her back home, that no matter what Howard had done, she would never abandon him. They'd only really ever had each other and she was going to see him through to the end, no matter what or when that might be.

Chapter Twenty-One

Raymond

Clark Hoover, the barber, was friendly enough to us kids, that's what I'll always remember about him. He would smile and laugh a lot when he was cutting hair, and took time, asking questions about how things were going in school, or how our parents were. That sort of stuff. And no matter what, he'd give us a penny in change after we paid him so we could run next door to the pharmacy and get a piece of candy. Howard had a different opinion, though. And he never shied away from telling me about it.

The two didn't like each other at all. The thing is, for the most part, Howard was quiet in his dislike, never saying too much to him or about him to people in town. Hoover, on the other hand, was squawking about Howard every chance he got. Other than the usual name-calling, Hoover would jump in Howard's way when he was walking, call him a Nazi because he walked straight and all. He'd block his path and flail his arms around. He'd take advantage of an audience and mock Howard when he walked by with his bible, just for a laugh. He'd scream all kind of things in his direction, even if Howard was walking on the other side of the street. It was just plain meanness for no good reason. And Howard never fought back, never said a word, until that morning of September 6, 1949.

I still see Howard's brown suit, the bow tie, the combat boots, coming through the door of the barbershop that morning. It's all in slow motion in my mind. Hoover took a second to figure out what was happening, then his face just dropped, turned white and he started shaking. That brush he was holding in his hand was almost vibrating. Hoover started dipping down and around the horse, then I heard the first pop. Sorg was maybe right about one thing. Hoover might've ducked down, letting little Orris Smith take a bullet in the neck meant for the barber. Orris slumped sideways off the horse. And then there was just screaming.

There were no words spoken. Nothing at all. Later I heard Howard had said, "I got something for you, Clarkie," or something like that, but that wasn't true. It was about fifteen seconds of just silent terror. I don't know what Clark Hoover was thinking during those last seconds between life and death. Whatever it was, he kept it to himself. The bullet hit Hoover behind the ear and I remember blood seeping down, reddening the entire collar of his white jacket. He fell back onto the floor and Howard stood over him and fired again into his forehead.

Howard turned to me and looked me dead in the eyes. They burned through me, I think. They were glazed over, doll's eyes. I can't say I stuck around long enough to describe what happened next. I ran. But when I circled back around the block, Clark Hoover was still lying on the floor. The hobby horse was smeared with blood, and the brush he'd been holding was about a foot away from his outstretched hand, as if grasping onto it would save his life.

That east-side stretch of River Road between 32nd and Bergen was still as closed up and empty as it had been months before, right after the killings. If you watched, most people would cross the street and walk on the opposite side of the road, pretending to look through the windows of the American Store or Engel's saloon. Anything not to have to look at those five stores on the other side where the dead bodies had fallen.

I wasn't going to avoid it. I made myself walk that stretch and see it all. I kept thinking if I faced it, the nightmares would go away, though I couldn't say it was working too well. My legs would almost stutter when I got to the barber's door, every time. Then all the details would come back to me in a flash, as if I were there again, sitting in that chair. My shirt was stuck to my back with sweat from the heat. Howard came in, just walked right into the middle where the hobby horse was. He raised his Luger and at that point my mind would go crazy trying to put the pieces together about what had happened.

No matter that months had gone by, I was still seeing Clark Hoover in my sleep. He was a little man. About an inch taller than me, maybe, and skinny. No more than 120 pounds or so. He had a face like an upside-down triangle with a forehead so wide and a chin so pointed, it took a minute to put all his features into place. He built the little shop at 3204 River Road sometime in the 1930s, but he had been there as long as I could remember, standing on the sidewalk outside, smoking and wise-cracking when he wasn't cutting hair.

He'd been married before and divorced, which in and of itself wasn't unusual, given the war and loss of life, and families being torn apart and separated. His two children, Ronald and William, from his first marriage, hardly came around. They were probably grown and had children of their own, but I don't ever remember seeing them around town. He married a second time and that's when Clark Hoover's story got really interesting.

My father took me to the barbershop and put me on top of that hobby horse when I was about four years old. This young woman with dark hair curling around her neck, her lips painted a deep pink color, came over to me, smiling.

"Oh, isn't he cute? What're we doing, just cutting it down? A number three blade or shorter?" she'd asked.

My father was smiling all goofy. "A number two is fine. It'll give him the summer to let it grow." She moved away, taking the scent of lavender with her.

Even at that age I understood that my father thought she was pretty. The first female journeyman barber. In our county, anyway. Barbering was a man's job, so it was something to see her there with her apron and clippers. Men came in to have her lean over them, put hot towels on their faces, lather and shave them, smelling that sweet scent that flowed off her. Her apprenticeship and eventual license was in all the papers and it drew a little notice. All the while, Clark Hoover was moving around like he was king of the world.

The thought on everyone's mind at the time was, how did Hoover manage this? The scrappy little man, who never backed off from a fight, who'd lost one wife because of his temper and habits, was shady. That's what my father said, anyway. Shady as a fifty-year-old oak tree. And from what I'd heard about his father, George Hoover, Clark came from a whole family of oak trees. George Hoover owned the saloon across the street before Engel, and bought the liquor license out of nowhere after years of just scraping by working as an automobile mechanic for different shops.

The father also bought a little jewelry repair shop next door to the tailor's where Latela's sandwich shop was now. Clark and his new wife lived in the apartment over the top. George even owned the house the Unruh's rented and sent Sorg around to collect the twenty-six dollars from Freda every month. Where this sudden cash came from was a mystery. But the biggest mystery of all was Clark Hoover's new pretty, young, barber journeyman wife, Rose Stiles Hoover. Never married before, no children, she was perfect and respectable in the eyes of Cramer Hill.

Clark Hoover was living large—multiple stores, a nice place to live, a new wife. But if you were paying any attention at all, it was easy to see something just wasn't right at Clark Hoover's barbershop during that summer of 1944. I was only seven at the time and might not have noticed, but my father did.

"I saw Hoover out last night with a pack of kids. Bill Morgan was there, and a bunch of other boys I didn't recognize," he said one night during dinner. Bill Morgan lived over on 32nd Street, just a few blocks from Hoover's shop. He was about sixteen or seventeen years old. "It's the second or third time I've seen a pack hanging at his door. Wonder what he's up to?"

"Maybe he's giving them work or something," my grand-mother said. "Cleaning around his shops or something. Or maybe helping George with the bar, unloading or whatnot."

"I don't know, they all piled into his car, two cars actually, with that wife of his too. All teens."

"Maybe they're all his apprentices, learning to cut hair," I offered.

My father shrugged and that was end of that conversation. I didn't think about it again, but every time I walked that way, I noticed the teenagers too, just hanging around. Most of them I'd never seen before. It didn't seem like a big deal, or even something to talk about until December 4, 1944. That's when all hell broke loose. It was one of those things that happens and you can't believe it, even when you know it's true. It had the whole neighborhood out on the sidewalk talking. Clark Hoover was arrested and his kingdom fell. The most interesting part about this was that his pretty, lavender-smelling wife was arrested alongside him. Both of them were dragged out of that shop at 3206 River Road in broad daylight and were shoved in the back of a patrol car.

I didn't see it myself, but I saw pictures in the newspapers, and I heard plenty of people describing it in detail. Hoover was in his dark coat, his brown hair in disarray, screaming at the cops the whole time. He might have hit one of them except he had his hands cuffed behind his back. His wife's hands were cuffed in front, and she had the sense to keep her head down and her mouth shut.

We all knew they weren't being arrested for a petty crime like driving drunk, or running numbers. We knew because of the number of police cars on the street when they hauled them out. Half the Camden police force was out to take down Clark Hoover.

"I told you something was going on," my father said. We were out in the front, clearing off the sidewalk. My grandfather was standing by the front door listening. "The Hoovers are something, I'm telling you."

"Is his father going to bail him out?" my grandfather asked.

"Can't. Heard there's no bail. He's stuck inside for a long while, I'd say."

My grandfather shook his head. "Robbing the Esso station? Robbery? For the love of God. I just don't understand people. I never will."

"More than just a simple robbery, Dad. It wasn't even one gas station. They're saying there were maybe over twenty. He was running a Fagin ring right in our town, using boys to do his dirty work. Stealing goddamned gas rationing coupons, money and oil. This wasn't the first or second time. God knows how long this has been going on. Maybe his father was doing it too. Maybe that's where they were getting all their money from?"

The rationing coupons was what upset them the most. Because of shortages of food and goods during the war, everything important was strictly rationed. To conserve important things like gasoline, butter, sugar and coffee, every house was given a rationing booklet that had to be registered and signed for. There were a bunch of numbered stamps in it that were good for so much of a particular product. It was a complicated system when I think about it. The stamps were different colors and had pictures on them—of an airplane, a soldier, a tank. Generally, the red stamps were good for meat, the blue ones for flour. But there was sometimes a mix and match. It was word of mouth—"Mr. Horner's taking two blue stamps for one red, hurry." Or you had to read the paper or listen to the radio to know a tank stamp was good for a pound of sugar that day. It's a wonder we didn't all starve.

Most people didn't own cars, but if you did, the stamps traded for gasoline were the most precious. A family might be allowed ten gallons of gas a week, depending on supply, and it might have been even less than that. That was it. Fuel was needed for the war effort, and for truckers to haul supplies. Not much was left for civilians. We were all in this effort to defeat Hitler together. Victory gardens, scrap metal drives, women's canning drives at the community centers to preserve every tomato. Everyone did their part. Except Hoover. He was stealing the rationing stamps at gas stations and selling them on the black market.

I didn't know what a Fagin ring was at the time when I heard my father talking about it. I learned later that Fagin was a character in Charles Dickens's novel *Oliver Twist*. The character Fagin had a group of boys stealing for him to make money and pay off debts. I'd say the name was perfect for Clark Hoover.

There's stretch of road called Admiral Wilson Boulevard that runs from the Delaware River Bridge through Camden, cutting it in half, and keeps going to the outlying towns. It's dotted with telephone poles, gas stations, cheap motels and liquor stores. It's the ugliest stretch of highway you've ever seen, and because it's a major thoroughfare to Philadelphia, it's always packed with cars, bumper to bumper. It also floods if there's more than an inch of rain on any given day and they have to close it down, creating a mess of cars crawling through Camden looking for a way out.

Hoover, his wife and the pack of teens had gone to the Esso station right there at Admiral Wilson and Baird Boulevard and had broken in. This wasn't an armed robbery with guns or knives or anything. It was a breaking-and-entering, smash-and-grab, after-dark kind of thing. The Hoovers had the sense to stay out of the way and let the boys do all the breaking in and stealing. They just coached them along, taught them how to pick a lock, or get the most loot in the shortest amount of time. They fenced all their stolen goods, and split the money with them. I imagined the two of them, eating a steak dinner late at night at Neil Deighan's night club up the street from the Esso station, Rose in her fur coat, and Clark in his dark dapper suit, clinking glasses, while those four boys smashed windows and cash registers.

While most of our men, including Howard Unruh, were serving our country during the war, stopping the axis powers from taking over the world, Clark and Rose Hoover were serving time in New Jersey State Prison. And they took four boys—Bill Morgan, Stanley Esposito, Victor Lundquist and Ray Lamoureaux—with them. They were all sixteen or seventeen years old.

Hoover spent two years of his seven-year sentence in prison and was released on parole in 1946. When he got home, everything had changed. The little jewelry shop was gone, as was their apartment, which went with it. George Hoover had sold the saloon to Engel. Rose had taken off after her release, not looking back even once at old Clark. But he still had his little barbershop, with the big plate-glass window and the hobby horse in the middle of the floor. So, he started over.

Clark Hoover's funeral was held the Friday after he died. My father and grandparents didn't go, so I didn't either. The only thing I heard about it was that it was quiet. There was no long funeral procession along River Road or throngs of people trying to get in. There was no circus at all. The obituary in the paper was only five lines long—a sad little tribute to Clark Hoover's forty-five years of life.

The shop stayed just as it was for the longest time until another barber came along and bought it, hobby horse and all, and reopened it. I never thought it was right. They should have taken down the horse and burned it. Orris Smith deserved better.

Howard's letter to Freda, April 1945

Small battle in Opfertshofen. It was maybe worse than the others. Krauts were hidden in a house behind our battery's position, caught us by surprise. Killed one of us and hurt a few others. I saw him die right in front of me. I thought I was done for. I was scared like I've never been. Rattling inside.

Chapter Twenty-Two

Raymond

I wouldn't have believed it if I hadn't seen it with my own eyes. I had to look twice. Leonard Cohen was coming out of the American Store with a sack of groceries under one arm and was waiting to cross over River Road. I watched him head around to the back of the pharmacy and go into the apartment through the back. If he hadn't moved in, he was at least staying in the apartment where his family had been murdered. Earl Horner, the grocer at the American Store, must have been having a hard time believing it too, because he followed Leonard out of the shop and stood there on the sidewalk next to me just watching him walk.

Not that there was anything wrong with Leonard staying on his parents' property, but it was odd. The pharmacy and apartments above it were like a mausoleum, maybe a shrine to the dead. Locked up, dark, creepy, almost like a clock that broke at the exact time of the murders. Nothing on that corner had changed, from the items displayed in the pharmacy window, to the small potted plants Mrs. Cohen had in the back. Time froze when the Cohens were killed, and it was like Leonard was rewinding the timepiece and we could all hear the loud tick-tick-tick and were bracing for what was to come next.

He'd ransacked the place that one night months before, looking for money, and that was bad enough, but now he was going right through the door again, through broken glass, and blood, and he was going to actually close the door behind him and live in it.

"Says he's going to pharmacy school. At Temple. Wants to open the store again when he's finished," Mr. Horner said to me.

"Is that so?" I muttered. "Has it been cleaned out? The last time I was in there, there was blood and—"

He shook his head. "Not that I've seen. Place hasn't been touched. Relatives are all over in Philadelphia. Nobody wanted to deal with this mess."

I looked up at Horner. "It's like a crime scene in there. Shouldn't somebody help him?"

"I helped him. Gave him two extra cans of Campbell's soup and a loaf of bread for free." With that he turned and went back into the store.

I went home, but it bothered me all night. Leonard could've stayed in Philadelphia and gone to pharmacy school—in fact, that made much more sense. Temple University was *in* Philadelphia. Coming back to Cramer Hill and choosing to live where his parents were killed made me wonder what was happening inside him and, maybe more to the point, what was happening with his family across the river.

Quite a bit, it turned out. The Cohens, between the three who were killed, left a good-sized estate, including the pharmacy, apartment and other personal monies they'd stashed away. I saw the very beginnings of the trouble when I was at the funeral—the two families separated, almost into camps, with the coffins lined up between them.

At the heart of it were the two sides of the family—Rose Cohen's brother and Maurice Cohen's cousin squabbling in the courts over control of the two boys and the money that came with them. Whoever had the boys controlled the estate, and Leonard and Charles were caught in the middle while lawyers squared off against one another.

As the older of the two boys, Leonard was forced into court, placed squarely in between the bickering factions, each wanting him to take their side. It was clear from his testimony that he didn't know what to do. He said that he finally escaped his mother's family's home because his grandmother had let loose on him one day, yelling at him, calling him selfish for not taking up their cause in the fight for the estate. I can't imagine what it would have been like to live in that war zone. I pictured Charles all hunkered down inside a bedroom in some strange house, coming to the slow realization that maybe the money that was now attached to him was of more importance to his relatives than his happiness and wellbeing.

And so I guess in the midst of all that constant bickering and stress, Leonard had decided he'd rather live among the broken glass and shell casings that ended his parents' lives than within the battlelines being drawn by greedy relatives across the river. I just had a feeling none of it was going to end well for any of them.

It seemed that no matter who was telling this story of Howard Unruh, whether it was newspaper men or the magazines, or the radio, they kept leaving out one important piece. Leonard Cohen. He was a full five years older than Charles and eleven years younger than Howard. All the papers had to say about him was that he was in the Air Force, that the Red Cross coordinated his leave so he could fly home for the funeral of his parents and grandmother. We all saw the photographs of his arrival at an

Air Force base in San Francisco California, saluting. There was a collective feeling of sorrow for him. Nobody looked beyond that.

The truth was that Leonard had only been in the military a few months before the shootings. Two months to be exact. Before that he was there, living in the house, sometimes sharing that back bedroom with Charles when he wasn't at military school. Whatever was going on within the walls of the Cohen home was in the whispers that rose from little gossip circles in the neighborhood. He didn't just up and randomly decide to enlist in the military. He was given little choice by his parents. What had happened? Was Leonard violent? Did he do something to Charles? Hit him, or something much, much worse? Leonard was almost being whitewashed from the retelling, as if he didn't exist before 1949. That was far from the truth.

Howard and Leonard had dueling insanities going on, on that corner of River Road before that summer of 1949, that was true. Leonard didn't like Howard, and would do the normal things to bother him—bang on the walls, make noise, call him names. Howard would throw Mrs. Cohen's laundry into the dirt, play his music louder. Howard told me not to turn my back on Leonard, that there was something of the devil in him, that he could hear the Cohens' fights through his walls, that Charles sometimes slept in his grandmother's room to get away from his brother.

So, when I saw a few pages of Howard's diary ripped out and reprinted in the newspaper, I thought it was interesting that nobody could decipher the code. It wasn't a code at all, or maybe it was all so familiar to me that I knew exactly what Howard was saying. The police, investigators, the reporters had all misinterpreted those Ls to mean Mr. Latela. I knew better. I knew at least some of them referred to Leonard.

L—Let's give him lots of noise when his mother's asleep.

L—Crackpot

L—Retal (retaliate)

Those were the only pieces reprinted, but I knew there was much more. Howard's kill list, which was either found, or more than likely recreated by the police or psychiatrists, was missing one key person, Leonard. That "retal" printed after one L meant Howard fully intended for Leonard to be a target of his revenge. It might have been the only time in history when enlistment in the military lifted someone out of the line of fire.

If you were to try and paint Howard and Leonard's mental illnesses onto a canvas they would look very different. Howard was aloof, paranoid. His mind could take the truth and bend and twist it until it became something else. He lived in fear of life, of people, even of himself and what he was. Leonard, on the other hand, was a sociopath, cut and dried. Part of him was dead inside, unable to feel anything for anyone, including his deceased parents or his only sibling, Charles.

The Cohens enlisted Leonard into the military because they'd run out of other options for him. He was only seventeen when he went in. He was only seventeen when his family was killed, not eighteen like the papers said. He was in a special military school for troubled boys before that, not public school like the rest of the kids in the neighborhood, and I'm not even sure he graduated. I think his parents pulled the plug, found the closest enlistment office around and just signed the papers. I imagine that the day that Leonard went off to the Air Force, his parents sat down and lit cigarettes with trembling fingers, and took big gulps of whiskey—it was that bad.

I once saw Charles waiting for the bus to Philadelphia by himself. I was kind of surprised. He was only around eleven at the time, and my father never would have let me loose in the city by myself at that age. He said he was headed to the pharmaceutical distributor to pick up medicines for the store. I asked why Leonard wasn't going instead—it seemed like an errand for an adult or an almost adult, but Charles just shook his head. "Leonard can't." That's what he said, "Leonard can't." That became the mantra for everything involving his older brother.

I don't know if his parents were worried Leonard would sell all the medicine before he got back on the bus to come home, or if they were afraid he'd wander off to the wrong part of Philadelphia and get lost, but it was clear from the time that Charles was small that he was the trusted one, the rock, the stability, that Charles had to be the adult before he even finished grade school. Now he was gone, and Leonard was there in the house alone, peeking out through the blinds, sleeping in the bed of a dead relative.

We all saw him around, in his backyard after he moved back, puttering not too far from the spot where his father died. There was tape up across the broken windows; the glass was swept into a pile. He'd walk with books in his arms, like he was in school even after it was rumored he'd flunked out. He'd sometimes sit out front on the pharmacy steps where James Hutton fell after being shot, always with a far-off look in his eyes. He didn't really talk to anyone that I know of, but he seemed like a man suddenly freed from a cage, who was paralyzed by the fear of suddenly being able to move.

One day the heavy pharmacy door was hooked open, just like Mrs. Cohen used to do, so people could just walk in. It made the neighbors stop when they were walking by and look. It was creepy. Mr. Engel thought maybe Leonard had hired a pharmacist, was going to try and keep the business going. Life had to go on. It wasn't unusual. Not really. But when Mr. Engel walked in, the place was dirty—the counters and everything were coated with dust. The ice-cream freezer had been turned off; the contents of the bins had turned to liquid and were moldy. Cough syrup and aspirin bottles were scattered, some on the floor.

Engel found Leonard sitting at the kitchen table in the back eating a ham sandwich. "Are you open?" he asked.

Leonard stood up and nodded. "What did you want? I can't mix compounds yet."

Engel just watched him, thinking the boy must be confused. Mixing compounds? He hadn't finished pharmacy school and all the compounds on the shelves were probably outdated. He bought a bottle of aspirin from Leonard, who stood there at the register, the front of his shirt dotted with breadcrumbs from his lunch, and handed him his nickel in change. Leonard only had the door open for two days and then it was shut for good.

I don't know if he cleaned up the upstairs living quarters or not, if he was still living in the debris of murder. The only thing I know from what I saw through the dirty pharmacy windows was that the contents inside the store looked more in disarray as the days passed, items scattered, moved around, rooted through, as if Leonard had decided that living off the snacks was better than selling them. It was all a mystery. Until one day, Leonard just disappeared.

People worried that he was inside, maybe hurt in some way. Mrs. Rice went and rattled the pharmacy door, and then went around the back and knocked for half an hour. She was a bony woman with a hawk-like face who lived above the Hamiltons' apartment. She had been hospitalized for hysteria after one of Howard's bullets missed her by inches that day. As she stood pounding at that back door, you could almost see her knees knocking together in fear, her head trembling on her stalk-like neck. The police came out, but Leonard wasn't huddled inside or hurt in any way, he was simply gone. The "For Sale" sign went up in the side window some months later. I don't know if it was Leonard's choice to move or if the executors of the Cohens' estate wanted to sell the property. Either way, we never saw him again.

Leonard's comings and goings from the apartment at 3200 River Road did help produce a piece of evidence in the case that might not have been found otherwise. A police car showed up outside the pharmacy one day, parked, and the officers went into the apartment through the back. The neighbors, already anxious and shell shocked, waited to see what had happened. It turned out that Leonard hadn't done a thing.

He'd found a bullet under a chair in the middle bedroom—his grandmother's bedroom. It was a 9 mm with a steel jacket, fired from Unruh's Luger that day. Officers analyzed where the bullet had landed, the line of fire, and concluded it had probably passed through the body of Minnie Cohen and then nestled itself in the corner underneath the chair. They bagged it and logged it as evidence. Leonard stood by the back door with a smile on his face, as if he'd helped move the investigation along. The circumstances didn't seem to bother him at all.

The last time I saw Leonard Cohen in person, he was just standing by the side door of the apartment on 32nd Street, hands in his pockets, looking up and down the road like he was waiting for someone. I don't know if he purposely sought out trouble in life, but trouble sure found him. The story of his life twisted through hospital wards after a suicide attempt: broken relationships, stints on the run from the law, stealing from his brother, hiding away in dingy apartments in Florida and yes, maybe the inside of more than one jail cell.

Chapter Twenty-Three

Freda

She watched the sun disappear into the night sky from the chair in her bedroom at her sister's house. She had the boxes opened from her apartment that contained her photograph albums, the books scattered across the floor. She had to see them, her sons' lives as they grew up. She had to find something that would pinpoint when things started to go wrong with Howard, but after hours of looking, there wasn't one particular picture that made things clearer. Howard had always been different.

He was quiet, kept to himself, just liked to be alone from the time he was small. He liked to read. He liked to tinker with things. He had a hard time bringing other people into his world. He'd never been able to slip into easy chatter with anyone, even at church. He'd told the psychiatrists that when he started middle school, he knew he was attracted to boys, but didn't know why, or what was wrong with him. And that it conflicted with his religious upbringing, making him withdraw from people even more.

She closed her eyes and thought about Maryanne, about how they'd dated for so long, holding hands, going to bible study or to picnics together. Something was missing in their relationship but she hadn't noticed at the time. The eagerness of it all, that's what had been missing. Howard hadn't seemed eager to see her, eager to spend time with her, eager to touch her, to steal kisses or private moments together, eager to marry her. It was everyone else that had held the eagerness for them.

The door opened and Louise looked around. "Goodness, look at this mess." Albums were on the floor, pictures scattered everywhere. "Bob's going to be late coming home. It's just you and me for dinner when you're hungry."

"Did you know Howard was different? Did you see it, Louise? Did you know it?"

Louise hesitated at the door, and seemed to be weighing the option of leaving the room without answering. "I think I saw what you saw."

"But when did it start? That's what I've been looking for in the boxes. When did it start? That he was strange." She wasn't talking about his activities with men, she was talking about his entire demeanor.

Louise came in and sat on the bed. Her hands were folded in her lap. "I don't think it ever started or ended. It just always was. Remember when we took the boys down to Hurley's to see Santa Claus and Howard wouldn't talk? He got so upset at the crowds he wanted to leave?"

Freda nodded. "And James was crying because he wanted his turn. I couldn't make the both of them happy at the same time. Night and day. But when did he get like this, that he could do something like this?"

Freda saw her sister rub her hand through her hair. She didn't want to have this conversation. "I hadn't seen him so much anymore. He wasn't coming to church the way he had been. I don't know what else to say."

It dawned on Freda that her sister had said these words before. To other people, to separate herself from her murdering nephew. "But you saw him not even a week and a half before this happened. Did he seem… more upset, or changed somehow?"

"No. But then I didn't talk to him for long that day."

"Well, other people saw there was something wrong with him. I spent my time just trying to keep going, make sure there was food. And a roof. It wasn't like I turned around one day and Howard was paranoid and angry, distorting things in his mind, making a tangled mess of our lives. It was gradual."

"I know."

"I mean, so gradual it all seemed normal. And the war changed him. He wasn't the same. When he came back. The boy who went over to Europe wasn't the same boy who came back."

"Look—"

"He was angrier. I think that's when he started questioning church. Like he was angry at God for making him kill. He'd have these nightmares, and I'd hear him screaming in his room at night." She put her head down and tried to stop her eyes from filling up with tears. "I told those reporters when this first happened that he wasn't the same. I told them. That's the truth."

"Freda, honey, come downstairs now. Let's put all this away. Okay?"

"It's when he started with the diary. During the war. He had it when he came back. He'd been writing in it the whole while. He told me. Each killing, so he wouldn't ever forget them. He wrote me letters, too, about it." Freda stood up from her chair. "The letters. I have them somewhere, all his letters he sent me when he was away. Where are they?" She went to a box in the corner and started rummaging through the contents.

She pulled out a stack of worn envelopes. "Look at this one. December 26, 1944."

They got us good, Ma, and we had to retreat. It's so cold, it cuts you in half and there's a wetness that soaks your bones. You would have had a laugh, we decorated our helmets with lace curtains yesterday, not to be pretty, but it's good camouflage in the snow. I sat in the pulpit for over ten hours yesterday, not the preaching kind of pulpit, the pulpit in the tank. My hand froze solid firing that gun. A few fingers are black, I might have frostbite. Not much at all to eat. Why does God want me here killing people? I saw a man's head explode yesterday. His brains blew across the snow. If you hear about Chenogne, don't say I wrote to you about it. It never happened.

But there was more than one Chenogne. All I see is blood and snow and body parts. All I hear is the sound of the clip clicking into place, the bullets leaving the chamber, and the sounds of screaming people. All I smell is smoke and burning bodies and blood. Blood has a smell too. You might not know it but it does, and that warm metallic scent goes up into your nose and never leaves. All I feel is cold and death, and the heavy kickback of the Garand against my right shoulder after I fire off a round. The only thing I can do is write it down and pray to God to forgive me if I get out of here alive.

"There are pages and pages of this, Louise. He wasn't the same after this."

"What was Chenogne?"

Freda waved her hand. "Killing prisoners of war. He told me that when he got back. Just shooting them in cold blood. Can you imagine? Do you know how long it takes for warm blood to freeze in the snow?" Louise shook her head. "Howard knew.

He told me, but I don't remember. He watched someone die and all he could do was record that. Something terrible was happening to his mind then, Louise."

Louise came over and took her gently by the wrist. "It's true. He changed. I saw it the first time he came to church when he got back. Tom Campbell made a noise, I don't know, he dropped his hymnal on the floor, and Howard went white. He started to sweat a little. I saw it then, that he'd changed. Lots of soldiers struggled with shell shock. Did he ever go to the Department of Veterans Affairs and tell them he was having problems?"

"I don't know what he told them. I know he went to get his GI bill money to go to pharmacy school, but I don't know what he might have told them. But this whole thing with guns started when he got back, too. He had souvenirs. And he was buying them in stores, collecting them—"

"That Luger?"

"He bought it. He didn't bring it back. The Army did this to him, Louise. If he hadn't gone off to war, he never would've shot all those people. Never. I saw it in his eyes that morning. The Army made him like this and set him loose."

Louise looked down. "It doesn't matter if he was always different or if the Army made him into a killer—"

"It was probably both. He never had any friends. Never. I didn't think about that until I went through his high school yearbook just now." She waved her hand towards a box in the corner. "Hardly anybody signed it. I just thought he was shy—"

"It wasn't your fault."

"I lived with him. I saw how everybody treated him. He had problems with everyone, not just one person. I should've told him to stop shooting in the basement. He had a whole target down there. I'd hear it, bam, bam, bam. I should've taken his guns."

Louise moved to the door. "There's a million pieces to this story, a million what-ifs, not just one. Not just your piece, or your what-if. There's enough blame to go around. It's been six months now, Freda. Six months."

"No, almost five." She felt water stream from her eyes. "It just feels like longer."

"Five months then. The answers aren't getting clearer. They're getting further away. Come down and eat with me. Before things get cold."

Freda nodded. She was glad Bob wasn't home. It was getting harder and harder to see him, to look him in the eye. He had surely heard the stories about Howard being with other men. He never said much, but Freda knew her welcome in his home might be growing thin. Louise turned and headed down the hallway, her shoes making tapping sounds against the hardwood floors.

She was at the table when Freda got downstairs. "It's just leftovers. Sit."

Freda pulled out a chair. "Louise, I think it might be time for me to move. I've been thinking about it for a while. I just don't know how to do it. Where to go."

Louise put a pork chop onto Freda's plate. "There's some corn, and rolls. That's all I have. But I can make you a sandwich instead, if you want."

"Did you hear me?"

"Where would you go, Freda? Do you want me to call Roberta? I can see if she has some room?"

"No." Roberta was Louise's grown married daughter. "No. I don't see why I can't go back to the apartment. I mean, it's where I lived for so long. Bob put the furniture up. See if I can get my job back."

Louise put her fork down. "Are you serious? With the buildings empty all around it, the people gone because Howard killed them? The windows are broken, the building is pitted with holes from gunfire. You think you could live in there, sleep in there? What is wrong with you?"

Freda pushed her plate back. "I want my life back. I want my job. I need money. I can't go on living with you, expecting you to make me sandwiches for the rest of my life."

"We'll figure it out. Bob was saying we should call Fred and Carrie and Estella, and come up with a plan."

"I don't need the whole family to solve my problem." Of all the siblings, Freda was the youngest. The baby. Estella, the oldest, had nine years on her, Louise had six, Fred three. They babysat her when they were growing up, practically raised her.

"It's a pretty big problem, Freda. And I'm just going to say no to going anywhere near that apartment. Someone has a place for you. It'll work out. Might be better to get you out of this area anyway."

Freda folded her arms in front of her. "I was thinking of moving up north, nearer to the hospital where Howard is. Nearer so I can visit him. I could stay in a rooming house. Fifteen or so dollars a month. I'll see if I can find work somewhere. Enough to pay my rent. A little food, that's all I need."

"And what about James?"

James hadn't called her in weeks. Her younger son wanted as much distance as he could get from his brother's deeds. "James has a life that doesn't include me. Moving up to Trenton is the best plan."

"We'll see."

The front door opened and Bob walked in. Freda felt her body stiffen. "Freda, you got a letter." He put the envelope by her plate. "Don't worry about dinner for me. I ate already," he said.

"Who's the letter from, Freda?" Louise asked.

She picked it up. "The *New York Times*. They probably want to interview me or something. I'm not talking to anyone. I told them that before. Can you write them for me, Bob? Please. I can't right now."

The envelope was long, legal sized. "Seems like they'd come down here and knock on the door if they wanted an interview. Not send a letter," Bob said, taking the letter from her hand. He ripped it open and pulled out a newspaper clipping folded in thirds to fit into the envelope. "It's an article from the *New York Times*, September 6. A Meyer Berger wrote it. I remember he was here. Remember, Louise? He was running all over the place trying to get a story. He had a couple hours to put it all together."

"There were a million reporters running around that day," Freda said.

"There were, but I talked to this one. I remember his name." He handed Freda the article.

"Why did he send that to her? It makes no sense. She doesn't need to go over this again," Louise said.

Bob was reading a letter that came with the article. "He won the Pulitzer for that article. He wanted you to see it. And to give you this." He put a piece of paper in front of her.

It was a check. "What's this?" she asked, looking up at her brother-in-law.

"He's giving you his prize money. The Pulitzer comes with prize money. He says he can't imagine what you're going through and he wants you to have it," he said.

She stared down at the check. It was for a thousand dollars. Years and years of rent and food at a boarding home. More money than she'd ever seen in her lifetime. "Why would he do this for me? I don't understand. People blame me for what happened."

"He doesn't, Freda. Maybe other people don't either," Bob responded. "It's just incredible."

She squirmed in her seat. Nobody had ever been that kind to her before. This man she didn't even know, hadn't even so much as written or called her before. The fact that he'd been thinking about her silently moved her in some way she couldn't explain. The tears that came to her eyes weren't happy or sad. They were somewhere in between. Meyer Berger had just given her a pass to a new life.

Chapter Twenty-Four

Raymond

For all the people who were involved in Howard Unruh's life, who took part in tormenting him in some way, there were many more people hurt on the day of the shootings who had never even met the man—or who only knew him in passing. It stuck in my brain like a scratch on a record, skipping over and over again. I'd seen people try and explain the whys of it—people with education, who had degrees in psychology or psychiatry, who had theories about what was happening inside Howard's mind during those twelve minutes he was pulling the trigger.

I don't think they understood much at all; not that I did, but I had the advantage of seeing it play out first hand, of knowing the man. I wasn't just guessing. I know when Howard started his rampage in the cobbler's shop, he had no interest in killing Ronald Dale. It wasn't on his mind. He didn't set out that day to wipe out everyone in his path. He had his list. When he came into the barbershop and shot Orris and Clark Hoover, he didn't kill Orris's mother, who was screaming at a pitch that could have broken light bulbs. Catherine Smith picked her son up off the floor. She was there, not running away. Howard didn't shoot her, or even try.

When he headed to the drug store next, to get the Cohens, he ran into James Hutton on the steps of the pharmacy. Mr.

Hutton was in his late forties with thinning brownish hair and little round glasses, looking pretty much like you'd expect an insurance man to look. He'd parked his car right on the street in front of the pharmacy, as he often did, to run in and grab a Coca-Cola before doing his rounds door-to-door collecting on policies. Mr. Hutton and Mr. Cohen were friends and you could find them chatting away lots of mornings, if you happened to stop by the pharmacy for something.

Mr. Hutton got to the pharmacy around 9:20 that morning. I don't know if he heard the shots and knew something was wrong when he got out of his car, or if it only occurred to him when he was at the front steps. I only know he was on the steps when Howard walked up to him. Howard had already shot three people, and the one thing he was probably thinking was that his time was running out. The clock was ticking and the police would be there any minute.

The two people he wanted to kill more than anybody else on his list were Maurice and Rose Cohen. James Hutton turned around when Howard approached. He had to have seen the gun in Howard's hand. Maybe he was confused as to what was happening. Maybe it didn't make sense to him and he was trying to figure it out. Maybe he thought he could talk to Howard and calm him down. Or maybe he was giving Mr. Cohen time to run away. The only thing that's certain is that James Hutton stood on those steps, in Howard's way, chewing up precious seconds. Howard walked up to him and said, "Excuse me, sorry," and tried to pass.

When I think about that, it makes me want to cry for some reason. Howard Unruh and James Hutton knew each other. They weren't strangers. Hutton was Howard's insurance man too, sold him at least one Prudential policy. He'd sat at Howard's kitchen table many times, just like I had, with Howard and his mother. He knew Howard had struggles and he'd tried to help him out by asking around about a job for him; he'd always given Howard his time and a smile.

But now the man wasn't budging from those concrete steps to let Howard through with his loaded Luger, and so Howard asked him to move in a polite way, like he was blocking his exit from a church pew. You couldn't make this stuff up. Mr. Hutton was only around five foot three inches tall and was on the thin side. Howard was six foot, easy. He could've pushed him out of the way without much trouble, but instead Howard shot him and James Hutton fell dead right there on the pharmacy steps with his head in towards the door and his legs splayed across the two concrete steps. Howard marched over him without looking down and entered the drug store to complete his mission.

James Hutton left behind a wife, Ethelyn, who was celebrating a birthday the next day. Mr. Hutton had planned an elaborate surprise birthday party for her with their two grown-up children. His wife was given the news that her husband had been killed while she was at her job at the W.T. Grant company in Philadelphia. When I was looking at pictures in the newspapers after the shootings, the one thing I couldn't take my eyes off, right there, in the middle of the frame, was James Hutton's 1947 black Chevy parked right outside the pharmacy where he'd left it.

After killing Hutton, Howard continued through the pharmacy in his pursuit of the Cohens. Something in him seemed to spiral after finishing off that task. He reloaded his clip, coming back down their stairs—they found the empty clip on the fourth step down. He'd spent nine bullets by that time. He came back out onto River Road, treading over James Hutton again on his way out, and his mind at that point slipped into another gear. He had gone from wanting to make a few people pay, to all-out war on the whole community.

A man he'd never met before in his life had the misfortune of driving down River Road right as Howard was coming out of the drug store. He was traveling north, crossing through the light at 32nd Street, and slowed to see why James Hutton's body was just lying there, with blood splattered across the steps. Howard went right up to the car and shot Alvin Day in the face. A few minutes later, I came back around the block and saw his head back, the blood dripping down his chin. Alvin Day was a television repair man and had agreed to do a job in Camden, driving all the way from Mantua that morning. He was twenty-four years old, a decorated veteran, and a married man with a two-year-old son.

After Howard shot Mr. Day, he went across the street in a frenzy and tried to get into the American Store, but the owner, Earl Horner, had had the good sense to lock it. Howard fired a few bullets into the door but then moved on. He turned around and saw another car, right there going southbound on River Road, waiting at that same light.

That car contained three people. Emma Matlack was in the driver's seat, on her way to a doctor's appointment in Camden that morning. I read in the papers that her husband had just died only a month before. As Emma was alone and reeling from the loss, her daughter, Helen Wilson, had convinced her it would be best if she moved up from Wildwood to live with her and her husband, Garland, in Pennsauken.

Emma didn't know it, but she had cancer. Her daughter Helen had been given the news by Emma's doctor, and she was trying to find appropriate treatment with a specialist in Camden before breaking the news to her mother. Emma was sure she was just having sinus issues, that she'd be fine, and thought the specialist in Camden was just fussing too much over nothing.

After being promised lunch downtown and some shopping, Emma agreed to go. Helen's ten-year-old son John climbed in with them, to be dropped off with a tutor downtown for English and spelling lessons. School was starting the next day and John had done particularly poorly in both those subjects the year before. None of them really wanted to be there when they pulled up at that red light at 32nd and River Road.

It's possible they thought that the loud banging noises they heard were firecrackers, or a car backfiring. Even when Howard was right there, with the gun in their faces, people said it didn't seem to register with them what was happening. Howard shot all three. The two women died instantly. John Wilson hung on for some hours at Cooper Hospital and died overnight. Garland Wilson lost his whole family that day.

Howard then crossed back over River Road, shooting Tommy Hamilton through the window of his apartment and then Helga Zegrino in the back of the dry-cleaning shop. That was thirteen people. He'd exchanged some gunfire along the way with Engel, hitting eighteen-year-old Charles Peterson in the leg, and took a bullet to his own buttocks, before scooting back down that alley and through his own yard to the Harrie home, his last stop before going back to his apartment.

Twelve minutes from the first shot fired, he was back in his house, staring out of the front window. Twelve minutes to kill thirteen people. He'd finished his war, expending both clips, plus the sixteen extra loose bullets in his pocket, and probably didn't even know or care about the casualties. Scores of people's lives were changed forever.

The randomness of it all bothered me. At the time, I couldn't put exact words to it, but that's what it was. Alvin Day's wife said out of dozens of possible service calls to make that morning, he had chosen to go to Camden. He had also decided to drive up River Road, rather than taking Westfield or Federal. What if one of the red lights along the way had kept him idle for a few minutes longer? What if he'd stopped for a cup of coffee or something to eat that morning? What if he'd noticed a block earlier that something was really wrong and made a U-turn? What if he'd run Howard over in the street?

The twist and turns and what-ifs kept me up thinking. Emma Matlack had only driven down River Road because of roadwork underway on Federal Street. What if she'd just dealt with the construction and traffic delays of the other route? What if she'd left five minutes later, or ten minutes earlier, not waited for the red light, but plowed right through it? What if John had begged his way out of spelling lessons? Any tiny change would have made all the difference in what happened.

The worst what-ifs came to mind when I thought about James Hutton. Howard had the presence of mind in that moment in his killing spree to say excuse me, and try to pass him. If Hutton had moved, he wouldn't have died. If he'd shifted three feet in any direction, if he'd gone into the pharmacy or out, if he'd walked back down onto the street, if he'd done anything at all other than just stand there, he'd be alive. It bothered me. Why didn't he move? He saw Howard's gun. He had to have seen it. Howard had it in his hand. A moment of indecision had cost him his life.

But these thoughts would always circle around to the same thing. If I hadn't been in the barbershop, if I'd waited across River Road, watching that napkin spin in the air in the exhaust fumes a little longer, or if I'd just hung back on the corner talking to one of the other kids, and maybe bumped into Howard when he came across the street, when he had spiraled down into full-blown killing mode, would he have remembered me, all our afternoon conversations, our friendship? Would any of that have mattered to him in that moment? Could I have stopped him or would he have shot me dead right there? I don't know. They're what-ifs that will spin and float in the clouds forever.

Chapter Twenty-Five

Raymond

Change, big and small, was happening all around me. Cramer Hill was no longer the little town in a larger city filled with immigrants and first-generation Americans making an average of five hundred to a thousand dollars a year at blue-collar jobs: factory work, shipbuilding, warehouse and clerical work. We weren't a community strong with the boys' club, or scouts, the auxiliary and rotary, or people that kept our houses nice, knew each other and had a sense of community. We were the town that had born and bred the first spree killer in the United States.

The world was watching and we knew it. As the months went by, we went from just another community reeling from the war, to the small crosshatch of streets a little north of downtown Camden where Howard Unruh had lived. In a blink of an eye, everything seemed different. My grandfather said changes were happening every day and always had been, and I was just noticing it now. People had hunkered down, eked out a desperate existence during the depression; they'd sacrificed during the war. Now, tired of this bleak city showing the cracks, they were looking towards Audubon or Haddon Heights, to Oaklyn or Haddonfield—nice little quiet places, suburbs outside the city, a better place to nestle in and raise a family.

As far as I was concerned, Camden was a beautiful city. We had restaurants good enough to bring people over from Philadelphia. We had shops of every kind, department stores—Lit Brothers and Hurleys. We had ice-skating rinks and theatres that were so crowded it was hard to get a seat on a Friday or Saturday night. Camden was just across the river from Philadelphia but we were really just an outgrowth, connected by one bridge.

In Cramer Hill, we'd go duck hunting by the cove, or swimming down by the 36th Street bridge, ice skating at Baldwin's Run in the winter, or hang around by the boating club, or go to the pictures at the Rio. There was an ice-cream fountain every few blocks, tucked away inside a pharmacy. We could walk to downtown Camden in a good thirty minutes, or over the bridge to Philadelphia in forty-five. A car or bus would get you there in ten. I didn't see any good reason to move anywhere else, but my grandparents had different ideas, always eyeing houses on the outskirts of the city. So did a lot of other people.

All these thoughts hit me in the gut one day when I was walking down the street and saw the moving van. It was perched at an angle out into the middle of River Road, creating a bottleneck for the cars for two blocks in both directions. Mr. Latela was standing near the vacant lot, his hands on his hips, watching it all. He owned the little luncheonette right on the other side of Zegrino's dry-cleaning store. Once a jewelry repair shop owned by Hoover, it was snatched up by Mr. Latela in 1944 when Hoover was serving time.

His real name was Taglialatela, but he laughed that his name had too many letters to put on a sign so he shortened it. Mr. Latela was a short man, in his mid-thirties, with dark brown hair, and a little belly that advertised his wife's cooking. His shop did a nice little business selling all kinds of sandwiches, soup, homemade pasta, and frozen food. He lived above the store with his wife, Dora, and their daughter. I wasn't really shocked when I saw he was moving. Though Howard hadn't hurt him or any of his family, he'd given his wife Dora quite a scare.

Mr. Latela peeked out of his doorway that day when he heard the gunshots and saw Mrs. Smith carrying her son, Orris, out of the barbershop. Orris's head was flopped back, the blood streaming down onto her clothes, dripping onto the pavement. Mr. Latela somehow managed to pull his car up, get them both inside and drive them to Cooper Hospital. Unfortunately, that left his wife hunkered down inside their shop to protect herself and their six-year-old daughter when Howard came back down the street looking for her husband. He was number eight on his kill list. Howard kicked out some panes of glass at their shop either with his boot or the butt of the Luger, shot at the door a few times and then left.

Those few seconds left Dora undone, shattered. She hardly came outside after that day, and when she did, she seemed nervous, flustered all the time. Mr. Latela was on Howard's list for the same reason the other business owners were—whenever Howard walked by, Mr. Latela would say things to him. He also made a noise with his car coming up and down the street, and would sometimes stop in front of Howard's apartment and honk his horn, just to annoy him. Howard saw him, the Zegrinos, Pilarchik, Hoover and the Cohens as a solid wall along that street that had to be destroyed.

"Where're you going, Mr. Latela?" I asked. "You're moving?"

He nodded. "The missus doesn't want to be here anymore. Thinks we're never going to have business the way we did."

It was true. The only business on the street that still had a flow of customers was Engel's saloon. Engel said he ran a business for all seasons. If times were good, people drank; if they were bad, they drank more. Right about that time, his bar was stuffed full every single night.

"But where will you go?"

The moving men came out with a big china closet and slid it into the back of the van. "Out to the country. We're moving near Colestown, Delaware Township. Dora wants to look at reopening a shop there."

I nodded. I wasn't going to ask him where that was. I had an idea that it was somewhere east of Haddonfield. "So that's it? In the middle of all this, you're going to move?"

He frowned a little. "In the middle? It's not in the middle. It's the end. Over. People are coming here to count bullet holes and point at buildings. Nobody's looking to buy Dora's raviolis. And she doesn't even want to come outside, afraid someone's going to start shooting."

"They won't, Mr. Latela. It only happened once. It's never going to happen again," I said.

"Ha. Young and naive, you are. That was just the beginning of the end of this town. Eleanor needs more room to grow up. Some place cleaner, less dangerous." He backed up and ducked through the door into the shop. I followed. "We'll be far away when someone pulls out a gun again."

The counter was there, but all the chairs were gone, as was the sideboard where they'd kept glassware and coffee mugs. The lights were out, and I got a big knot in my stomach. "It only happened because someone took his gate. That's the only reason. I promise you it won't happen again." I was bargaining with him to stay and I wasn't sure why.

"The gate? Maybe he says it was about his gate. Maybe that explains it all. But if it wasn't the gate, that madman would have found another reason. I saw him only a few days before it happened, walking right past the shop. He wasn't right, something in his eyes. He hasn't been right since he broke up the shoemaker's lumber."

"Did you talk to him?"

He nodded. "I told him. I asked him what the hell was wrong with him, watching his mother slowly dying in that factory while he lounged around collecting guns, shooting in that basement. I called him a lazy bum, because he was. He wasn't a boy anymore. What was he doing with his life?"

I half closed my eyes. "What'd he say?"

"He told me to mind my business, that he was lookin' for a job."

I nodded. "Oh."

"I told him to look harder or when his mother dies he'd be out on the street beggin' for change. Then his head sprung back straight and he kept walking. I told him he'd better watch out because we were gonna give him a reason to use all those guns if he kept bothering everyone."

"You did?"

"Yes. He said nothing to that. He just kept going." I must've been staring at Mr. Latela hard because he jumped in. "Listen, I drove that little boy he shot in the barbershop to the hospital, you know," he continued. "Him and his mother. In the middle of all the gunfire, I got my car to them, looking over my shoulder, waiting to get killed, and we took off. Orris was still alive when I picked them up, did you know that?" I shook my head. "Shot in the neck. Every time he took a little breath, the blood sprayed out a little onto his mother, onto my car seats. He died in her arms. Somewhere around the Federal Street bridge. Damn bridge." He turned around and walked back out onto the street, motioning for me to follow. He shut the shop up behind us and locked it.

"I didn't know that," I said.

"Yeah, well. I scrubbed that seat, but Dora won't go anywhere near it, won't touch that car. And every time I even see that bridge in the distance, it gets me." He started to choke up a little. "Kid was only six, like my daughter. You think about that when you start talking about his gate."

"Okay." I felt properly chastised.

He softened a little. "Ray, listen… I know people gave him a hard time. I know people weren't nice to him. But he wasn't the easiest guy in the world to get along with. Bad memories here."

"Do you know who took the gate?"

He shook his head. "You looking for someone to blame? I took the gate, Pilarchik took the gate, Hoover took the gate. All of us did it, Ray. The Cohens too. All of us on this street did it together."

"Really?" I knew he was being sarcastic but I had to ask.

"What do you think?" he asked. "You best be getting home now. It's getting dark."

I turned to leave. "Bye Mr. Latela." Him leaving felt like one more nail in the coffin for that street, for Cramer Hill.

"Tell your father and grandparents I said goodbye. They can come to my new shop sometime," he said. "First meal is free."

"Thanks." I waved and walked away, only looking back once to see him put a closed sign on the door.

I couldn't sleep that night, just lying in bed, imagining all of them, all crouched down outside the Unruh yard wrestling with Howard's fence. The Cohens, Mr. Hoover with his wide forehead and little ears sticking out to the side, Mr. Pilarchik, his dark curly hair poking out from under a cap, Zegrino and his son David, maybe dressed in dry-cleaned black clothing, Mr. Latela with his little round glasses, hands on his hips, Sorg and all three Harrie brothers.

I saw it all clear as day. Sorg would be the lookout—wise-cracking and telling them to hurry. Charles would just be hanging back watching with his hands in his pockets. Mrs. Cohen would be orchestrating the thing, telling them they were doing it wrong. Mr. Cohen would be quiet and watching, arms folded, weighing the pros and cons. The Harrie boys would be laughing, their fingers maniacally ripping at the wires. The Zegrinos would be there with cutters, and a hacksaw—the tacticians of the removal—and Hoover would be figuring out how to sell the gate to make some money.

None of that really happened. I knew Mr. Latela was just making a point that everyone had some part, however small, in what had happened in our town. As I drifted off, I wondered if the people in Cramer Hill, all of them good people in their own way, were any different—angrier, meaner, nastier—than anyone else across America. And if Howard was the sickest, most paranoid and evil person. And if they weren't, and he wasn't, then maybe Mr. Latela was right. This kind of thing might happen again at some point, but moving to Colestown wasn't going to help.

Howard's letter to Freda, December 25, 1944

Guarding POWs at this gas dump. Expecting German paratrooper raid. We're all on edge. I guess that's what you'd call it. Two POWs didn't get back to base on time. I watched it all, Ma. They were screaming the whole time. It was fast. They were lined up together facing us and got shot in the face. It's the first death I've seen since getting here. I wanted to write it down so I didn't forget—everything. What they looked like, how they fell. The taller one had brown hair, the shorter was darker in case you wanted to know. They looked alike when they were dead, though.

Chapter Twenty-Six

Freda

She saw him coming but hesitated too long, unsure of where to go, so she stood right in his path. She'd just taken a walk down 36th Street, to get out of the house, to take a break, and had just crossed over the train bridge nearing River Road and there he was, looking at her with his curious eyes. Raymond, his name was Raymond, but Howard always called him the Stamp Boy. He'd been coming to the apartment steadily for a few years, and on and off before that, scampering through the Cohens' gate or through the rough lot, with some wax envelope in his hand for Howard.

She never questioned why he stayed so long after he'd dropped off his little parcels, but he did, and he seemed to keep Howard company so she didn't say a word. He always seemed older than his age, talking to adults the way a child shouldn't—too comfortable and informal. He was comfortable around people in a way Howard never was. The way she never was.

She liked him well enough. He wasn't old enough to be hardened by life, or to be taken in and saddled with the gossip and opinions of the bitter adults who surrounded him. He didn't care what anyone thought. He just brought some rare stamp for Howard that would make his eyes light up. Then Howard would run up the stairs, grab one of his albums off the shelf and charge back, spreading it all out on the kitchen table, and the two of them would sit elbow to elbow talking about the history of it.

While Howard's conversations about foreign countries, or those little pieces of paper, bored her, the Stamp Boy seemed endlessly fascinated. He was always right in step with her son, asking questions, his big brown eyes roving all over looking for new bits of information—not about other people, never about other people, but about things. The two of them were a curious pair. And she'd thought about him after the shootings. She'd heard he witnessed it, was in the barbershop at the time. That Howard hadn't raised his gun to him. Now he was thirty feet away from her, his eyes crawling all over her, waiting for her to greet him in some way.

Pangs of guilt tore through her body. Shame that she'd let this happen, that she hadn't done something to stop it. The boy walked closer and she turned her back on him and started back up 36th Street.

"Mrs. Unruh?" he called to her. She could hear his feet on the pavement, behind her. "Wait."

She got to the bridge and stopped, leaning against the rail, looking down at the train tracks. He came up and took a place beside her, saying nothing. Neither of them moved.

"I'm not sure we should be talking," she said.

"Why not?"

"It doesn't seem right." She shot him a quick look. "The town blames me."

He just nodded. He wasn't going to disagree. "I heard you were leaving town. Is that true?" he asked.

"I guess news travels fast. I'm moving up near Trenton. Closer to the hospital." She put her head down and pulled off the hat she always wore so people wouldn't see her face. "My sister's driving me."

There was a silence between them but neither made a move to leave. "You've seen him, then? You've talked to him?" Raymond asked.

"Yes."

"How is he?"

She turned slightly to look at this boy. He was the only one who'd asked about Howard over the past six months, who even cared to know how he was. "He's not the same… I don't know if they have him on some kind of sedative—"

"But he's talking?"

"Yes. And he knows what happened." A train sped by underneath them and shook the bridge, drowning out all other sounds. "Please don't ask me any questions," she said when it had passed. "I don't have any answers."

"What's he saying about it? Anything at all?"

She was looking out into the distance towards downtown Camden. She could just make out the round top of the City Hall building. "Nothing anyone would want to hear. He's not sorry, if that's what you're waiting for. He said they had it coming to them. That they deserved it."

"Oh." The boy's head was down.

She'd hoped for something more from him, that he understood some part of it. She put her hands on the railing and squeezed. "He doesn't remember shooting the kids. He says he didn't mean to get them. I need you to know that. I know you were there… he never would have—"

"I don't know that. You didn't see his eyes." The Stamp Boy was staring at her now. "I don't even know for sure if he recognized me."

"I did see. He looked at me the same way that morning. He mighta killed me with a wrench if I hadn'ta moved. So I do know."

"If that's true, Mrs. Unruh, if he mighta killed you, then neither of us know anything about him. It's like someone just swapped his brain out for someone else's."

She cleared her throat. She could feel the heat rising up her back into her face. "Well, he's not the same, that's for sure. He says doesn't remember shooting Mr. Cohen either. He's confused. But the rest, he knows what he did."

"But he's not sorry for it?"

"No, he just isn't. He said he'd been planning on getting the Cohens for a long time now. Over a year. He bought a big knife, a machete—" She stopped talking; her throat felt as if it was closing. She took a few big breaths. "He had it in his closet—was going to use it to cut them, to cut their heads off—"

"Cut their heads off?"

"He said the Cohens had it coming for a long time. He couldn't hold back anymore. And he just said it like it was the most normal thing in the world. Stopped going to church. That's what it was." She wondered if this boy had heard about Howard being with other men. She wasn't going to bring it up. "You close yourself off from the Lord and the devil—"

"What's going to happen to him now?" he interrupted.

"I don't know and he doesn't care. He doesn't even read his bible anymore. He doesn't care if he dies. He asked to die in fact. He told them to hurry it up and get him over to the prison."

He didn't look at her when she said that. It was almost as if he knew it was easier having this conversation if he didn't look her in the eye. "But for now, he's stuck in the hospital until they say he can go."

"Well, I should probably go now, Mrs. Unruh."

"Wait. I need to ask you one thing. Did you see it, Raymond, when they arrested him? Did you see it all? I asked my sister and my brother-in-law, but they wouldn't say a thing. They're keeping certain things from me. And I can't bring myself to read the papers…"

He was shuffling his feet and she knew he might just turn and walk away. "I saw most of it. You know, people in the neighborhood were gathering along the Harries' driveway, all pushed up against the fence trying to see. The police were keeping them back."

"Before they even arrested him? They could've been shot."

He nodded. "When they had him barricaded inside. The police were crawling out of Charles's bedroom with tommy guns—"

"Machine guns? They had machine guns? How do you know that?"

"I just know. They were crawling across that back roof with tear gas and guns. There was smoke everywhere. The cops were screaming for everybody to stay back. Stay back, they said. But nobody listened. They all wanted a piece of him when they brought him out."

"They didn't have it blocked off or something?" she asked.

"They tried. And Mr. Cohen was lying dead right there out in the open in the street. The police couldn't be everywhere at once."

"Did they rough him up at all when they brought him out? Hurt him at all?"

"No. After the cops tear-gassed him, he put this white material out the window like he was surrendering and the cops went in and brought him out, had him right up against your outside door. But they protected him from the crowd. They just put him in the police car and took him away. That's it. The rest of it I just got from other people. Like the police asked him if he was a psycho or something, and he said no, I have a good mind, but I don't know if that story's true or not. Ambulances were blocking off the streets, getting all the bodies out. Police were walking all over with guns, yelling through blowhorns for people to get inside. Like a war zone."

"It was a war zone. That's what Howard wanted, a war zone."

"If you see Howard again, tell him you saw me…"

She frowned. This boy thought that Howard would care how he was doing. He didn't. He didn't really even care about how she was doing. His conversations were all shallow and superficial. His soul and substance were gone. He was just saying words he didn't mean. He'd found a way out of his miserable life and sitting right behind his eyes was a look of self-satisfaction. She'd asked him once if he'd do it again and he took his time in answering. He said that he'd failed. That if he could do it over, he wouldn't fail. That was his cryptic response.

"You were always nice to him," she said.

"I guess. I didn't mind bringing him stuff from my father. I never minded."

"But you stayed. You didn't just leave. And you listened to him. You two seemed to just get along somehow—I never understood."

Raymond shrugged. He was chewing at his bottom lip. This wasn't a good conversation for either of them. "He liked interesting things. It was something different every time. And I liked listening to his stories."

"He told me, I don't know, maybe a week before... that you helped him. I came home from bible study and he was all worked up. I asked him what was wrong and he said it didn't matter anymore, that you'd helped him to see what was really going on..."

Raymond looked up at her. He pushed off the railing and stood up straight. "I don't remember exactly how I might've helped him. Look, I need to be going now, Mrs. Unruh. I was just dropping something off for my grandmother at one of her friends', but she's expecting me back."

She nodded. "You better get going."

"Take care of yourself," he said, walking past her. "Good luck with your move."

"Thank you, Raymond." She was saying it to his back as he was heading down the street.

He didn't turn around. How could he after what Howard had done? She remembered the first time he'd shown up at their doorstep, this boy with medium-brown hair combed over to the side, wearing a long-sleeved light blue shirt, the ends of it frayed a bit, and dark-colored pants that were an inch too short. He looked clean but his fingernails were chewed and the skin was picked all along the cuticles. He was standing there with this envelope in his hand.

"My father, Raymond Havens Junior, asked me to drop this off for Howard Unruh," he'd said. He was so polite. Howard had been in the living room and came and took it right from him, barely giving him any notice at all.

"These are Jenkins' Camden. He said he had them. I didn't believe him. Tell him I have something good for him too. I need to go through things tonight. Can you come by tomorrow?" Howard asked him.

Instead of nodding and leaving, Raymond moved in closer. "What makes that stamp so different? My father said it was different."

He was so smooth and easy. Like oil, just greasing the conversation. And whatever it was about him, Howard dropped his guard. He ran up and got a stamp album and opened it on the kitchen table. The light overhead was dim and they were both hunched forward, staring down at the small squares of paper. Howard had on a t-shirt and his worn brown trousers, and he was leaning over so far, she could just see the top of his curly head.

"Oh." He seemed surprised. "It was issued by this private company—Jenkins' Camden Dispatch. In 1854 they were competing with the US post office, had an office right downtown, issued their own stamps and everything. I've been looking for this for a long time."

"So, they're rare?"

"Pretty rare. You don't see them around much. They went out of business, I don't know, maybe ten years after this was issued, if that. Thank your father for me. This is a gem."

Freda did the dishes, half listening to the conversation. At first, she thought that he might be the smart-mouthed kind of kid who was only staying and talking just so he could run back to his friends and make fun of Howard, like they all did, but as the conversation went on, and she watched his eyes, his expressions, the questions he was asking, the more she dismissed the idea. He was an unusual boy.

After that she couldn't count the comings and goings. Sometimes the Stamp Boy would stop by just to talk or to tell Howard something. It amazed her, because Howard was talking back. And he never said any angry word against him, never complained about him or twisted his words. He never asked her if maybe the Stamp Boy was against him, or did something to him on purpose to bother him, or thought he was talking about him behind his back. It never got complicated. He just took him at face value, maybe because he was so young.

One day, after a few bad days of rain and when their basement had flooded, Raymond was there visiting. Howard had showed him the mess. He was in a rage, because the smell of dampness and mold had filled the apartment, making both he and his mother sick.

"You want me to go to the pharmacy and get you some medicine?" Raymond had asked.

Howard was on his side lying across the small sofa in the living room, his long legs bent and tucked under him, so his body would fit. "No. I don't want anything from those people. I'm fine."

"So, what are you gonna do about the water? Are you going to talk to Mr. Pilarchik?"

"No," he'd answered. "It wouldn't do any good."

Raymond went to the pharmacy anyway, not to get Howard some medicine, but to ask the Cohens if they were getting water in their basement too. There was only a concrete wall separating the two spaces. It turned out, they were getting some seepage; not as much as the Unruhs, but enough that they were concerned.

Mr. Cohen said he would talk to Mr. Pilarchik and figure out a solution for everyone.

Before that could even happen, Howard went over and broke all of the lumber into pieces with a hammer and saw. Freda only knew Raymond had been to the pharmacy to see the Cohens about the dampness and mold because she heard Mrs. Cohen talking about it a few days later. She said the Havens boy had told them about it and they had plans to address it. After Howard broke the lumber, the whole issue then twisted into Howard's anger, Howard's irrational behavior, and not about the water problem that started it all.

She didn't know what Howard was talking about when he said the Stamp Boy had helped him the day that he was upset. He was a bit agitated when he said it. She'd brought it up, hoping Raymond would fill in those pieces, but he didn't. It just made him uncomfortable. The whole meeting was uncomfortable. Of all the people who'd witnessed the massacre, it was that boy who bothered her the most. The only memory he would ever have of Howard was of him raising his gun and killing people. Everything else about him would be forgotten.

She started walking slowly back down 36th Street to her sister's house. She had spent most of her life in Camden; three more days and she would be leaving it behind forever.

Chapter Twenty-Seven

Raymond

I was in my yard on my back on the grass, staring up at the clouds. I didn't care that it was cold and damp; the wetness of the ground underneath was seeping through my pants and jacket. I knew that as soon as my grandmother got home, she'd be telling me to get up, that I was going to make myself sick. I was already sick in a way. I'd planned to see Mrs. Unruh before she left, but wasn't sure I could actually just go to her sister's house uninvited. I was trying to figure out what to do when I saw her coming over the train bridge. It caught me off guard. I wasn't ready.

She looked worn and haggard, more than I'd remembered. Her clothes were just hanging off her, like she hadn't taken a bite in six months. She was wearing the same kind of big, drab dress she always wore. I recognized her by the hat with the tattered bow on it. I think she put it on so people wouldn't recognize her, but that hat was worse than wearing a big sign that said, *killer's mother*. She'd worn it every day that I could remember so I knew it was her when I rounded the corner.

Her skin looked paper thin and wrinkly, and hung from her bones like worn linen. Mrs. Unruh always was a little odd, like I said. Nervous, flustered all the time, even behind her own doors. She was afraid of people and what they thought of her.

My grandmother always said she was ashamed—of herself, her apartment that might have needed some new wallpaper or a lick of paint and a good scrubbing, of her clothes, which were old and needed mending. She was ashamed that she was poor, and would probably never have a better at life than she already had. But mostly, she was ashamed she was alone, that something was so wrong with her that her husband had chosen to leave her with their two sons to raise by herself.

I was there one day when she was trying to put a few groceries into the cabinet overhead; her hands were swollen and cracked, and a can of soup slipped from her grasp and rolled under the table. She steadied herself by holding onto the edge of the counter and I saw the red skin, raw, ballooned up over brittle bones. She couldn't even make a fist. When she went to lean over to fetch it, I scampered under the table and got it for her. The job at the soap factory was killing her. But it was the only thing keeping her in their apartment, with enough food for her and Howard to eat.

She was trying to thank me, for visiting with Howard, for talking to him; she didn't say it outright, but that's what she was getting at. I didn't know how to respond. When people bring it up to me now, I don't want to admit that I knew him. I say I was only there dropping off something—just a messenger. I deny we were friends. I can't admit how many times I sat in his living room or kitchen, letting him tell me about a book, or a map of the sky, or whatever bit of knowledge grabbed him by the shirt collar that day.

The truth was, I liked him. I did like him. He wasn't exactly funny, though he laughed once in a while, this sort of deep little chuckle from the back of his throat, but he was smart, and he was interested in everything. And he wanted to like people. That was the hardest part for me to reconcile. His wanting to fit in got lost as his anger swirled around him and took over everything else, but it was in there. But now I didn't know if that was real or if I'd just wanted it to be true.

Freda Unruh said I'd helped Howard in some way. I didn't want to talk about it. I didn't want to be standing on that train overpass talking about it with her. There wasn't enough time for me to put everything that needed to be said in a few sentences. A million words between us wouldn't be enough, but it felt like a hundred might be too many.

She was suffering, but there were people suffering more because of her. She only wanted to know if they'd hurt Howard when he was arrested. She didn't bother to ask how Mrs. Hamilton was, if the loss of little Tommy had killed her too. I thought about Charles Cohen every day, every time I walked past the apartment, every time I sat in class. She didn't seem to care that he was somewhere in Philadelphia being cared for by some aunt or another, because Howard had wiped out his entire family.

But mostly, I couldn't talk to her because she and I shared the same little seeds of guilt. I closed my eyes and felt the cold air on my face. The guilt kept me up at night sometimes, thinking about my last visit to Howard's apartment before he'd unleashed hell on the neighborhood. I put myself right there, over and over again. Standing in his kitchen, frozen in time. If I could just grab it and go back, everything could be undone.

That Wednesday before, August 31 to be exact, I had been helping my father most of the morning in the printing shop. I was on a stool in the corner watching him, learning. He thought lithography was a good, important skill to have. I thought that the minute he said I could go, I'd dash out of the door and find my friends. We only had six more days of summer left and there was a stickball game in the park waiting for us.

"Oh, ask your grandmother for the envelope I gave her. Drop it off for Unruh for me?" he asked as I was heading out of the shop door.

"Okay," I answered. But going to Howard's wasn't on my schedule. I always got caught up for at least an hour when I went there and I wanted to be with my friends, outside, while I still had the chance.

I got the bus home and grabbed the envelope and ran to 32nd and River Road. I was going to just stick it in the mail slot but Howard was there, in his backyard, when I got to the fence line. I can't explain what was going through my head. Maybe I'd watched him spiral down to this place I could no longer understand. Maybe I was tired of hearing about all the things the neighbors had done to him. Maybe I just wanted to drop off the stamps and not get sucked into the depression and sadness that surrounded him and his mother. I was getting older. My friends were more important. Whatever it was, I just wanted to go.

"Ray, come on in. I want to tell you something."

I followed him into the kitchen and stood there. He didn't seem upset; he was more excited, but in a bad way. Something had happened. His buttoned-up white shirt wasn't tucked in properly, and he was moving fast. I assumed it was another Cohen or Hoover story he wanted to tell me. Chewed, swallowed and digested already. I didn't want to bring it up again. He insisted I follow him to the sitting room on the second floor.

I hesitated in the kitchen. "I can't. I need to go. My friends are waiting."

His face fell a little. "Are you coming back? It's kind of important."

"Not today, Howard. School's starting in a week. I have stuff to do. My grandmother—"

"Oh. Tomorrow then?"

"Maybe tomorrow."

"I have this little problem. Something's happened; this thing I've been waiting to tell you, Ray."

I looked around. "Your mother's not here?" I thought he should be telling his mother whatever was going on.

He shook his head. "No. She's at work and she's going to bible study with Mrs. Pinner afterwards."

"Are you going to Philadelphia later tonight?"

He frowned at me. He probably thought I knew what he was doing there and was making a crack. Or making fun of him. I wasn't. I had no idea what he was doing in Philadelphia until afterwards. For the first time, I saw this suspicion towards me in his eyes. I didn't know what it was at the time.

"Philadelphia? No. Why would you say that?" he asked. "What did you mean by that?"

I shrugged. "Nothing. I didn't mean anything."

"So why'd you bring up Philadelphia?" he asked again.

"I don't know. I always see you waiting for the bus. I was just making conversation."

"Did someone say something about it, about me going to the city? One of these people that make up lies about me? What did they say, Ray? Tell me."

"No. They didn't say anything. I didn't hear anything at all."

"Oh." But then he was quiet. He was upset, as if I'd wounded him in some way.

I was going to ask him what was wrong, but I didn't want to hear it because if I listened to it, I'd be there for another hour and eventually he'd get around to telling me about his problem. That would cost me another hour. "Well, I have to go now. Maybe I'll see you before school starts, then."

I turned and left and that was it. When he told his mother I'd helped him with some problem he was being sarcastic. He was angry at me. I never went back. Those were the last words we ever spoke to one another. He might have thought I'd turned on him, writing about me in his diary, that I'd made fun of him or was mocking him. I'd seen him take a nothing little sapling of a thing and turn it on its head and feed it with his paranoia until it grew into an enormous tree. I don't know if that's what he'd done with me.

It's plagued me, what had been upsetting him that afternoon. I had a small inkling of an idea what it was. Somebody had seen Howard in Philadelphia in that Family Theatre that mostly homosexual men frequented. A neighbor two blocks over was sitting three rows up from him one night and saw Howard with another man. So instead of Howard looking at this neighbor and figuring they were both there for the same reason and it would be best if they both kept quiet, Howard had been petrified the man would tell everyone and his secret would be out for sure. I'd heard bits about it over the following months, and couldn't even imagine what kind of conversation we'd have had if I'd stayed that afternoon and let him talk.

He only looked me in the eye for a split second in the barbershop on September 6, after he'd shot Hoover. I tried to take that look and put words to it to describe it, draw some meaning from it—if it was a look filled with hatred or fear. But it wasn't. His eyes softened a little when he saw me. But it's possible there was no meaning or feeling in his eyes at all.

I almost told Mrs. Unruh to tell Howard I was sorry. The man had shot and killed thirteen people, and I was sorry. I felt I'd let him down. If he hadn't done this thing, of course I would have gone back to see him again. I would have listened to his problems. I would have listened to his stories, absorbed whatever project he was working on. All of it. I hadn't turned on him.

I might be stuck forever on August 31, 1949 in Howard Unruh's kitchen, my back against the counter, going over that conversation each time, saying something different, hoping the outcome would be different. But I couldn't go back. That last conversation between us was sealed forever in time. Unchangeable. And I was going to have to find a way to live with it.

The one thing I did know for sure was that something about Mrs. Unruh bothered me. For all her bible studying and worship, when it came down to the end, she only cared about herself and Howard. She was packing up and leaving to go north so she could be closer to her son, leaving all the rest of us here to live in the mess they'd both created, without a word to the community or the victims' families. All of us were in a sort of hell with no release. It would only fade a little with time. And I was going to have to learn to live with that too.

"Raymond, it's time for dinner. Get up off the ground. If your clothes are filled with mud, you're going have to wash them out yourself. Do you hear me?" My grandmother's words brought me back to my feet.

Chapter Twenty-Eight

Freda

She felt small, seated in a corner out of the way. Ignored. Forgotten. She wanted to leave this hospital, but promised herself she wasn't going home without answers about her son, about what they were doing to him. She'd heard horror stories about patients being placed in boiling hot baths, or in cages and sprayed with freezing water, about inserting an ice pick into the corner of the eye and chipping away at the brain, or dosing them with insulin until they became comatose. Howard didn't have anyone else fighting for him, so she forced herself to stay in the seat and inhale the strange combination of disinfectant and human filth, no matter how much she wanted to run.

"Mrs. Unruh? I was told you were waiting. What can I do for you?" the psychiatrist asked. It was the same Dr. Garber she'd talked to before.

She stood up suddenly, pulling herself to full height. "What kind of treatments are you giving my son? How is he doing? I need to know." Her eyes were on the floor, examining the speckled patterns in the tile.

Dr. Garber moved a folder from one hand to the other. "I appreciate your concern, but please know, we haven't started any real treatment on Howard other than narcosynthesis sessions."

"Narcosynthesis? What's that?"

"It's simple, Mrs. Unruh. We just sedate him with sodium amytal during a therapy session. It's… a form of truth serum. It helps to get him in touch with unconscious thoughts—"

"I don't want you doing anything to him that might hurt him in some way. I know I don't have much say in what happens to him. I know I don't. But it's been worrying me, keeping me up at night. I know people think he deserves whatever you give him, but he's just a boy."

He stared at her for half a minute without saying anything. "When is the last time you slept?" he asked. Her eyes grew watery and she shook her head without answering. "You don't look well."

"I'm not. I've been worried sick—"

He seemed to be looking anywhere but into her eyes. "This isn't usual, Mrs. Unruh, but we have a session scheduled with Howard at ten o'clock tomorrow morning. Let me talk to the team, and if everyone agrees, perhaps you can sit in. Though I can't promise anything. Maybe you can lend some understanding to all of this."

"How will I know?" she asked. "How will I know if I can come?"

"We have your sister's number. I'll call you later on this afternoon. Do you have a family doctor looking after you?"

"Dr. Hammett. He's been coming to my sister's house since… since this happened."

"I would give him a call. He might give you a sleeping pill. I think it would help."

She nodded. "Chloral hydrate. They make my head swim." She turned and wandered down the hallway towards the exit. The bus had not even pulled out of the hospital parking lot when Freda closed her eyes and fell into a deep slumber, only waking two hours and twenty minutes later when it arrived at the Mickle Boulevard station in Camden. The message was there, on a pad by the telephone, when she walked through her sister's front door. *Visit approved. Dr. Garber said to be at the hospital tomorrow morning by nine thirty.* She sighed, and fished the bottle of pills from the kitchen cabinet, putting one at the back of her tongue and swallowing. She needed all the sleep she could get tonight.

*

She saw Howard, though he didn't see her. He was flat on his back on a table, wearing street clothes; it surprised her that he wasn't in a hospital gown. There was a metal stand near him with a clear bag hanging from it. She sat down in a chair, partially hidden by a curtain. She kept her purse in her lap. Her lips were pressed together. Dr. Garber had given her strict instructions to stay out of sight, to say nothing, and if he motioned for her to leave, she needed to do so quietly through the door behind her.

Dr. Garber, Dr. Spradley, Dr. Magee and Dr. Bennett sat around the examination table, tablets in their hand, waiting. Howard put his right arm out to the side.

"I don't like doing these narco sessions," he said. "This truth serum doesn't help get at the truth. I've told you everything a million times already."

"Just relax, Howard. We're going to start the IV drip of sodium amytal and then we'll just ask you some questions. You've done this before," Dr. Garber said. His voice was low and smooth. "The medication just helps you to release some of your unconscious mind. I'm going to lead this session. I'll be asking the questions. These doctors are just here to observe. I want you to close your eyes and listen to my voice."

"I know I've done it before, and I don't like it any better now than I did then. I don't know what I'm saying when you drug me up. I don't think I like the things I say." He flinched when the needle went in and his whole body relaxed. "It feels warm," he added.

"Yes, it will. So, tell me, Mr. Unruh, are you relaxed?"

"Yes," he said. "My head is filled with cotton, just how you want it."

"I want to start by asking you your name and date of birth."

"I am Howard Unruh and I was born January 21, 1921."

"And Mr. Unruh, do you know why you're here in the hospital? Can you tell us?"

"I killed some people. I killed my neighbors."

"And how many did you kill. Do you know?"

Howard shook his head back and forth a few times. "Ten or so."

"Thirteen. You killed thirteen. Now, can you tell us when you started having thoughts about hurting your neighbors?"

"About two years ago. But I wasn't just having thoughts of killing them the whole time, maybe to just hurt them for the things they were doing to me."

"Did you feel this way towards them before you went into the Army?"

"No. The Lord was with me before I went into the Army, so I would feel peeved but I didn't do anything about it. After I got out, the Lord left me. He actually deserted me as soon as I got overseas, I think."

Freda squeezed her hands together; the water sprung up again in the corners of her eyes. She wanted to say, *no, the Lord didn't desert you. He never did.* But instead she pressed her lips together and shifted in her seat.

"You think you were a different man when you came back from the war?"

"Yes."

"How so?"

"Before I went in, I was steady. I saved money, I was dependable, I saw a regular life for myself. I worked, I wanted to someday get married. I wasn't bitter."

"And what changed that, do you think?"

"Being in combat. Learning about guns. Killing people. Seeing terrible things. I felt different when I got back. And I stopped going to church. I stopped wanting any of those regular things."

"Has the Lord forgiven you for what you did in the Army or for what you did to the neighbors?"

"You have to ask to be forgiven. I didn't ask. I won't ask."

Freda put her head down, feeling the tears rolling onto her cheeks. Religion, the Lord, had been a part of their lives every day, every breath they took. She hadn't known he'd felt this way.

"But do you feel remorse? For instance, do you feel remorse for killing the two women in the car? Or the man in the car, whom you'd never met?"

"No, no. I don't feel badly about it at all."

"But you didn't know them. They'd never done anything to you. Why'd you kill them?"

"I don't know. They weren't even looking at me. They were just looking straight ahead, like zombies. I don't know why, but I shot them."

"Howard, do you think your shooting just got out of control at any point, where you didn't know what you were doing?"

"Yes."

"At what point in the shooting do you feel you lost control?"

"When I shot the insurance man, Hutton, on the pharmacy steps. I didn't want to kill that man. He was in the way. But after I shot him and I saw him fall, I got pleasure out of stepping over his dead body. I liked it. It did something to me."

Freda knew Hutton personally, but hadn't allowed herself a minute to really think about any of the victims. Hutton would come and sit at their kitchen table, have a cup of coffee with her, talk about his wife, Ethelyn, and his two kids, Barbara and Blaire, about how Barbara was a nun, and how proud he was of her calling. They'd talk about religion until he'd wind his way to a discussion about life insurance or whatnot. Like clockwork, he'd appear at their back door every month to collect his policy money and have a chat. Howard had stepped over his dead body as if it was nothing.

"So, you're not sorry about any of it?" Dr. Garber asked.

"I'm sorry I killed the children. I wasn't aiming for them. I didn't know I'd shot them."

"Why do you feel sorry about killing the children?"

"Because they were so small."

"Did you kill the women in the car because you hate women?"

"No. But I dislike women."

"Why is that, Howard?"

"Because they use you and are naggers."

"What about your mother? Do you hate your mother?"

"Yes. I hate my mother. I love my mother but I hate my mother, too."

Freda wanted to get up from that chair, to sneak out of the door and not look back. But she stayed firm, clutching the arms of the chair with her fingers.

"Was your mother worried about you over the past two years? Did she nag you?"

"Yes. She nagged me every day. She thought I was leading a mysterious life because I wasn't going to church and she wanted me to get a job."

"Now Howard, you had a girlfriend when you came back from the service, didn't you?"

"Yes, for almost three years. But I didn't love her."

"You didn't have any feelings for her at all?"

"No. She would kiss me, but I didn't really notice."

"You did not have sexual relations with her, is that what you're saying?"

"No. I've never had sexual relations with a woman."

"But you had sexual relations with men? Is that right?"

"Yes."

"And when did that start?"

"In 1946, after I got out of the service. I went to the Family Theatre by chance and I had this contact there. It was the first time."

Freda knew instantly when that had happened. Not the exact day, but she remembered the change in him. Something was so different about him. And it was sudden, like someone had hit a switch in him. On, off. That had to be it. He wouldn't talk to her, was spending more time alone. She thought it was war that had changed him.

"And you wanted to do that, Howard? You wanted to have sex with that man?"

"Yes. I knew from when I was in middle school I was attracted to boys, but the Lord took care of it. I didn't act on it until the Lord deserted me."

"So, you've had sex with many men?"

"Yes."

"Now Howard, were you just receiving sexual gratification from men or were you giving it? Was it oral gratification or was it anal?"

Dr. Garber glanced back at Freda briefly after saying this. She caught his eye and then looked straight ahead. He probably thought she should leave, that the questions were too delicate, too intimate, but she was going to hear it all.

"It was all ways. Giving and receiving. But I slowed down a little when I got gonorrhea and had to be treated for it at Cooper Hospital."

"Okay, let's move on. You're doing fine. Now tell us what happened that night, the night before the murders. If you could walk us through it?"

"I left my house around seven thirty at night and got to the Family Theatre. I was supposed to meet someone, a man named Van. He was supposed to wait for me. We'd been together almost three weeks and really got on together well. But I was late because of the bus and he was gone. He was leaving town and went off without me." Howard's voice started to shake and he broke down in tears.

"Why are you crying, Howard?"

"Because I'm upset."

"You're upset about Van? When is the last time you've cried? Do you know?"

"I cried about my mother. About this whole thing because of my mother, six months ago, after the shootings."

"You cried because you knew what it was doing to her?"

"Yes."

"Okay. So what did you do when this fellow Van wasn't there when you got to the theatre?"

"I stayed at the theatre and watched the movies, a double feature, three times. Then I left and came home."

"And what happened when you got home?"

"I came around the back and saw my gate was ripped out and my fence was broken in three places."

"And that upset you?"

"Very much. It upset me very much."

"And when did you decide you were going to kill all your neighbors?"

"I decided to kill them right then. I made a plan right then that I was going to go to bed, and get up in the morning and wait for the shops to open and I was going to kill them."

"And you decided that you were going to do that when you got home around two thirty in the morning?"

"I decided I was going to do it when I got home and went through the gate."

"Now Howard, you killed thirteen people—five women, five men and three children. If you could do this all over, if we could take you back to September 5—"

"If I could go back to September 5, I would have left earlier and not been late in getting to the theatre."

"But other than that, would you have done this all over again, if we could take you back?"

"Yes. I would kill the people who deserved to die, and I would make sure I killed the ones who got away. I would do it all over again. I might bring more ammunition with me. I only had thirty-three bullets and I would make sure I got the Sorg boy, the man who owns the luncheonette, the man and wife in the apartment building, and the tailor."

"But you had more ammunition in your room, when you got back to your room, and you didn't shoot at anyone else, including the police when they showed up, even though they were shooting at you. Can you explain that?"

"I didn't want to hurt the police. I liked the police. They tried to help me in the past. I didn't want to hurt them."

"Is it maybe you only wanted to hurt people who couldn't fight back, and the police had weapons, more weapons than you and could have hurt you? Is that why?"

"No. I didn't care if I died. I didn't care about myself. I didn't want to hurt the police. I had a direct shot at Officer Ferry, and I didn't take it. I could have. I'm a pretty good shot, but I didn't take it."

"You let some people live, that's true. You let boys who were in the shops live—"

"I didn't want to kill them. I... didn't want to hurt the boys. They never did anything to me."

"And you let the Harries live. Both the mother and the son—"

"I might've shot the Harrie boy, Armand. My gun jammed, but I let him live. I only shot him in the arm."

"Why would you have killed Armand?"

"Because he came after me when I shot his mother. I didn't like him."

"Do you hear voices, Howard?"

"No."

"Do you feel that the television is talking to you?"

"We didn't have a television, only a radio."

"Okay, is the radio giving you secret messages?"

"That's stupid. No. I don't have any of that."

"So, you feel you're of sound mind."

"Yes, I have a good mind."

"But if you could, you'd do this all over again. You would shoot thirteen unarmed people again?"

"Yes. I would get the people on my list. I would shoot them again for talking about me and bothering me all the time. For disparaging my character. I told you all this already. I don't know why you keep asking me the same things. I decided it that night when I came home and I walked through the gate. The missing gate, I mean."

"Do you know who took it?"

"No. But I decided to just kill them all to make sure I got the right one."

"And you think you killed the right one?"

"I have no way of knowing. I really hope I did. I hope I got them right in the head."

"Howard, what if I told you someone put your gate right back where it was, a few days after the shootings? It's there now, leaning up against the fence line. What would you say about that?"

"I don't know. I'd say someone felt bad for taking it in the first place. I'd say that maybe they won't bother anyone again or they'll think about it next time."

"Okay Howard, just a few more questions. How did you feel after you'd done this thing? Right after? When you saw the carnage."

"Numb."

"How else?"

"Very indifferent."

"How else?"

"Like it was routine."

"How else?"

"Like it was part of a job I was doing."

"Anything else at all?"

"Well, there was pleasure in seeing them fall. That's all I have to say."

"And do you think it's because of your Army training that you feel this way, that maybe you felt like you were in a war? Is that possible?"

"Maybe. I don't know. I felt numb when I was in combat. It felt the same to me."

"So you don't care if we sign the papers tomorrow saying you're sane and send you off to jail? You'd face possible conviction and the death penalty."

He shook his head. "No. I deserve it. You should do it."

"All right. I think that's all for this session, Howard. I think we're going to stop here and maybe schedule another session for next week. Okay?"

The nurse pulled the needle out of his arm and Howard rolled over and assumed a fetal position. "How many times do we have to do this before you leave me alone?"

"We can't leave you alone, Howard. That's not the way this works. We need to talk some more about your relationship with your parents. Your mother in particular. Your feelings of love and hate. Your resentment towards your father. We want to take you back to your childhood. Talk about some of those early memories. We have work to do, but we're making progress."

Dr. Garber motioned for Freda to leave and then the four psychiatrists followed her out of the room and went into an office across the hall and shut the door. They all took seats around a table.

"Mrs. Unruh, this is actually a conference about the session, about what your son said. About his condition, our thoughts about his treatment. As a family member, you're welcome to stay."

Freda nodded but didn't say anything.

"I'd say dementia praecox fits. The bizarre flattening of emotions is disturbing," Dr. Garber said.

"Yes. Quite bizarre. He has no remorse. None whatsoever, as if he doesn't fully understand what's happened. And he has such a shallow emotional range," Dr. Bennett remarked. "An almost monotone delivery, except when he was talking about that man, Van."

"Even so many months after the incident, he has no pangs of conscience. Even when it's presented to him in detail, he shows no signs at all of guilt. And no sense of self-preservation. It's as if he doesn't care what happens to him at all," Dr. Garber added.

"Do we have his service record?" Dr. Bennet asked.

"Yes. Tank gunner—342nd Armed Artillery Unit, 7th Army Division. Battle of the Bulge, heavy combat. Exemplary service. No issues. Given high mark by the section chief Norman Koehn. Won several marksmen awards. Honorably discharged. No mental health issues during the service, and none reported afterwards. There's nothing here. It's as if this seemingly normal fellow by all reasonable standards, at just the age of twenty-eight, descended into madness. So, what should be the course of treatment?"

"He's very bright. Very smart. I suggest we do some more psychological testing. What was his IQ?" Dr. Magee asked.

Dr. Garber flipped through some pages. "We should have this repeated. On the Wechsler-Bellevue Intelligence Scale he was tested at 141. They also did a Rorschach."

"And?"

"They found a tendency for over-bizarre and incomplete organization. Also deep-seated feelings of inadequacy, inferiority and depression, with a surface anxiety. He also had many signs of inner conflict and lack of inner control."

"Is it possible he's feigning all of this apathy to prolong his stay in the hospital? To avoid the exact thing he says he doesn't care about? Death by electrocution?" Dr. Spradley asked. "I am just throwing it out as a possibility."

"I don't think he can feign anything while under the influence of sodium amytal. Impossible. No. I suggest we repeat the IQ testing, get an MMPI[1], and continue narcosynthesis sessions, as well as psychoanalysis. Agreed?" Dr. Garber said.

"Agreed."

"Agreed."

"Agreed."

"Good, we have a consensus. We'll convene again next week then, gentlemen. Do you have any questions, Mrs. Unruh? Anything at all?"

---

1 The Minnesota Multiphasic Personality Inventory was developed in the 1930s to help mental health professionals evaluate people with psychiatric disorders. It is not an IQ test but more of a "personality style" inventory. It is widely used today in both clinical and non-clinical settings.

She cleared her throat. "And this narcosynthesis is the only treatment you're going to give him? No hot water baths? Or… shots of insulin… this is it?"

The four men looked at each other. "For now, this is it. He may take part in group at some point, but for now, just individual sessions. Psychoanalysis. And these sodium amytal sessions, like the one you just witnessed," Dr. Garber said. "We may have you come in for a family session too, later on."

She wiped at her eyes. "No icepicks in his eyes? None of that?"

"A lobotomy? Is that what worries you? Oh no. Our goal is to make him fit for trial. That's our goal. We would never consider anything like that at all, don't you worry."

Freda felt her heart soar, and then sink, all within the space of a few seconds. She knew then that this was to be her life. She was going to be alone, with nothing left but hospital visits, psychiatry sessions, endless questions about how this had happened with her son. That is, until they found him sane enough to put him to death.

Chapter Twenty-Nine

Raymond

With all of the people I knew struggling in all sorts of ways in the months following the shootings, I wanted to remember the small details from a time from before all of this had happened. Something I could grab onto and hold close, that would remind me that things weren't always bad. It was funny that the last full day we all had together before everything fell apart was a holiday. It was hot. That's what I remember about that Labor Day, September 5, 1949. Much hotter than I ever remember it being in September—almost 90 degrees by noon. My grandmother had pulled down the paper shades in all the rooms to keep the sun out, except for one window in the living room. She'd balanced a pan of ice on that window ledge and set a fan behind it, hoping it would bring freezing air into the house. It worked a little and then the ice melted. Our freezer only had two little metal ice-cube trays and those cubes melted faster than we could make them.

"Hey, little Ray, run down to Latela's and see if he has any ice he can spare," my grandmother yelled to me.

She had her hair pinned up, and was wearing a pink house dress made out of some light material, and the sweat was still rolling down her hairline onto her cheeks. "Ray, I wish the ice man was still in business. Remember those days when he'd bring that huge chunk in and slide it right inside the icebox? I could use a big slab right about now," she said to my father. With three generations of Raymonds living under the same roof it sometimes got confusing.

"That old icebox we had in the kitchen, the tray leaked and made a mess," he said.

"He delivered on Tuesdays. I remember that. We had to put a sign in the window when the ice had all melted off and we needed more. A sign!" She laughed.

"Get going to Latela's. Offer him this," my father handed me a nickel and a penny, "if he asks for money. The penny is for you to get a piece of candy."

I ran the block and a half up to River Road, and then slowed down and walked the rest of the way. Latela ran his little luncheonette—the last shop on River Road—between 32nd and Bergen Avenue—from nine in the morning until six thirty at night, like clockwork. It was a holiday but a lot of the stores were open all along that street. People were out, sitting on their steps, sipping iced tea or lemonade or anything cold they could get their hands on. It was an end of the summer party in Cramer Hill.

I walked past the pharmacy and saw Mr. Cohen behind the counter. I figured I'd better get my candy while I could in case he closed up shop. It was a good thing I did, because he was talking about just that with Mrs. Cohen when I pushed my penny across the counter.

"Hurry up, Maurice. I want to get the noon train," she said.

I figured they were headed to Atlantic City to the horse races with friends. That's where they always went—every Thursday they'd hire a pharmacist to come in and handle prescriptions and they'd grab the first train to the shore. Going to the Jersey shore was big deal for most people I knew. The train went right from downtown Camden all the way to Atlantic City. You could change trains, or grab a bus and get anywhere along the shore you wanted—Margate, Ocean City, Wildwood. But mostly we went to Atlantic City.

Especially at Easter. Just when the sun was starting to shine again, and the air was getting warmer, it was time to hop on the train to Atlantic City for the parade on the boardwalk. Everyone who could go was there. The men wore suits, but the women were dressed in ridiculous ruffled dresses and all kinds of hats decorated with flowers or feathers sticking out all around the sides. Then we'd promenade all along the boardwalk for everyone to see. It was a social affair. There were food stalls cooking up burgers and meat skewers, the salt water taffy rolls were all stacked in the shop windows, there were ice-cream carts—it was all there. My grandmother would pack some bags with a change of clothes and we'd make a day of it. After the parade, we'd sit on the beach and breathe in the cool salt air, or swim in the freezing ocean not yet warmed by the summer sun. The Cohens, I think, went to Atlantic City for the race tracks.

Horse racing, dog racing, card games and any sort of gambling you might want were there long before they built the casinos. That's what the Cohens loved. I figured Charles was spending this Labor Day holiday at home with his grandmother rather than heading down to the ocean because I saw him—the side of his face anyway—peering out from the back of the store before he disappeared from sight again. Considering what was to come the next morning, he would have been better off far away from that backyard and that gate that night.

I took my piece of candy and ambled down the street. The barbershop was closed, and so was the shoe repair shop next door, but I found both Hoover and Mr. Pilarchik outside the dry cleaners with Mr. Zegrino, just smoking cigarettes and chatting. All of them were in their plain white t-shirts and light trousers, leaning against the wall. They were talking about the Phillies. They'd just won a double header against the Giants at the Polo Grounds in New York the day before and it was all anyone had been talking about. It was the first season they might be in the pennant race in twelve years.

"They'll be in the race. You'll see. They've only got—how many games left to play?" Hoover said. "Twenty at the most? They're having a streak."

"Three of those are against the Cards. It's gonna be tough," Pilarchik jumped in. "And all those games are on the road."

"As long as they keep Borowy off the mound. I give him one more season, tops. Arms going." Hoover again. "Stick with Meyer or Heintzelman."

All three nodded at me as I passed by. There were two doors to Engel's bar across the street. One was the ladies' side; one was the men's. There was music playing and it looked lively inside but it was only the men's door that was opening and closing. The women were all home making potato salad or getting the hamburgers ready. Latela's was open and I saw his wife, Dora, moving behind the counter. I hurried in.

"Hi, Mrs. Latela. My grandmother wants to know if you have any ice. She used all of ours up," I said.

She had three fans going inside her little restaurant but it was barely moving the air. "I'd like to live inside the freezer right about now. Let me ask Dom. I'll be right back."

She came back with a big metal bowl filled with cubes. "It's the best I can do. Can't spare anymore. I don't have anything else to put it in. Tell her to just bring the bowl back tomorrow."

I pushed the nickel at her and she took it. She popped the top off a bottle of Coca-Cola and handed it to me. The condensation was dripping down onto my hand. I just stood there, holding the bowl in one hand, and the bottle to my lips with the other. I don't remember anything tasting so good.

"Ice was free," she said. "Hey listen, tell your grandparents and your father, a few people are coming over after the sun goes down, just to sit out and have a few drinks if they want to come over. Let 'em know, okay?"

"Okay. Thanks. I will."

I hurried back, watching the ice cubes swirl in the bowl and start to melt as I went. The Hamilton boys, Joe and Jim, were in the back of their yard. I could hear them squealing. Every house I passed had people outside, on the steps, or in their yard; the sounds were almost like a hum, drowning out the noise of the trains, the boat horns from the Delaware. I didn't know what content sounded like until afterwards, but that was it.

We had a little picnic out back that afternoon, which was nothing more than a few hotdogs thrown on a little flat grill my father had just bought, with ketchup and relish and my grandmother's pasta salad. Only a few years before, cooking outside was something you did when you were camping or at a state park, but more and more of these Kook-Out flat grills with wheels on one side were popping up in people's backyards. The men manned them and the women handled the other food in the kitchen. That afternoon, Milton and I ran around the yard in our bathing suits, spraying each other with the hose, getting my father and grandfather wet too.

After the sun went down and the stars came out, my grandparents, my father, Milton and I took a walk after things cooled off, talking about nothing in particular. The crickets were chirping and every so often a firefly would light up. I had only one day left before school started. That's what I thought anyway, and I wanted it to last forever. My father stopped walking when he got near Sharp School and pointed up at the sky.

"Look boys. See that star? The bright one. Riiight there." He was pointing and we were looking but the sky was full of dots of light. "That's the North Star. It's there all year round. Sailors used it to guide them."

We looked and we looked and pretended we knew what he was talking about, but it didn't matter. We kept walking and knew we were getting close to River Road because we could hear the music. The streetlight lit up part of the Cohens' backyard. It was empty, though I saw a light on in the upstairs back window—Charles's window. Sorg was standing on the sidewalk in front of the pharmacy with two friends.

"Havens," he said. "Little Ray. Milton."

"Boys," my father responded. Sorg just nodded and backed up and sat down on the steps of the empty store front.

I could see the Latelas outside, sitting in lawn chairs on the sidewalk half a block up; the Zegrinos, all three, were next to them forming a circle. They seemed to be drinking beer but I couldn't tell. I could just hear the laughing. I could see the back of Helga Zegrino's head, bobbing as she talked. The American Store was closed and locked up tight. The bar was hopping.

We didn't stay long that night. Only a half hour or so. The adults took seats and Milton and I ran to play with friends we saw at the end of the street. Sorg and his friends had little firecrackers and we heard the loud pop and saw little sparks of light. But mostly it was just quiet.

I keep trying to remember the feeling I had that day, of standing on that street and hearing those people talking about the heat frying an egg on the sidewalk, and whether Shibe Park was going be demolished or restored, and how the summer went by so fast, and how the mosquitos were particularly bad this year, how in another month it might be cold and we'd all be wishing it was warmer, how RCA was hiring a few hundred people back to work soon, how the street light two blocks south was blinking, and about the sales on lawn mowers at Sears.

I would lie in bed sometimes and picture that day in my mind—the conversations, the people and how relaxed everyone was—and I wished more than anything to go back in time and do that all over again. The feeling in our neighborhood would never be the same after that day. If I'd known that only twelve hours later everything in my life, on that street, in the city of Camden, was going to change, that half the block would die, I might have stayed out and looked at the stars a little longer.

Chapter Thirty

Raymond

The days wound around one another, twisting forward, and there was only one question left to answer. The central question and maybe the most important one, to me anyway. I took out an article I'd clipped and re-read it. *Lost Gate Linked to Killings is Brought Back. Reappearance gives probers another mystery to solve.* That article in the *Courier Post* had been written months ago, yet there was no follow-up about it in any newspaper I could find. So, I figured maybe Sorg was right. Either the police had only half probed and then forgot about it, thinking it wasn't that important, or they knew who did it, but didn't want to announce it for some reason.

I had no one to hash this out with. My father and grandparents had closed the topic of the murders, forever and permanently. They didn't want to hear a peep, not from me or from anyone else. They thought it had become, in their words, a morbid fascination. My friends didn't have much interest either. Ironically, the one person who would have loved this kind of discussion was Howard. He'd have taken all the angles of it, pulled it apart and then gone back to the beginning and pulled it in the other direction. He would have gone over it for hours, or for as long as I liked, because it was a riddle with no answer, and that would have made it interesting.

I considered writing to him in the hospital to ask his opinion, I was so curious, but I knew I couldn't. If anyone in my family found out, I'd be done for. I was on my own. I was going to have to try and figure this out just by putting the little bits and pieces together the best I could. I wouldn't know the truth for years to come, but I came pretty close there with my sleuthing, in the spring of 1950.

I closed my eyes and remembered walking up 32nd Street that Labor Day night, right past the Cohens' yard. The street light was on; nobody was out. Not then, at around eight o'clock. I know the time because my grandfather was listening to his favorite radio show, Edgar Bergen and Charlie McCarthy, which came on every Monday night. My father told us we were going to walk down and see the Latelas for a little bit, but we had to wait for my grandfather.

While the Latelas and Zegrinos and my family were all sitting outside on the sidewalk in front of the luncheonette, Milton and I ran down the street. Sorg was out. His friends, Paul Hurst, Bill Clawell and Bill Brustel, were with him, standing in front of the Cohens' home. They were jumping around, as usual, in and out of the empty store in front of Unruh's, setting off these sparklers. I thought I heard Joe and Jimmy Hamilton in their backyard, but I didn't actually see them. Mr. Hamilton came outside for a few minutes before disappearing again.

That's all I saw that night. My family didn't stay too long with the Latelas. They mostly went to be friendly. My father had to work early the next morning. We all started walking back down 32nd Street at around quarter to nine and walked right past the Cohens' backyard again. This time I saw the Harrie boys in their own yard, all three of them, but they were nowhere near the fence line; they were back behind their own house.

I kept thinking about all the people who lived in the neighborhood who might have done this thing, and kept coming back to Charles Cohen. He had a funny look on his face at the funeral when I mentioned the gate. He was *there*. I mean, he was home that night—I saw the light on in his window. That window looked out over the backyard with a direct view of the fence line.

Charles Cohen wasn't the sort of boy to vandalize like that alone. He just wouldn't have. Maybe as part of a group, he might have watched, but that's it. The other problem I had with naming Charles as a suspect was that he was taken from the house right after the shootings and never went back. He couldn't have put the gate back. That left only the Harrie boys. It fitted. They could have ripped it out as a prank, stashed it right there in their shed, not even fifteen feet from the fence, and put it back afterwards. I came to that conclusion then, that the three brothers, Armand, Leroy and Wilson, had done it together and never said a word to anyone about it afterwards.

It made sense too, that the police wouldn't have given that information to reporters. The Harries had suffered. Howard had gone into their home, shot Madeline Harrie in the arm, choked Armand and shot him too. Just seeing them afterwards, you could tell they'd paid a huge price and would never be the same. Putting their names in the paper would have almost pointed a finger of blame at them in a terrible way. It would have provided a place for all the rage in the community to land, and they just didn't deserve it. I imagine if they did do it, it was only done as a prank. Nobody could have imagined people would die over a few pieces of wood and some wire.

If Charles knew who took it, why didn't he say anything at the time? That would have made sense. Every article done at the time, including Meyer Berger's Pulitzer Prize-winning piece for the *New York Times*, talked about the gate. It would be a normal thing to say, "Hey, I was outside or watching from my window and I saw what happened," but he never did. He never said a word. I can only guess that the reason for that was guilt. Did Charles take it himself? Probably not. But what if he was a sort of passive accomplice, laughing as the Harrie boys did their thing, all four of them imagining Howard's face when he saw what they'd done, thinking Howard deserved it?

He deserved it for making a racket with his music at night, for throwing Mrs. Cohen's clean clothes from the line into the dirt, for making such a big stink about not being able to use their property as a pass-through, for breaking up the lumber that didn't belong to him, for complaining about the trumpet playing, for getting the Cohen parents so upset they sent Charles away from home for hours at a time. For bickering with every single neighbor on the block, for making their very existence living next to him so difficult, he deserved it. They'd make him mad, then they'd put the gate back. What harm could there be, really?

If any of what I suspected was true, I felt terribly sorry for Charles. If he was involved or even witnessed it in some way, he would carry that horrific quiet guilt with him for the rest of his life. He was never mean, never vindictive that I knew of. If Charles was involved at all, it was probably some sort of horrible accident of timing—that he was in the backyard when it was happening and got caught up in it. But he lost his entire family over something so random. And then he just disappeared into the rest of his life and wasn't seen or heard from again for many years.

I didn't know how to reach Charles, but I knew exactly where Howard was, and the urge to talk to him about all of this was always there, just a phone call away. I could write or visit. I could have an adult conversation with him, ask all those questions that hung in the air like storm clouds ready to burst. I could clear my conscience, match my childhood memories against his adult ones. I imagined what that would be like over and over again. It might provide a salve for an old wound, or be the flicker of fire that would light the fuse to an explosion inside me. I didn't know which. But the visit would never happen. It couldn't.

One cold evening, the winter after the shootings, my grandparents and father were lingering around the table after dinner, in one of those moments that seem like magic when I think back on it. We were just there all together, dirty dishes still on the table, but there was no rush to push away from each other and hurry to clean up. The conversation drifted to Howard and his legal situation.

"I believe something good has to come from all of this. I don't know what, but it does," my grandmother said. "We need to make sure this doesn't happen again."

"What're the chances it's going to happen again? Almost none," my father said.

"Well, good or bad, there's a big push to get guns off the street. I saw it in the paper. In Philadelphia. They're going around collecting them from people." My grandfather added his piece. "George Thomson told me the same thing the other day.

They're calling on the veterans to lead the way in this, bringing in all their souvenirs."

"I doubt it's going to make a difference," my father said. "They'd be taking the guns from the wrong people."

"George said if there's enough push and support that maybe they'll bring it to the legislature. Some sort of limits or something on buying guns because of Unruh. He said people have already volunteered to hand over ten thousand guns in Philadelphia alone."

"It's all just talk. Because people wanna feel like they're doing something after what happened. If we can't electrocute him, we gotta do something." My father was always cynical. "So now they'll come after law-abiding citizens and try and take our property away from us."

The conversation drifted on to something else that day, but it got me thinking. The situation with Howard was a perfect storm of yards with no exits, endless teasing, paranoia and access to guns. It couldn't happen again. I went to my room that night and started rummaging through my papers, reading and discarding until I found the article my grandfather had been talking about. A first-page piece in the *Philadelphia Inquirer*, written only four days after Howard Unruh unleashed hell on our little community. This was maybe the good thing my grandmother was talking about.

September 10, 1949, Philadelphia Starts Move to Control Guns

As Camden buried its dead from across the Delaware River at Philadelphia, today came another warning to guard against another street slaughter by doing something about guns. Francis V. Willis, chairman of the War Trophies Safety Committee of Philadelphia where Unruh bought his death-dealing weapon, declared, "It's time to take drastic action in stopping this wholesale unnecessary slaughter."

Chapter Thirty-One

Dr. Garber

He had just agreed to present at the American Psychiatric Association conference as a favor for an old friend—The Classification of Personality Disorders, New Developments, his favorite topic. He didn't know it would stir up old obsessions, but it had. So much so that he'd been poring over files for days. It was Unruh that consumed him—he was still confined to Trenton Psychiatric Hospital after so many years, though the murder indictments had been dropped. The current director of the hospital, Dr. Howard Blechman, slid into the seat next to him after one of the lectures had concluded.

"Dr. Garber, do you have a minute? I'd like an opinion on an old patient of yours."

Garber nodded. "Which one?" he asked. He took a sip of white wine and waited.

"Unruh. You remember him well enough—"

Garber put both palms up. "I couldn't forget that man if I tried."

"So, let me tell you what happened. Do you have a minute to listen?"

Garber did, but he almost wished now he hadn't, or that he'd cut Blechman off. Or that he'd never gone to the conference at all. The story had him rethinking everything he thought he knew about the murderer.

Blechman told him he'd walked through the dayroom and stopped in his tracks one afternoon. Patient 47,077 was there at a table, talking to someone. Howard had dressed neatly for the occasion in a black shirt and slacks as if he could get up at any moment and go to work in an office. Blechman had been treating Unruh for several years and said he had read all information on him from the day after the rampage. He knew his clinical chart intimately and he'd never known him to have any visitor other than his mother. This man sitting next to Howard was not familiar.

He saw a nurse coming towards him. "Who is that?" Blechman asked, pointing towards Unruh. "Who's visiting?"

"That's Harry," she whispered. "He's been coming in for months."

"But who is he?"

She shrugged. "They seem to get along well. It's the first time I've seen Unruh laughing. It's strange."

Blechman said he'd watched the two of them interacting. Unruh's affect had brightened; he was leaning in, chatting. "Is he family? Someone related to his father? A cousin?" he'd asked. They looked to be close in age.

"He's just Harry. That's all I know. Howard writes letters to him too. Watch. Howard'll be sitting out here tonight. He writes to his mother and brother too, but he'll drop post to Harry along with them," the nurse told him.

"Do we ever look at those letters by any chance or are they sealed?"

"Mary reads outgoing mail sometimes. She said his are all straightforward. Jokes, riddles. How are yous. Nothing interesting. Harry apparently knows the Unruh family in some way. Communicates back and forth between them, giving information."

Blechman assumed he was a relative. He decided to watch them for a bit. It was the most intriguing thing he'd seen since he met this killer. Bright, articulate, sensitive, paranoid, forthright, lucid, organized, withdrawn, bizarre, alone. All those adjectives fit Howard, he thought. The Rorschach they'd done, where he'd examined ten ink-blot images, had revealed the personality of a man perched right on the brink of psychosis, looking down into the abyss. This Howard was nowhere near an abyss. He was fully in the folds of humanity.

He imagined Howard would find someone to talk to here or there, but not a friend. He moved closer to listen.

"Okay then, How. Next week. And I'm going to bring my wife and grandson. He's only ten, you don't mind?"

"No, it'll be good to see them," Howard had answered. "I'll try and find something for him. A little gift."

The man had a wife and children, grandchildren. A family. For an instant, Blechman thought he might be the friend, Van, Howard had spoken of in regards to his visit to the theatre so many years before. That was the only person ever mentioned who had brought Unruh to tears, who had likely set his mind in a place where he was able to kill. Their friendliness made him consider it. But to come here like this would be very bold. Improbable after so much time.

Harry was walking towards the door when Dr. Blechman said he'd intercepted. "May I speak to you a moment?"

The man straightened up. Six foot easily, he had bushy brown hair covering his head.

"I'm Howard Unruh's psychiatrist. I just wanted to ask a few questions, if you don't mind?"

Harry looked over his shoulder at his friend briefly and then nodded. "Is everything okay?"

Blechman said he'd wished he had more than a minute to talk but they were waiting for him upstairs. Time was pressing and he had no idea when he might see this visitor again. If this was Van, then he was living a double life with a wife and children. He'd given a fake name then and maybe now. Either way it was fascinating.

They moved to a corner. "How do you know Howard? I'm interested because he hasn't had any visitors, other than family, since he came here."

"Oh." He assumed a defensive posture, arms folded, back to the wall. "We're friends," he said. "I don't mind coming to see him as often as I can. It seems to make him happy."

This Harry hadn't answered his question. "You know his family, then?"

He shook his head. "Only a bit. I've talked to his mother. She may have a hard time getting out here as much as she has done. I told her she can call me. Between us, we'll see that he gets a visit."

"Doctor, you're needed in the conference room," a nurse had called to him. "They're waiting for you."

Blechman heard her but didn't respond. There was an awkward moment where neither moved. "Well, listen, you go. Take care now," Harry said. He turned, waved to Howard and headed towards the door. Blechman stared after him. The ear-to-ear grin on Howard's face made him look like a different person. The usually sullen chap who shuffled into his office weekly and assumed a prone position was gone. It was as if Howard was two people.

*

That night, the office light was casting shadows across his small office, but Blechman hadn't even noticed the sun had set. He heard the rain beating against the glass but he was far too consumed with the Unruh file to pay any attention; he was reading and reading, feeling he'd missed something. Interview after interview, with sodium amytal and without, Howard presented as a primitive individual, who didn't clearly fit into one category or another. He was flat, incapable of empathy, remorseless, detached. No evidence of delusional process, yet so paranoid, any real attachment to another human being would be difficult. Dementia praecox as a diagnosis fit back then, he was convinced, though all Unruh's symptoms weren't always present. Schizophrenic. It was just that visit from Harry befuddled him.

It wasn't the visit alone, and it wasn't the fact that Unruh conversed with Harry—it was the intangible connection they had, the reciprocity of human emotion, the mirroring. That was innate in most people, but in Howard it was lacking. It couldn't be feigned or reproduced. Some psychopaths had enough insight into the human condition to mimic, but Howard seemed to lack even the basic understanding of the pretense, or even why he should bother with it at all.

And this man felt comfortable bringing his grandchildren to visit Unruh, who'd aimed a gun at a child's head and fired. It was a mystery. Blechman shut off the light, grabbed his briefcase and headed out for the night.

He passed the nurses' station and saw the bin filled with outgoing mail. The letters were unsealed, often read by one of the nurses before posting only to ensure the patients weren't threatening to harm themselves or someone else. On a hunch, he flipped through the first few envelopes until he saw Howard's familiar writing. Three letters. His mother, his brother and the last was to Harry. Harry Rosell. He pulled it out, threw his brief case onto the counter and dropped down into the nearest chair. The letter was just one page, Six lines. But those six lines had twisted everything he thought he knew about this man into a bunch that might never be smoothed out.

Dear Harry,

It was so good to see you. I was so sorry to hear Betty was hurt in that robbery. And they dragged her just to get her purse off her arm? I pray her ankle is on the mend. Terrible what's happening in the world. All for a few dollars. I know you won't be in for a visit anytime soon, but don't worry about it. Write when you can.

Howard.

He sat there reading and rereading. Harry's wife, Betty, had been robbed. Someone had presumably attempted to snatch her purse; she fell and was dragged, hurting her ankle in the process. Terrible what's happening in the world? He stared at those words. This man had gunned down half his block. Killed three children, aged ten, six and two. It was as if it hadn't happened or he wasn't the person who did it, yet if Blechman were to ask him, Unruh would readily admit he did. He had so severely compartmentalized that part of him, that he was no longer in touch with it.

Howard had always been superficial in discussing September 6, gliding over it, trivializing and rationalizing it, blaming the victims for their part, discussing his hatred of the Cohens. He wasn't angry or tormented. He almost seemed content. Blechman felt he needed to find out more about this Harry.

*

He had to wait a month for the opportunity to present itself. Harry Rosell was there along with a boy of about ten, sitting in the visiting room, waiting for Howard. Blechman had no rounds pending, no conferences, nowhere to be. He wandered over to the table and sat down.

"We met before, some time ago. I'm Howard's psychiatrist. I'm curious how you know him," he said.

Harry hadn't even taken off his overcoat and he struggled to get his arms out and at the same time maintain some composure. "This is my grandson, Jonathan," he answered. "He agreed to come along and keep us company, didn't you?" The boy nodded. "Do me a favor, go over to the window and count all the cars in the parking lot for me. Can you do that?" The boy nodded again and bounded away.

Blechman waited for something more but it didn't come. "I ask because in treating Howard, I find it helpful to know as much as I can about him. He hasn't had many visitors—"

"Howard and I were both in the war, both in combat. We talk a lot about it. We've shared some experiences. It's sort of good to talk to someone and not have to explain every little thing. I started writing to him but it took a bit for him to open up again. He thought I only wanted to talk about what happened on River Road. That wasn't it at all, really."

"Then what was it? You must know the whole story, what he did, what happened?"

Harry had his head down, thinking. "He's a gentle soul. He is. Good sense of humor—"

"But—"

Harry put his hands up. "No buts. I'm not going to speak about what happened in Camden. I don't have to defend anything about him. Whatever he chooses to tell you, he will. What he doesn't, he won't. I'm not getting in the middle of it."

"Don't. Just tell me what I'm not seeing. If I'm missing a piece of this puzzle. Because it is a puzzle."

"There's a kindness in him, a concern. And he's interesting to listen to, if you take the time to hear him. He's not River Road in Camden. He was a person before then. He's a person after—"

Blechman was dumbfounded. "I appreciate that. I do. But what he did doesn't live a separate existence outside the Howard we see here. Howard took the gun, and shot people. Thirteen. Three children."

Harry nodded. "That's true. But the story of what happened is more than just Howard and his mind. It was a combination of everything—the people around him on that block, his own circumstances at the time, his mother, even. His father, too. His brother. It's a mixture. You're trying to make a cake with just flour. Find the eggs, butter and sugar."

Blechman smiled at the analogy. "You're comfortable bringing your grandson here, after all of that? Because what happened wasn't just a simple vanilla cake, it was a triple-decker loaded cake. That exploded."

"I'm comfortable bringing my grandson here. My wife is comfortable with Howard too. She'd be here if it wasn't for her ankle."

"And you've known him for how long?"

"Long enough to know exactly what he went through in the war and that he sees dead bodies in his sleep, because I do too. Long enough to know he really struggled afterwards, with everything. He's in a struggle. What you're seeing is a struggle."

"Does he see the dead bodies of the people he killed? That's the question. I don't think he does."

Just then Howard came into the room and bounded to the table, slapped Harry on the back and took a seat across from him. "Good to see you. I have a book," he said. "I got it to read to Jonathan."

Harry took it from him. "He'll like this. Dr. Seuss. *Horton Hears a Who*. Jonathan, come here."

Blechman watched them for a minute before getting up and waving his goodbyes.

"There were thirty-nine cars that I could see, Grandpa," the boy said.

"That's good. Listen, Howard is going to read you a story. Or do you want to read it to Howard? Okay… that's fine…" The voices faded away.

Blechman had studied them for another ten minutes, he said. Howard was smiling, pointing to the pictures, leaning in to speak to the child. Laughing.

Blechman finished telling the story to Garber and took a long drink of water. "And that's it. That's the story, Dr. Garber.

You know this patient. You studied him for years. You saw him at the very beginning." Garber saw equal parts concern and curiosity etched into his colleague's face. "So, in telling you all this, I'm asking for your help. How is this possible? Has he been faking all this time? Was he misdiagnosed? Is he just smart with a personality disorder that helped him evade the electric chair? Did we get it wrong?"

"Have you seen any other changes in Unruh? Anything else different, maybe when he thinks no one's looking?" Garber asked.

"Not really. He's a model patient. Smart. Picks and chooses who to talk to. Watches television with the other patients, reads his books. Writes his letters. Takes his medication. He says he's hearing voices occasionally, which is a new development, but there's no evidence he's experiencing any sort of hallucinations. He's always remarkably clear, very organized in his thinking."

"And Harry has continued to visit? He wasn't visiting as a curiosity?"

Blechman shook his head. "Harry visits. Quite often. They enjoy each other's company. I've had the opportunity to speak with him a few more times, but it's just as simple as it seems. He's a friend."

"And it's not a dalliance of some sort, you don't think?"

"No. I'm positive it's not."

Garber started remembering all the sessions he'd had with Unruh after the shootings, how he was remorseless, even when staring at photographs of faces of the children he'd killed. "Interesting. These patients can be complicated. Keep an eye on him," was all he said.

Blechman left him at the table that day with a half-empty glass of wine and the never-ending mystery of Howard Unruh to ponder. He'd pulled out his old notes when he got home and started reading. And rereading. If the man had been feigning, it was the best, longest con he'd ever seen. Could a person be one thing one day and another thing another? Was Unruh different than the thousands of other schizophrenics he'd seen during his career? The presentation was certainly unique. What Garber did know was that a mind could break into a million pieces, and he realized he could spend his entire life trying to find them all and put them back together, but he'd never get it exactly right.

Chapter Thirty-Two

Raymond

Of all the books on Howard's shelf, the one that I loved the most was the book on Greek mythology. It was a big red book with a hard cover, the pages filled with pictures and stories of the gods and goddesses. He would never let me borrow it, but I could sit on the little couch in his living room for as long as I liked and pore over the pages.

The biggest picture was of Zeus, the king of the gods, with his crown and lightning bolt. Sometimes Howard would sit and talk about one of the stories, or he'd flip pages and talk about the pictures. The story Howard liked the most was about the phoenix.

The phoenix was an immortal bird that had to enter our world to be reborn. First it flew west until it reached the spice groves in Arabia. It collected the finest herbs and spices before continuing on to Phoenicia. When the phoenix arrived there, it built a nest from the herbs and spices and waited for the sun to rise. The next morning, when the sun god began to drag his chariot across the sky, the phoenix turned east to face him. It then sang the most beautiful melody—so beautiful that even the sun god had to pause and listen. When the phoenix finished the song, the sun god readied his chariot and continued his journey across the sky. This caused a spark to fall from the sky and ignite the nest of herbs and the phoenix in flames. All that was left in the ashes was a tiny worm. After three days, a new phoenix rose again, flew away and began the next cycle of a thousand years.

"Why do you like that story, Howard? There's better ones in there," I asked.

"I like the colors on the bird," he said. It was painted in colors of yellow, orange and gold. "And I like that it means nothing ever really ends. It doesn't. We keep going and it cycles around again. From where we're sitting, it looks like a straight line, but that's an illusion because you can only see a few feet in front of you at any given time. It's really an oval, like a race track, and we just go round and round."

"I don't like that," I said. "What's the point in that, going around and around?"

"The end is just the beginning. It's never over. You'll see."

"I don't know what you're talking about. I like this story better." I took the book and started flipping through the pages until I came to the picture of Hercules. "The twelve labors of Hercules. It's like a *Superman* comic. He slayed the lion and the hyena—"

"The only lesson in that one is don't trust women. If you follow the story of Hercules, he does all those things to get his freedom and in the end his ex-wife gets him, kills him."

"Deianira wasn't his ex-wife. She was still his wife."

"That makes it even worse. Read the story of the phoenix again…"

Like phoenixes, we all went on in our own way after those few years of sorrow. We weren't exactly reborn but we reinvented ourselves into something a little bit different. In the fall of 1951, my family finally packed up and moved out to Audubon, a little town that was only fifteen miles away but felt like a whole other world. I wasn't sorry to leave it all behind. Reliving Howard Unruh's walk of death everyday was taking a toll on me. That's what journalists were calling it, the Walk of Death. Cramer Hill would never live it down.

The lesson in the phoenix story wasn't that things would get better, just that they would go on. And maybe that's the moral of this story too for most of the people who lived on the street. Leonard didn't finish his pharmacy course at Temple University, and eventually lost the store and apartment at 3200 River Road. I wasn't there to see it, but he sold it to another pharmacist sometime in 1951 and moved all of his and his parents' things out.

He moved back to Philadelphia and was looking for odd jobs. There was something in the paper about him needing to work, bringing up the fact that his parents were killed in the infamous shooting. People were moved by his plight and he got something—working in a grocery store, or in a factory. Whatever it was, it probably paid the bills but otherwise he seemed kind of lost, with no direction, wandering.

It was about a year later, the day after Christmas in 1951, that my grandmother saw a story in the paper. I was a few years older, fourteen, and so I suppose she thought she didn't need to hide things from me so much anymore.

"Sad," was all she said, putting the paper down near me. "Just very sad."

Leonard's face was on the page, unmistakable. The story was like something out of *The Guiding Light*, a soap opera that my grandmother listened to on the radio. Leonard had got married to a seventeen-year-old woman named Anna Gittman. Not even nine months later he and his now eighteen-year-old wife had attempted to kill themselves in a suicide pact after days of arguing. Anna was eight months pregnant with their child. She chose to drink cleaning fluid with lye, while Leonard took some sleeping pills and then ran to the neighbor Mrs. Kanafsky, and told her what they'd done. By the time police arrived, they were both unconscious. The baby was delivered by C-section and was doing fine, but Anna was in a critical condition. Leonard, it seemed, would be okay. I just looked at my grandmother in disbelief.

"I don't understand why. He had a job. He had an apartment. His wife was going to have a baby," I said.

"If you read on to page three, it says they did it after arguing for days because Leonard was spending most of his time with Charles. She was jealous. They're both so young. Suffering seems to follow that family."

Leonard and the baby survived, but his wife Anna didn't make it. Tragedy seemed to cast a long shadow over the Cohen family.

Other people continued on as if the shootings were just a little bump in life. The Hamiltons weathered their storm for years right there on the bottom floor of 3208 River Road, in the wake of their son's death, with their three remaining children, Joe, James and Maryanne. I would see Mrs. Hamilton around from time to time. She had this sort of faded look about her, as if the most important thing in the world to her was just putting one foot in front of the other and getting on with it. I never heard that anything terrible happened to them after that, but I'm sure continuing on every day, staring at that window where the bullet had passed through, piercing Tommy's head, shaped their lives. They finally got enough money and moved out some years later to a new apartment in Blackwood.

Thomas Zegrino kept his dry cleaners open, doing a good business, eventually taking down the sun-faded trousers in the window and throwing them away. He had a new and better drama to fill his days. His first wife's brother, Angelo Errichetti, became the mayor of Camden. I only know that because his name was in all the papers for some big corruption scandal—Abscam—with the FBI, and wiretaps and the whole bit. David Zegrino popped up again too, when he was caught getting paid by the city during his uncle's reign without really showing up to do any actual work. His supposed job was all on paper. Thomas Zegrino stayed out of most of it, went on, married again and faded back into the fabric of the dry-cleaning world.

Mr. Latela moved to what would become Cherry Hill and opened his luncheonette there. I saw his name in the papers too, many years later when he was being interviewed about his restaurant and was offering up recipes for cream of cauliflower soup. He looked older and a little rounder, but happy. Every so often on the anniversary of the shootings, he would pop up in an interview, talking about how he'd driven little Orris Smith to the hospital and how the boy's blood had squirted all over his car.

Carl Sorg stayed in town, got married and started a successful roofing business in Cramer Hill. He had two sons and a daughter, rarely talked about the incident and refused interviews. He was devoted to his wife and children and became an enormous asset to the community. Whatever information he had about that night before the murders, whatever he might have seen or witnessed, he kept to himself.

Engel's saloon continued to serve people through good times and bad for many years to come. Frank Engel would sit on his bar stool and tell his stories about the day Howard Unruh shot up the neighborhood, and how he got him in the backside with his .38 pistol from across the street.

What was left of Clark Hoover's family disappeared. The children from his first marriage floated around in Collingswood and Haddon Township, maybe even picking up arrest records of their own for fraud, but they never reappeared or gave interviews about their father or the events of 1949. Mrs. Catherine Pilarchik, the cobbler's wife, lived out her life in Pennsauken and was never interviewed or appeared again in the press regarding the death of her husband.

But the biggest phoenix of them all in this story was Charles Cohen. His whole family was wiped out that day in the space of thirty seconds. And it doesn't matter if he was in the hallway witnessing it, or if he was in a closet the whole time or even on the roof. He was there in the apartment when Howard came up the stairs with his gun.

He survived it. Maybe at that point, depending on how you looked at it, he was the worm in the story, and everything around him was burned to ashes. And then being sent to live with family who were squabbling over money, and having a brother who seemed destined for destruction and havoc, was probably crippling. Charles was left having to put all the pieces of a life back together by himself.

Charles disappeared after that day on September 6, 1949, and I never saw him again after the funerals, so it was the strangest thing when I opened the newspaper in 1982 and there he was. When I saw his face thirty-three years later, he was much bigger, his hair was darker, but he carried the exact same expression in his eyes that I remembered from the last time I saw him out in front of Levin & Sons funeral home on the day of the funerals. I could have picked those eyes out of a line-up—sorrow, fear, the fog of war sitting just behind the brown irises. He'd come out of the anonymity of his quiet life to show up in court for a very special hearing.

Howard Unruh had spent all those years in the hospital trying to regain his sanity. In 1965, he wrote a well-worded letter to the Camden County prosecutor's office asking that the charges against him be dismissed. It was pointed out to him that by writing that letter, he had illustrated the point that he was now competent to stand trial. He quickly withdrew the letter. In 1979, he petitioned the court to be moved to a less restrictive setting in order to be closer to his mother, Freda, who by this time was ill and in a nursing home. The request was denied. In a surprise move in 1980, his lawyer filed a motion to dismiss the murder indictments against him on the grounds that he had been entitled to a speedy trial and didn't get one. The motion was granted and all thirteen indictments were dropped. Howard Unruh, by all standards, was a free man, and was only confined to the hospital on the basis of his mental status. Everybody went crazy. It was true that thirty-one years had passed, but the people lost were still remembered.

"If he's not being charged with murder, then are they saying my parents and grandmother never died? They were never murdered? Are they still alive somewhere? No," Charles Cohen said. "This is terrible."

What was more terrible was that Howard Unruh was ordered to be brought to court every year, as was his right, to appear before the judge and see if some restrictions could be lifted. He wanted to be moved to a less secure setting since all his charges had been dropped and there was nothing holding him legally within the confines of the Vroom building in Trenton. His mother was still visiting him regularly, and his wish was to be moved to a hospital closer to where she lived.

Every year, Charles Cohen would appear in court, and sit and listen to the testimony of Howard Unruh's public defender, about how he'd been a model patient, non-violent, compliant with medications, spending his days reading his beloved books, writing letters and watching *Star Trek*. Cohen showed up to make sure Unruh stayed where he was and was not released to some cushy setting, where he'd get day passes to go shopping or out to eat. In 1993, he was moved from the Vroom building to the less restrictive geriatric wing of Trenton Psychiatric Hospital.

Charles Cohen's family went to court with him, always by his side, enduring the dog and pony show, watching Unruh morph from tall and lanky with brown curly hair into a gray-haired chubby older man with glasses, barely recognizable. Unruh didn't say much and appeared sedated most of the time. He'd sit there in his street clothes, his hands folded in front of him, gazing off into the distance, frowning or on rare occasions flashing a disarming smile.

Each year his petition to be moved to another setting was heard, and every year it was dismissed, and Unruh would shuffle back into the hospital, never giving Charles so much as a backwards glance. Charles had built a solid wall around himself, with a supportive wife, three daughters, a career, friends. He was in a place to start talking about that day. And he did multiple times; in multiple ways, he told his story. It was because of this that I stumbled across the interview with him that appeared in

The Philadelphia Inquirer in March 1982, which shed light on many of my long-held suspicions.

Horror of Thirteen Slayings Recalled

I do remember the night before the tragedy, kids who lived directly in back of us said they had broken the fence.

Thirty-three years later, Charles Cohen was pointing a finger directly at the Harrie brothers as the culprits who had stolen the gate. Maybe that was the truth, maybe the truth was much more complicated than Charles would ever admit, or maybe the truth about the gate was lost forever.

I thought about Howard and the story of the phoenix over the years. I wished I'd asked Freda the last time I saw her, when we were standing at the train bridge, if she had that book, if I could have it. Everyone who witnessed the shootings, everyone who had a family member killed, our whole town, was a phoenix, pushing on, creating something new from the rubble, trying to forget just enough to survive.

In light of the bell tower sniper shootings in 1966 (fourteen dead), and the Howard Johnson Hotel shootings in New Orleans in 1973 (ten dead), and the Easter Sunday massacre in Hamilton Ohio in 1975 (eleven dead), and the California State University Fullerton shootings in 1976 (seven dead), and many more too numerous to mention, I think Howard might have been right. Maybe the end was just the beginning.

Epilogue

Florida, February 14, 2018

Carly Novell thought about her grandfather, Charles Cohen, that morning. He'd passed away nine years before but her mother had placed his photographs on the wall in the hallway and in the living room, so he would be a constant presence in their lives even after he was gone. Living only fifteen minutes away in Tamarac, Florida, sometimes she'd come home from school and find him sitting there in the living room.

A big man with big brown eyes and gray hair, funny and kind, he'd filled the house with his presence. He worried a lot about his wife, his three daughters and his grandchildren. She remembered that; he was always worried when they were out late, wanting to know where they were going, what time they were expected to return, telling them to be careful, to call if they needed him.

It sometimes caught her off guard how much she missed him. The little things, like how he'd eat all the food in sight. If she left anything on the coffee table and went to another room, she knew it'd be gone when she got back. Food was a running theme between him and Grandma. He'd sneak it, and she'd pretend to be angry, because he was supposed to be cutting back. They'd take trips to Chilis when Grandma was out of town. He'd say, "What happens at Chilis, stays at Chilis." And they'd watch him devour his plate of ribs and laugh.

He was corny, bursting out into that old Doris Day song, "A Bushel and a Peck"… *hmmm hmm hmmm.* She could still hear the melody, his deep voice belting out the tune. But there was always something else about him. Something distant and sad and far off that should she couldn't name and, at that age, she didn't know what to call it.

She couldn't remember the day she knew. She was maybe eight years old when her mother took out an old black and white photograph of a couple and put it in her hands. The man with black hair was standing behind the woman, leaning against her, his chin resting on her shoulder. She was smiling, his arms wrapped around her waist. They were vaguely familiar, family members who had passed away long ago. People connected to Pop-Pop somehow. They'd died in a car crash when he was a boy, that's what she'd thought. Or had she been told that? It didn't matter, they were gone.

That's when she learned the truth about her grandfather, about that little corner in Cramer Hill, Camden New Jersey, the second floor of the apartment where he'd hid, while a gunman hunted down and shot his mother, father and grandmother. He'd never told her the gruesome details, the horrible nitty-gritty of dead bodies and police gunfire, of being taken to the police station after being ferreted out of the apartment, to wait for relatives from Philadelphia to fetch him, of seeing the killer being brought in in handcuffs. Of them locking eyes briefly. She'd found that out on her own, later.

After hearing the truth of it all, everything seemed to make more sense—his excessive worrying about little things, how her mother, Merri, seemed hypervigilant, and whatever room she was in, be it the airport or a store, she'd immediately start looking for potential places to hide in an emergency. Reporters seemed to find them every so often and she'd never known why, if he was a famous salesman or if it was because of the work the family did for victims of crime. Now it all made sense—it was always on that day, September 6, that the media would descend.

That little bit of sadness in him had a reason and a name. She didn't want to remember him so much as a victim but a survivor. The things that stuck with her were that their dog Lucky loved him, and loved to sit on his stomach, and how he always made them change the channel no matter what they were watching, so he could follow his stocks. Channel 31. He'd made a good living as a master salesman. Beauty supplies. Linen. Doing so well, he'd purchased property at the shore in Ventnor, New Jersey, only a few minutes' drive from his parents' beloved Atlantic City. Solid marriage, three successful daughters. He had survived. *A bushel and a peck…*

Carly got dressed in a navy-blue, short-sleeved homecoming t-shirt from the year before with the little nautical symbol in the upper left corner, and her black jeans. After combing her long dark blonde hair, she pulled a scrunchie onto her wrist. She had to get to school, to the school newspaper office, so she could finish some pieces she was working on. They were going to print in two days and she had so much work left to do. There were only three months left at this place and she'd be graduating. Three more months. Prom, an ex-boyfriend, a senior trip and problems, problems, problems. She was hoping to get into George Washington University, go to DC and start the next chapter of her life up north. Journalism. That's what she wanted.

The school bell was ringing when she arrived on campus. Marjory Stoneman Douglas High School was a whole complex of buildings; some were whitewashed stucco and some were industrial gray and peach. The high school was comprised of fifteen separate buildings, all spread out over one square mile, bordered by canals and palm trees, idyllic. She pulled her car into the student parking lot and got out, making sure she had her backpack and coffee.

Just another day of school. Class after class, lunch. Back to the school newspaper office. That's all she was thinking about. Meeting up with friends after school. And then going to see her grandmother later on, who still lived in the same house.

That afternoon she was in the school newspaper office working against a deadline to get an article finished. She glanced at the clock, typing away at her laptop. Fifteen more minutes and school would be over for the day, and she had so much more to do. A shrill siren went off at exactly 2:20, the fire alarm. The loud ringing ricocheted off the walls, getting louder by the second. They'd had a fire drill earlier that day, and everyone had filed out into the courtyard, milling about for half an hour before being allowed back inside. Two in one day seemed a little ridiculous. She was in the media center, building number two, and the sudden blast of noise distracted her, pulled her away from her thoughts, irritated her.

"I'm not going outside again." She said it loud enough for everyone to hear, but to no one in particular. "I need to finish this."

There was a buzz of commotion behind her, movement in the hallway, cell phones dinging. "Oh my god, there's a shooter somewhere in the school," someone yelled. "We have to hide. Get the lights, get the lights. Computers off."

She whirled her head around, not really understanding what was happening. A hand slapped her laptop shut and grabbed her arm, pulling her into the darkness of the closet. There was no noise, no gunfire within earshot. Cell phones were providing all the information they needed to know. Building twelve, it was building twelve. That was two buildings away. Gunshots on the first floor. Bodies, blood. No death count yet. The Parkland school shooting was underway.

Carly took the girl's hand next to her. "Breathe. Just breathe," she whispered. It was hot and stuffy in the closet. They were quiet, waiting for the sounds of shots fired, or footsteps. People were muffling their cries, covering their mouths to keep from being heard. All she could think about was that sixty-eight years, six months and twenty days before, her grandfather had sat in a closet, probably much smaller than the one she was in, alone without the comfort of a hand to hold, or a cell phone to communicate, while his entire family was being murdered within earshot.

The minutes ticked by, turning to an hour. Fifteen dead, at least fifteen. He got to all three floors of building twelve. Bodies in the hallways. He was still on the loose. So much information was coming in, a lot of it jumbled and contradictory. The calls to 911 from others sitting in the closet were increasingly frantic. *Stay put. Stay calm. We know you're there.*

While others were calling their parents or crying, Carly was praying to her grandfather to give her the strength to get out of the small space without losing her mind. The stories she'd heard from family members, his stories, about the crazy man who lived next door, it made her wonder if she knew this shooter, if she'd ever talked to him, if he'd sat next to her in English or History. And if she would know the victims when they were named.

The lights in the room flicked on and they all held their breaths, squeezing each other's hands, waiting. "Police. Kids?

Is there anyone in here? It's all clear. Walk out slowly, put your hands on the shoulders of the person in front of you. Stay together. It's all clear." As they filed out, she heard the death toll. Seventeen. Seventeen people had lost their lives. The shooter was still on the loose. Her mother was waiting outside, had organized things for the other parents, bringing water, trying to help calm and pacify as the minutes went by.

When she got outside, Carly hugged her mother and didn't let go. "I'm so glad Pop-Pop didn't see this," she said. "It would've gotten him so upset," she said.

"He might not have survived it," her mother responded.

Afterword

Raymond Havens III passed away in 1995 and didn't live long enough to see the Howard Unruh story to completion. He went into the United States Air Force and was stationed at McGuire Air Force base and then at a base in the United Kingdom where he met his future wife Sylvia Cheeseman. After some time living in the States, and Laon, France, they settled in the United Kingdom, where he remained until his death in 1995. He had two children, Andrea and Norman, who reside there today. He never spoke to Howard Unruh again after the day of the shootings.

Charles Cohen had a different fate. "I want Howard Unruh to die. I want to spit on his grave and be able to get on with the rest of my life." Those were his words during an interview after a special court hearing to determine if Howard Unruh should be allowed to go to the hospital greenhouse to take part in horticulture therapy. "This has to end sometime."

It didn't end as Charles Cohen had hoped. On September 4, 2009, Charles Cohen suffered a stroke and passed away. He battled the courts until his death to prevent the lessening of restrictions for Unruh. Ironically, his funeral was held sixty years to the day of the massacre. At the time of Cohen's passing, Howard Unruh was still confined to Trenton Psychiatric Hospital, as patient number 47,077, in the geriatric wing. He died a month later on October 19, 2009 at the age of eighty-eight, after suffering a long illness. He received visits from his friend, Harry Rosell, up until the end.

Howard Unruh discussed all aspects of the case with Rosell, saying that he was sorry he'd killed children, but nothing else. "They took my gate," he'd said. "I wasn't going to take anymore from them." He refused to discuss his sexual orientation, stating that he wouldn't talk about his activities in Philadelphia, and that the things he did there were probably a mistake. It is noted that he developed a crush on a much younger male patient, but nothing came of it.

He outlived his father, Samuel Unruh, who passed away in 1953, only four years after the massacre, and his brother, James Unruh, who died in 1998. Freda remained in central New Jersey for the rest of her life. She continued to visit her son every week until her passing in 1985. She refused all interviews throughout her life and continued to emotionally support her son. She is buried in an unmarked grave next to her son in Whiting Memorial Park in Whiting, New Jersey.

Throughout his many years of hospitalization, Howard Unruh never exhibited any signs of violence or anger. He never reacted, even when assaulted by another patient. When a riot erupted in his wing in 1954, patients raged for over two hours taking hostages and setting the furniture and part of the building on fire. Unruh was one of the only patients who did not get involved. He sat in a chair and watched calmly.

He was officially diagnosed with dementia praecox (another term for schizophrenia) in 1949. At the time, there were no medications available to treat mental illness, and psychiatry was heavily influenced by the works of Freud. Patients were treated with electric shock therapy and hydrotherapy, where people were confined to tubs of either very hot or very cold water in an attempt to stimulate parts of the brain. Insulin shock therapy, where large doses of insulin were administered over a period of months to induce coma, was also used. Sodium amytal, a form of truth serum, was given via intravenous drip during therapy sessions to help the patient access their unconscious thoughts. The use of sodium amytal, called narcosynthesis, was discontinued in the early 1950s as psychiatrists felt it was unreliable, since patients blurred fact with fantasy.

There is no indication in any of his hospital records that Unruh was subjected to any treatment during hospitalization other than narcosynthesis and psychoanalysis. He was treated with various antipsychotics as they became available. There is debate among psychiatrists as to whether the diagnosis of schizophrenia is correct. It has been suggested he may have had a combination of post-traumatic stress disorder from the war coupled with a personality disorder.

What is clear from his records is that over a period of sixty years, his story never changed, never wavered. He never talked about it in more detail, or expressed real sorrow over what had happened. He never reached out to the families of the victims, he never wrote them letters, or even kept a diary of his thoughts after the shootings.

The diary that he'd kept years before, which chronicled his military experiences and his growing resentments towards neighbors, was turned over to the psychiatrists at Trenton Psychiatric Hospital, then presumably was logged into evidence at the Camden County prosecutor's office. When the evidence against Unruh was made available to reporters from *The Philadelphia Inquirer* in the 2000s, the diary was gone. Only several ripped pages have survived.

Although the Vroom building in Trenton, and the prosecutor's office received many requests for information as to its whereabouts over the years, the diary, save for those several ripped pages, is presumed lost. Dennis Wixted, prosecuting attorney for Camden County, who represented the State vs. Howard Unruh in the KROL[1] hearings in the 1980s, doesn't recall whether the diary was in evidence during his tenure. "It might have been there. I might have read it. I just don't remember," he said. "There were no murder indictments against Unruh at that time, so I wasn't prosecuting his case, reviewing all of the evidence."

It stands to reason that if the diary was logged into evidence, someone removed it. If it wasn't logged into evidence, it disappeared during the early years of Unruh's hospitalization. The prosecutor's office refused to produce the indictments, the contents of the file on Unruh or any of the items in evidence.

The Luger used by Unruh to kill thirteen people on September 6, 1949 was not booked into evidence after the murders and was found in 1990 at the home of a retired police officer, Vincent Conley Sr., when his children were sorting through his belongings

---

1 KROL is a term used in New Jersey based on the case State vs Krol. In 1975, Stefan Krol stabbed his wife to death and was found not guilty by reason of insanity. A number of stipulations were placed on Krol that mandated court supervision should he be released from a psychiatric hospital. It was mandated he live in a certain place, have supervision, and appear in court regularly for review. In New Jersey, the term KROL now refers to any stipulations placed on a person found not guilty by reason of insanity. When the murder indictments against Unruh were dropped, he was placed on KROL status, which mandated he be brought in front of a judge for a yearly review and that no restrictions could be released without a judge's consent.

after his death. There were multiple envelopes containing shell casings and evidence envelopes tucked in the with the gun. It was all promptly returned to the prosecutor's office.

Unruh spent years in therapy talking about his ambivalent feelings towards his mother, stating he had an Oedipus complex, wanting to have sex with his mother, and kill his father. He seemed compelled to talk about this in therapy sessions. It was noted he had an entire set of books by Sigmund Freud in his room.

Leonard Cohen survived his suicide attempt in 1951, though his wife Anna did not. The baby she was carrying was delivered by C-section and was placed up for adoption. Leonard lived out his later years in Florida. He had one step-daughter who resides in Germany, and a wife, Estelle, whom he left behind when he passed away in 2007. He did not have a close relationship with his brother Charles and they were completely estranged at the time of his death.

The stretch of River Road between 32nd Street and Bergen remains largely the same after seventy-two years. The pharmacy and store front under the Unruh and Cohen apartments have merged into one shop. For years, the building was riddled with the pockmarks of the gun battle of that September morning. People would often stop and point and remember. The apartments in the back where the Cohens and the Unruhs lived were sealed for over sixty years, the windows and some doors cemented in, preventing anyone from entering. It's been said when the owner was asked why he sealed up the back, he responded with one word—ghosts.

Those apartments were unsealed when the building was purchased by Maritza Gomez in 2019. They remained almost a time capsule, with the original fixtures in the bathrooms and kitchens and wood finishings throughout. The closet doors were original, including the one where Rose Cohen was hiding and lost her life. There were patches on the wood where bullets had passed through.

Both back windows of the apartments, the one that Maurice Cohen had used to escape when he fled onto the roof in an attempt to save his family, and that police had used when they crawled onto the roof to toss tear gas to flush Unruh out, have been cemented over and not reopened.

Maritza Gomez is aware of the history of her store and the apartments above. She seemed unconcerned, but was very helpful in allowing access to the apartments and the basements below. The Unruh basement is only now accessible from the street, and in the process of waterproofing, all remnants of the shooting range and all the bullet holes have been covered up.

Hoover's barbershop was demolished in the early 2000s. The cobbler's shop that John Pilarchik and his brothers built from scratch in June 1949 still stands. It is now a barbershop. The apartment house where the Hamilton's lived is a Chinese restaurant, Thomas Zegrino's dry cleaners is now empty and the luncheonette once owned by Dominic Latela is a mobile phone shop.

The Unruh and Cohen apartments were remodeled and rented out. It was the first time in seventy-two years that both apartments were occupied at the same time. The family living at 3202 River Road—the Unruh apartment—discovered there was a problem. They had no easy access to the street when they exited their back door. The owner of the building finally solved the problem by creating a cement path around the back of the garage that leads right to 32nd Street.

There was no need for a gate at all.

A Letter from Ellen

Dear reader,

I want to say a huge thank you for choosing to read *Murder in the Neighborhood*. If you enjoyed reading it as much as I did researching it, I would love it if you could write a review. It makes such a difference helping new readers to discover my book for the first time.

I love hearing from my readers—you can get in touch on my Facebook page, through Twitter, Goodreads, or my website.

If you did enjoy it, and want to discover more true crime stories, just sign up at the following link. Your email address will never be shared, and you can unsubscribe at any time.

www.thread-books.com/sign-up

This story of Howard Unruh and the River Road murders seemed to fall into my lap in the most coincidental way when I was driving through Camden one day with my mother. She spent many of her childhood years in East Camden and was familiar with all the stories, all the lore. As we headed down River Road, she talked about living on the other side of the railroad tracks, of playing with her friends near the tracks and getting trains to smash their pennies.

It was just then that we approached 32nd Street and pulled up at the light. Gomez Shoes was right across the street and I had no idea it had a history hidden within its walls. "That's where Howard Unruh lived," she said. "He killed all these people right here when I was a kid." I had heard the story before but hadn't put all the pieces together of where it happened, and what exactly had happened. "I remember it so clearly. My mother told me to stop collecting those newspapers and looking at the pictures of the victims. She said I was morbid. Nothing like that had ever happened before."

When I got home, I looked it up. The images of a young Unruh popped up, along with a smattering of crime scene photos. I was mesmerized. I found it incredible that the story of what happened that Tuesday morning on September 6 had never fully been told.

I started doing research, making phone calls, digging up names long forgotten, finding children or grandchildren who might have a memory or story to share. The fact that I could almost reach back and touch these pieces of the past fascinated me. I dug up court documents, interviews, hospital records. I interviewed prosecutors and family members of the victims until the story started to take on a life and breath of its own.

My mother guided me with tales of taking the bus down Westfield Avenue by herself when she was eight years old to buy a pair of shoes she'd seen in the shop windows somewhere along Federal Street. They cost a dollar fifty. Or going downtown to Ferry Terminal to catch the boat across to Philadelphia with throngs of people on their way to work. She told me of the smell of tomatoes always in the air from the Campbell's soup factory, and the smoke rising from the stacks of the RCA building. Of a truck filled with potatoes that had tipped over in the middle of Westfield Avenue, scattering spuds everywhere. Women were scooping them up with pans or their aprons and rushing back to their homes. She had potatoes for dinner—boiled, mashed, fried—for weeks. Of blackout drills, rationing coupons and victory gardens during the war.

This story became personal for me. My grandfather and great-grandfather both had stores along Federal Street in the early part of the century. My grandmother worked near the RCA building. I had worked within the correctional system in the city of Camden for nineteen years. Both my children took the PATCO line into the city for college every day.

Some say the Howard Unruh shootings paved the way for the decline of the city, forcing people to look towards the suburbs for a brighter, safer future. Or that the mass Jewish emigration from Camden into areas of Delaware Township (now Cherry Hill) can be directly attributed to the brutal slaying of the Cohen family. I think both are an oversimplification of a complicated issue. Most major industrial cities saw a post-war mass exodus as industry and jobs shifted.

What the Howard Unruh incident did do is strike fear into tight-knit communities where fear had never existed before. How well do we know one another? Can we trust people we don't fully know? Are we safe? Can the government keep us safe? How do we protect our families from this? What do we do about gun violence? In the past seventy years since the shootings, there are still no clear answers.

The thirty-three bullets fired from Howard Unruh's gun that day in Camden may have been followed by thousands more over the years, but as much as the city has changed, so much of it has stayed the same. The history is everywhere, with buildings and streets virtually unchanged, the neighborhoods filled with hard-working people fighting to make a better life for themselves and their children. The landmarks that anchored the city seventy years ago—Cooper Hospital, Campbell's Soup, the City Hall building, RCA—are all still there. And on a breezy day, if you're facing in the right direction, you might just catch a hint of tomatoes cooking in the far-off distance.

Ellen J. Green Author

@EJGreenBooks

EllenJGreen.com

@EJGreenBooks

Images

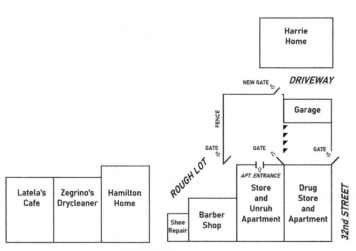

A plan of the neighborhood

Howard Unruh's enlistment photograph

Howard Unruh displaying his gun collection after his return from the Army (Photo: Getty Images)

Howard Unruh arrested at his back door. His bedroom window can be seen above where police shattered glass to lob tear gas (Photo: Getty Images)

Howard Unruh in the police car immediately after his arrest (Photo: Getty Images)

Unruh's Residence

1. John P. Pilarchick
2. Orris Smith
3. Clark Hoover
4. James Hutton
5. Mrs. Rose Cohen
6. Maurice Cohen
7. Mrs. Minnie Cohen
8. Alvin M. Day, Jr.
9. Mrs. Helga Zegrino
10. Thomas Hamilton
11. Mrs. Emma Matlack
12. Mrs. Helen Wilson
13. John Wilson

The crime scene map

John Pilarchik's funeral. The cars went past the shop at the family's request (Photo: Getty Images)

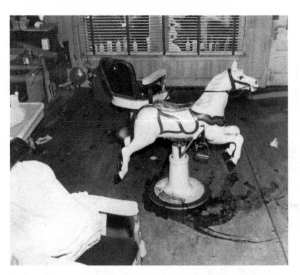

The aftermath in the barbershop where Clark Hoover and Orris Smith were killed (Photo: Imagn Images)

Freda Unruh

Raymond Havens, one month after the shootings
(Photo: Andrea Havens-Forsdick)

Carl Sorg (Photo: Carol Sorg Neumann)

Acknowledgments

This project came together with the help of numerous people. I could never have done it alone. Bonnie at the Camden County Historical Society took on my many research requests and opened up her archives to me. All of the Howard Unruh hospital records, court orders, and commitment papers are housed there, along with magazines, interview statements and police reports. CCHS is a fantastic organization. The history of Camden should never be lost.

Many thanks to Jessica Alvarez at BookEnds Literary for taking on this project (and me) and seeing the potential in this story after reading just a handful of written pages. Without your encouragement and presence of mind, all of this would have been much more difficult.

Claire Bord and the team at Bookouture were fantastic in pulling all the threads of this project together. I appreciate all the time and attention, telephone conferences, discussions and re-discussions, poring over every tiny detail. This story was put onto the page because of the team at Bookouture, and I am so happy *Murder in the Neighborhood* found a home with you.

Andrea Havens-Forsdick (daughter of Raymond Havens), I will never be able to express my gratitude for your help and cooperation. As I started reading all the Howard Unruh material I could find, the name Raymond Havens kept coming up again and again. I wasn't sure how I'd be received when I reached out but you have been gracious, patient and just wonderful all the way around. Your family is the backdrop for the telling of this story, and I hope I did your father justice.

Maritza Gomez, the owner of the property at 32nd and River Road, and owner of Gomez Shoes, tolerated and understood my every little fascination with her store and the apartments above. I walked in one day without warning and plied her with questions about murders that had taken place there so many years before. She was fantastic in letting me look around, explore, get a first look at the unsealed Unruh-Cohen apartments, climb down the ladder into the basement even when she had customers to attend to. You welcomed me back many times and were patient beyond belief. You have no idea how much your kindness lent itself to the telling of this story. I am beyond appreciative!

Many thanks to the families of the victims that responded to my emails and questions and encouraged me along the way. Jenna Zegrino, Carol Sorg Neumann, Joseph Hamilton, Maryanne Hamilton Purvenas, Tom Harrie, and especially Marian Cohen. I am in awe of the entire Cohen family and the legacy Charles Cohen left behind. You are all wonderful people, able to move forward from tragedy, taking on causes of victim's rights and gun control. I am sorry I was not able to meet Charles Cohen and hear his story firsthand.

Carly Novell, I will always appreciate that you took the time to speak with me when I know it brought back painful memories. Your story launched the telling of this tale to another level. You are a gifted writer and I look forward to watching you soar.

John Pallone, Mayor of Long Branch, New Jersey, made a documentary about the Howard Unruh incident in 1979 when he was a film student at NYU. He was able to interview the survivors of the shootings, family members, and witnesses, many of whom have since passed away. It was through his kindness and generosity that I was able to see Carl Sorg, Ron Dale and Mitchell Cohen, Detective James McLaughlin and Dominic Latela interviewed about the incident. Many thanks for your help and patience.

To my friend Christine Martinelli, thanks for research Sundays, finding relatives of victims, trips to Cramer Hill, and cold calls to strangers. I appreciate all your help on this journey.

To Dr. Peter Brancato and Shelley Brancato—this story couldn't have been told without you. Peter, your information about psychiatry transformed this book—our discussion about Unruh's confessions, psychiatric reports, testing information, all of it helped me to better understand exactly who Howard Unruh was, and paint him onto the page. And to both of you, from reading chapters, to line editing, to helping to put the chapters in order, all of it was invaluable. Shelley—you have a unique gift for editing and structure. I really enjoyed working on this with both of you and will always treasure our friendship.

To my children Eva and Ian, many thanks for sitting up and listening to one more Howard Unruh story, or enduring another trip to Cramer Hill or to the Historical Society to read and scan pages of documentation. You were there for me every step of the way. I love you more than you know.

GET CURIOUS.

Join our community

www.thread-books.com/sign-up

for special offers, exclusive content, competitions and much more!

Follow us for the latest news

 @Threadbooks

/Threadbooks

@Threadbooks_

/Threadbooks

CPSIA information can be obtained
at www.ICGtesting.com
Printed in the USA
LVHW022204280922
729514LV00003B/161